# The Glory & the Dream

## L.M. Montgomery's Writing Life

BENJAMIN LEFEBVRE

Publisher and acquiring editor: Meghan Macdonald | Editor: Jess Shulman
Cover designer: Karen Alexiou
Cover image: Archives of Ontario, M.O. Hammond fonds
Images on pages 76, 105, and 220 courtesy Benjamin Lefebvre; all other images courtesy the L.M. Montgomery Collection, Archival and Special Collections, University of Guelph

**Library and Archives Canada Cataloguing in Publication**

Title: The glory & the dream : L.M. Montgomery's writing life / Benjamin Lefebvre.
Other titles: Glory and the dream
Names: Lefebvre, Benjamin, author.
Description: Includes bibliographical references and index.
Identifiers: Canadiana (print) 2025030175X | Canadiana (ebook) 20250307197 | ISBN 9781459755345 (softcover) | ISBN 9781459755352 (EPUB) | ISBN 9781459755369 (PDF)
Subjects: LCSH: Montgomery, L. M. (Lucy Maud), 1874-1942—Criticism and interpretation. | CSH: Novelists, Canadian (English)—20th century—Biography. | LCGFT: Biographies.
Classification: LCC PS8526.O55 Z768 2026 | DDC C813/.52—dc23

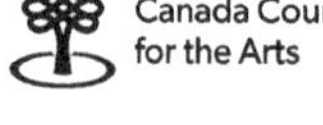

We acknowledge the support of the Canada Council for the Arts and the Ontario Arts Council for our publishing program. We also acknowledge the financial support of the Government of Ontario, through the Ontario Book Publishing Tax Credit and Ontario Creates, and the Government of Canada.



Printed and bound in Canada.

Dundurn Press
1382 Queen Street East
Toronto, Ontario, Canada M4L 1C9
dundurn.com, @dundurnpress

# The Glory & the Dream

*In loving memory of Elizabeth Hillman Waterston*

"Oh, I must write, Aunt Elizabeth," said Emily gravely, folding her slender, beautiful hands on the table and looking straight into Aunt Elizabeth's angry face with the steady, unblinking gaze which Aunt Ruth called unchildlike. "You see, it's this way. It is *in* me. I can't help it. And Father said I was *always* to keep on writing. He said I would be famous some day. Wouldn't you like to have a famous niece, Aunt Elizabeth?"

"I am not going to argue the matter," said Aunt Elizabeth.

"I'm not arguing — only explaining." Emily was exasperatingly respectful. "I just want you to understand how it is that I *have* to go on writing stories, even though I am so very sorry you don't approve.... Teddy can't help making pictures and Ilse can't help reciting and I can't help writing. *Don't* you see, Aunt Elizabeth?"

— *Emily of New Moon*

Such moments come rarely ... but when they do come they are inexpressibly marvellous and beautiful ... as if the finite were for a second infinity ... as if humanity were for a space uplifted into divinity. Only for a moment, 'tis true ... yet such a moment is worth a cycle of common years untouched by the glory and the dream.

— "The Woods in Winter"

# Contents

Introduction: The Glory and the Dream ..... 1

1 Things Readers Want to Know ..... 23

2 The Visionary Gleam ..... 39

3 Such Simple Little Tales ..... 65

4 In Lands Afar ..... 83

5 The War at Home ..... 99

6 With Hamlet Left Out ..... 117

7 A Fiction Writer on Fiction Writing ..... 143

8 A Writer and Her Critics ..... 165

9 The Scarce Hints of Love ..... 181

10 Returns to Anne ..... 201

Conclusion: After Life's Fitful Fever ..... 219

Acknowledgements ..... 223

Appendix: Books by L.M. Montgomery ..... 225

Notes ..... 229

Index ..... 249

# Introduction

## The Glory and the Dream

— 1 —

On September 20, 2008, amid a year of international celebrations of the centenary of *Anne of Green Gables*, the *Globe and Mail* published an essay by L.M. Montgomery's granddaughter Kate Macdonald Butler. Stating that a series of articles about mental health appearing in that newspaper during the preceding months had prompted her "to reflect upon [her] own family's history with depression," Butler revealed a secret that had long been kept in her family in spite of the intense scholarly and media scrutiny of her famous grandmother's life and work, particularly in the decades since Montgomery's death on April 24, 1942. "What has never been revealed," she wrote, "is that L.M. Montgomery took her own life at the age of 67 through a drug overdose." Writing eloquently about Montgomery's struggles to keep private her experiences of depression and mental instability within a life of public visibility (nationally and internationally as a famous author as well as locally as the wife of a Presbyterian minister in rural communities), Butler added that "I wasn't told the details of what happened, and I never saw the note she left, but I do know that it asked for forgiveness."[1]

Sympathetic and supportive responses to Butler's courageous decision to break her family's silence poured in. A week after her essay appeared, the *Globe and Mail* published two columns of letters from readers across Canada, a mere sample of the dozens of comments left on the newspaper's website.[2] But what those comments revealed was that the readers who were most shocked by Butler's revelation were those who'd known Montgomery solely as the imagined author of *Anne of Green Gables*. This view of the idealized author is one Montgomery herself confronted in letters sent to her by adoring fans, including one from "some pathetic ten-year-old in New York who implores me to send her my photo because she lies awake after she goes to bed wondering what I look like." Highly conscious of the contrast between fantasy and reality, she reported in a journal entry dated February 27, 1920, that she nevertheless had sent this reader "a reprint of my last photo in which I sit rapt in inspiration — apparently — at my desk, with pen in hand, in gown of lace and silk with hair just-so — Amen."[3]

Moreover, Butler's article went entirely against the grain of that year's widespread coverage of the *Anne* centenary, which touched on everything from the book's continued appeal with readers of all ages to Prince Edward Island as an ideal vacation spot. A *Globe and Mail* article by James Adams the preceding February had highlighted the range of ways in which the centenary of the "seemingly inextinguishable red-haired girl" would be celebrated worldwide, including new editions, supplementary titles, and book-length studies, as well as conferences, lectures, and exhibits.[4] Yet in most of this coverage, Montgomery was barely present *except* as the author of *Anne of Green Gables*, continuing a media pattern that is as old as the book itself: As Faye Hammill noted in her book *Women, Celebrity, and Literary Culture Between the Wars*, published the year preceding this anniversary, "[Montgomery's] fame has always been contingent on the much greater renown of her character Anne Shirley," who "might be considered a celebrity sign in her own right."[5] As though proving this point, Butler's revelatory essay appeared under the headline "The Heartbreaking Truth About Anne's Creator."

Soon after the publication of that essay, a colleague asked me how far I expected readers and critics would be willing to fold this revelation about

Montgomery's death into their understandings of her life, her work, and her legacy. This proved to be a complex question, since anyone who'd read Montgomery's journals, which by that point had been published in five selected volumes between 1985 and 2004, couldn't have been that surprised by Butler's revelation, given how frequently Montgomery wrote in that record about her struggles with depression and especially given her final journal entry, dated a month before her death, which comes across as nightmarish in its intensity: "Since then my life has been hell, hell, hell. My mind is gone — everything in the world I lived for has gone — the world has gone mad. I shall be driven to end my life. Oh God, forgive me. Nobody dreams what my awful position is." The carefully vague phrasing of the annotation for this entry by editors Mary Rubio and Elizabeth Waterston — "The 'primary cause' of death on her death certificate was 'Coronary Thrombosis'" — clearly indicated that there was much more to this story.[6]

The final volume of Montgomery's selected journals had promised to conclude tensions and conflicts that had been brewing throughout her life and that had captivated readers of the earlier volumes — as Laura M. Robinson put it in her account of skipping to the end of the volume as soon as she received a copy, "I had to know once and for all how the story ended"[7] — but the final entry in particular only prompted more questions. Did

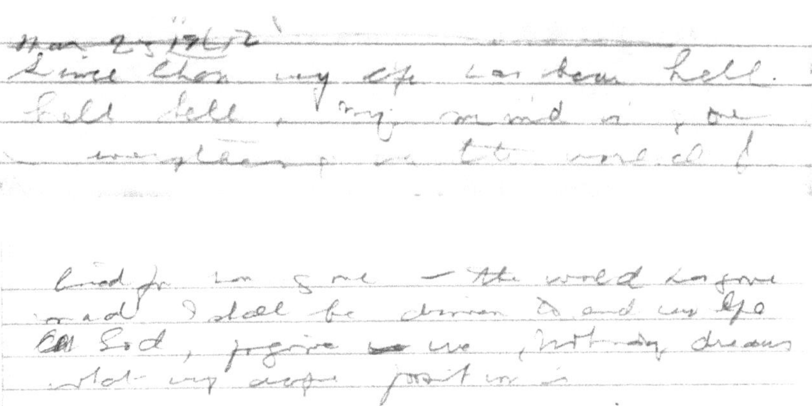

Montgomery's final journal entry, dated March 23, 1942, and written in pencil, on pages 478 and 479 of her tenth ledger.

Montgomery really die of coronary thrombosis, the clinical term for a heart attack? Who signed the death certificate? Were any secondary or additional causes listed? Can coronary thrombosis occur as a result of external factors such as, say, a drug overdose?

To the best of my knowledge, the circumstances surrounding Montgomery's death were touched on in print only a few times prior to the publication of Butler's 2008 article. Stuart Macdonald, Montgomery's youngest son and Butler's father, had written a letter to the editor in response to inaccuracies in a 1977 article, also in the *Globe and Mail,* that profiled the burial places of prominent Canadian authors. Even though this article went only so far as to mention that Montgomery had "suffered in her old age from severe depression and poor health," Macdonald evidently felt the need to set the record straight: "She died of a stroke." In a 2002 *Saturday Night* essay about the Montgomery phenomenon, Cynthia Brouse posited that "what actually caused her death ... is a little murky, and suicide rumours may or may not be quashed when Mary Rubio of the University of Guelph publishes her long-awaited biography." For Irene Gammel, Montgomery's final journal entry and its cryptic annotation opened up several possibilities. "Did she actively commit suicide or did she will herself to die? The journal leaves the question open, but what is clear is how conscious the writer was of her impending death." Even so, Gammel's question could easily have been asked of Montgomery's final letters to two men she'd met as part of a literary correspondence club in 1903 and with whom she'd been exchanging letters for almost forty years. "I am no better and never will be," she wrote to G.B. MacMillan of Alloa, Scotland, in a letter dated December 23, 1941, signing the letter "yours in all sincerity and perhaps for the last time." In a letter to Ephraim Weber of Alberta dated three days later, she added, "I do not think I will ever be well again," echoing a statement she'd made in a letter dated a year earlier: "I do not think I will ever recover."[8]

Within days of the publication of Butler's article, the Charlottetown *Guardian* published an interview with Elizabeth Rollins Epperly, co-editor of a 1980 volume of Montgomery's letters to MacMillan, who revealed that she'd been told thirty years before that Montgomery had taken her own life, but (in the words of reporter Jim Day) had "never wanted to be the one to make the shocking revelation." As Epperly recalled of what she'd told Butler by telephone concerning Butler's *Globe and Mail* article, "People need to hear that from the family."[9] And so, it looked like Butler's article would answer the lingering questions of those who'd read Montgomery's published journals and letters, at the same time that it raised a possibility that readers who were unfamiliar with that body of work were much less likely to contemplate.

— 2 —

It turned out, though, that Butler's answer about the circumstances of Montgomery's death led to several more questions.

On September 24, 2008, four days after the publication of Butler's essay, an article entitled "Is This Lucy Maud's Suicide Note?" appeared on the front page of the *Globe and Mail*, consisting of the full text of a short note — excerpted from a major biography by Rubio released the following month — that allegedly had been found on Montgomery's bedside table at the time of her death:

> This copy is unfinished and never will be. It is in a terrible state because I made it when I had begun to suffer my terrible breakdown of 1940. It must end here. If any publishers wish to publish extracts from it under the terms of my will they must stop here. The tenth volume can never be copied and must not be made public during my lifetime. Parts of it are too terrible and would hurt people. I have lost my mind by spells and I do not dare to think what I may do in those spells. May God forgive me and I hope everyone else will forgive me even if they cannot understand. My position is too awful to endure and nobody realizes it. What an end to a life in which I tried always to do my best in spite of many mistakes.[10]

The note that appeared in the *Globe and Mail* was supplemented by a follow-up article by Adams, which revealed Rubio's interpretation of the note as being "the final page of a 176-page account of the years 1939–1942 that Montgomery expected one day to transcribe in more writerly fashion into her official journals," the term "tenth volume" referring to the last of ten handwritten ledgers that provided the basis of the five published volumes of selected journals. Stressing that her stance should not be interpreted as a contradiction to Butler's statement, Rubio nevertheless cautioned that the note — clearly bearing the date April 22, 1942, two days before Montgomery's death — does not point conclusively to premeditated suicide. The note confirmed Butler's assertion that Montgomery had asked for forgiveness, but this request clearly pertained to her realization that her

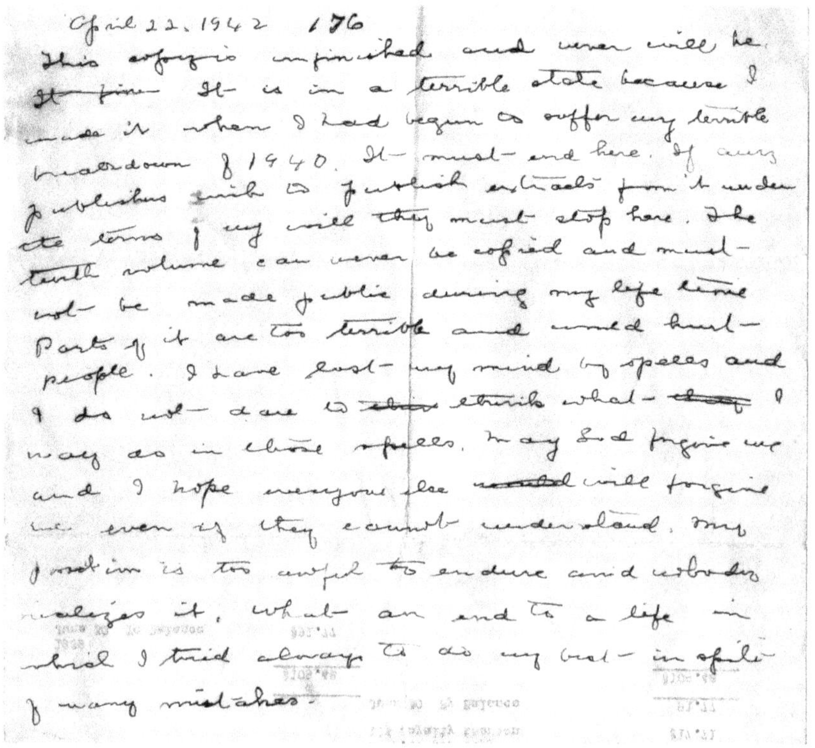
April 22, 1942 176
This is unfinished and never will be.
It is in a terrible state because I
made it when I had begun to suffer my terrible
breakdown of 1940. It must end here. If any
publishers wish to publish extracts from it under
the terms of my will they must stop here. The
tenth volume can never be copied and must
not be made public during my life time.
Parts of it are too terrible and would hurt
people. I have lost my mind by spells and
I do not dare to think what I
may do in those spells. May God forgive me
and I hope everyone else will forgive
me even if they cannot understand. My
position is too awful to endure and nobody
realizes it. What an end to a life in
which I tried always to do my best in spite
of many mistakes.

The handwritten note, dated April 22, 1942, found on Montgomery's bedside table after her death.

mental instability had caused her to be uncharitable to people in this record of her life. During a talk given at the University of Guelph on October 25, 2008, as a projected image of the handwritten note loomed before us, Rubio revealed that Stuart Macdonald had entrusted her with the note before his death in 1982.[11]

Although Rubio doesn't state in her biography how she obtained the note, she does report that Stuart Macdonald and Montgomery's attending physician, Richard Lane, both "took her death as a suicide" upon discovering her body in her bed on April 24. As Rubio notes, "The death certificate lists Maud's primary cause of death as 'coronary thrombosis,' and Dr. Lane attributed it to 'arteriosclerosis and a very high degree of neurasthenia,'" adding that "the box that listed suicide as a possible cause of death" remained unchecked. Rubio conjectures that Lane and Macdonald were too caught up in their fear of scandal to read the note carefully or to think twice about the "176" located at the top of the page; in her view, given the absence of the preceding 175 pages, it was easy for them to see the single sheet of paper as a stand-alone suicide note.[12]

In the end, Rubio's biography echoes her interview with Adams in terms of declining to make any definitive statement about the cause of Montgomery's death and whether or not it had been deliberate. Even so, further pieces published in the *Globe and Mail* went to great lengths to show that the possibility of suicide shouldn't be discounted completely. The very day after Adams's interview with Rubio appeared, Butler's side of the story was staunchly defended in an unsigned editorial: "In revealing her belief that Lucy Maud Montgomery committed suicide," Butler "kept faith with her late grandmother's deepest instincts as a writer." The following week, Paul Tiessen, co-editor of a volume of Montgomery's later letters to Weber, noted in a letter to the editor that Montgomery had expressed to Weber in 1922 that she "never felt the horror in [regard to] suicide that some feel" — as long, of course, as such an act does not leave "any burden on others." And as Gammel reminded readers in her review of Rubio's biography, Montgomery had "an ingenious way of always speaking through indirection" and "had placed the note with provisions for her journal on her bedside table where it had to be found.

(Given that she was highly protective of her personal writings, is this not evidence of volition?)"[13]

And so, while these revelations provided some crucial answers about the circumstances surrounding Montgomery's death, they also prompted a slew of follow-up questions, as did later discoveries. When book antiquarian and appraiser Vanessa Brown examined the note found on Montgomery's deathbed alongside additional documents housed at the University of Guelph archives, she realized that the "176" appearing at the top of the page did not point to a missing 175 pages of handwritten notes for the period after mid-1939, as Rubio had surmised; she speculated that Montgomery had meant for this sheet of paper to be the final page of her edited typescript of her ninth journal ledger, which ends at page 175.[14]

My objective here isn't to try to "prove" that Montgomery died by suicide or that she didn't, nor is it to suggest that the way she died is in itself a reason to re-evaluate her work. It's clear to me that Montgomery's descendants have believed sincerely that her death was premeditated suicide prompted by depression and that they struggled for decades with the weight of this knowledge, and I'm fully conscious that my perspective on how she died is constrained by the fact that I was not present at the scene and had no opportunity to discuss this event with anyone who was. As such, I also take the evidence as circumstantial, given that the note found on Montgomery's deathbed does not point explicitly to suicide; even without Brown's discovery of the link between the handwritten note and the typescript version of her journals, the "it" that "must end here" refers unambiguously to a written record of Montgomery's life that she intended to leave behind as a major component of her literary legacy, rather than her life itself. Given Macdonald and Lane's fear of scandal (which would have been entirely understandable in 1942), it's impossible to piece together decades after the fact what really happened or how closely the death certificate reflects what happened. Besides, even if an autopsy had confirmed that Montgomery had died of a drug overdose, the results couldn't have proven whether that overdose had been premeditated or caused by years of addiction to mood-stabilizing prescription drugs and exacerbated by a recent weight loss, as Rubio suggests.[15]

While all these revelations add crucial pieces to the puzzle — Macdonald's role in the aftermath of his mother's death, passed down to family members; the note on Montgomery's deathbed, entrusted by Macdonald to his mother's biographer; and the careful work of dedicated scholars who have prepared and contextualized these archival pieces for public consumption, for the benefit of us all — the broader picture remains incomplete, because Montgomery left no clear record of the "awful position" she claimed to be facing at the end of her life. The woman whom Gammel refers to as "Canada's most enigmatic literary icon" remains as unsolvable in her death as she did in her life.[16]

Montgomery's final letters to MacMillan and to Weber; her final journal entry, dated March 23, 1942; and the single sheet of paper found on her bedside table after her death may not constitute suicide notes in the conventional sense, as what Jerry Jacobs considered to be "an unsolicited account of the victim's thoughts and emotions regarding his intended act and, often, what he felt was responsible for it."[17] Yet, as Edwin Shneidman noted in *Voices of Death*, the meaning of a suicide note can be found in the note itself as well as in the context of the life that has ended:

> Suicide notes, written, as they are, as part of the life that they reflect, can have a great deal of meaning … when they are examined in light of the details of the full life history of which they are the penultimate act. By putting a suicide note within the context of the life history of the individual (who both wrote the note and committed the act), one can find that many words, ideas, emotional proclivities, styles of reaction, modes of thinking, etc., that characterized that life are reflected in the specific details of the suicide note. And conversely, many words, phrases, ideas, passions, emphases, etc., contained in the suicide note are extensions of those very same threads that had previously characterized the life. Living or dying, a particular individual has a certain consistency,… a certain "trademark," which he or she will show in work style, in play style and in life style,

> whether celebrating life in a poem of love or contemplating death in a note of suicide.

As though echoing Shneidman's remarks, Rubio notes in her biography that "the ability to face the world through a composed, inscrutable mask, while deciding how to respond to a situation, would become her trademark in later life."[18] While Montgomery's journals come across as spontaneous, in-the-moment observations about her life, her relationships, and her problems, they also include recurring patterns of delay, silence, and indirection. For these reasons, it's no surprise that the note found on Montgomery's deathbed doesn't point directly to premeditated suicide, even if that was the cause of her death.

— 3 —

There's no one else like L.M. Montgomery.

From the time she published *Anne of Green Gables* in 1908 to the end of her life in 1942, she occupied a unique place in Canadian literature, given that her work was widely popular, critically acclaimed, *and* enduring in its appeal. She published twenty-four books in all, including nine more that featured Anne Shirley, her celebrated Emily trilogy, fan favourite *The Blue Castle*, a volume of poems, and a co-authored book of biographical essays. But her literary output was even more extensive than this, since starting in 1890 she'd also published over one thousand short stories, poems, and miscellaneous pieces, in venues from leading cosmopolitan magazines to daily newspapers all across North America. And while she shared the spotlight during her lifetime with many fellow Canadian writers whose books were popular — including Ralph Connor, Nellie L. McClung, Mazo de la Roche, Robert Stead, and Stephen Leacock — she's one of the few Canadian authors from that period who continues to be recognized by the general public *and* whose work is still widely available in multiple formats.

In addition to her journals, Montgomery kept a handwritten ledger of the income she earned as a writer and compiled more than a dozen scrapbooks of her shorter works and of the press coverage she and her books received. This included reviews — many of them sent to her by a clipping service — that had appeared in periodicals across Canada and the United States as well as in faraway places such as the United Kingdom, India, South Africa, Cuba, Australia, and New Zealand. These items — now part of major Montgomery artifact collections at the University of Guelph library, the University of Prince Edward Island library, and the Confederation Centre Art Gallery in Charlottetown — consist of Montgomery's personal archive of her writing career, supplemented by occasional marginalia in her often indecipherable handwriting.[19] But while her efforts have been a boon for researchers, these records aren't always complete. One of her scrapbooks contains the first half of a thrilling Gothic fiction serial she'd published in early 1907 but not the second half, and since copies of the issues in question haven't been found yet, this gap in Montgomery's record makes for the ultimate cliffhanger ending.[20]

In the seven decades since Montgomery's death, the conversation about her life, her work, and her legacy has continued to evolve, thanks to several initiatives that have kept her and her writing in the public eye. These include adaptations for stage and screen, biographies and other trade non-fiction books for adults or for young readers, university courses, academic conferences and scholarship, tourist sites in Prince Edward Island and Ontario, translations of her books into forty languages, creative works by new authors, and an endless array of memorabilia. *Anne of Green Gables: The Musical*, which premiered in Charlottetown in 1965, claimed the Guinness World Record for longest-running annual musical just ahead of its fiftieth anniversary, and although its yearly run was broken as a result of the Covid-19 pandemic, it continues to be performed today. Sullivan Entertainment's first two *Anne of Green Gables* miniseries (1985, 1987) starring Megan Follows, the television series *Road to Avonlea* (1990–1996) starring Sarah Polley, and the CBC/Netflix series *Anne with an "E"* (2017–2019) starring Amybeth McNulty have all attracted massive international fanbases, including viewers who have never read Montgomery's work.[21]

No other Canadian author comes close to matching the extent of this cultural reach (except arguably for Margaret Atwood), and the English-speaking counterparts outside of Canada are few and far between: Louisa

May Alcott, Emily Dickinson, and Laura Ingalls Wilder in the United States come to mind, as do Jane Austen, the Brontës, Charles Dickens, and William Shakespeare in the United Kingdom. And because so many Montgomery readers encounter her work (or its offshoots) starting in childhood, they end up nurturing attachments to this author and her work that last their entire lifetimes.

Like me, they never get tired of Montgomery's writing. Like me, they keep returning to this body of work because each time they do, they discover something new to appreciate.

Since 1960 and particularly starting in the mid-1970s, published volumes of Montgomery's letters, journals, short stories, and poems have expanded readers' knowledge about the author and her work. The one-hundredth anniversary of Montgomery's birth in 1974, for instance, saw the publication of three books of new Montgomery texts: *The Road to Yesterday*, billed as a late collection of short stories that featured an adult Anne and her family; a book version of "The Alpine Path: The Story of My Career," a 25,000-word celebrity memoir first published in instalments in 1917; and Francis W.P. Bolger's *The Years Before "Anne,"* which includes the full text of several of Montgomery's earliest publications alongside biographical and historical commentary. But some critics reacted to these new Montgomery texts with surprise, if not with hostility, in reviews with titles like "So Feeble. Why Do It Now?" and "Scrap from the Barrel." For many of these commentators, *The Road to Yesterday* departed too much from what they expected of the author of *Anne of Green Gables*, whereas, paradoxically, "The Alpine Path" conformed too much to those expectations in that it seemed to reveal little about Montgomery as a person.[22]

And so, when the first volume of *The Selected Journals of L.M. Montgomery*, edited by Mary Rubio and Elizabeth Waterston, appeared in November 1985, a month before the Canadian premiere of Sullivan Films' first *Anne of Green Gables* miniseries, it was a revelation both for people who'd known Montgomery personally and for readers who'd expected her to be just as sunny and optimistic as Anne herself. Because she used her journals as a place to record emotions and frustrations she didn't want to reveal in public, reviewers and readers alike were shocked by the discrepancy between the author they'd imagined and the woman they discovered in its pages — one who frequently chafed against enormous pressures to conform to societal expectations involving gender and class.

But for some, shock led to fascination. As Elspeth Cameron wrote in *Saturday Night* upon the release of this volume, "The journals present almost entirely new information and reveal a young woman whose tough carapace concealed the soft underbelly of human vulnerability." And as Janet Saunders noted in her review in the *Winnipeg Free Press*, "In [Montgomery's] journals it is *life* she is talking about, not fiction; and, while her joyousness, strong will and 'strange, deep, hidden inner life of dreams and aspirations' may color her account of the years, *these* joys and sorrows are real. And, for much of the period covered by this first volume [1889 to 1910], the sorrows outweigh the joys."[23]

That curiosity kept increasing with the release of four more volumes of selected journals between 1987 and 2004, but because this autobiographical account proved to be such a compelling narrative, it risked becoming interpreted as the sole site of the "true" L.M. Montgomery, much to the distress of her neighbours, extended family members, and friends who had difficulty reconciling the narrator of the journals with the woman they remembered. And so, Alexandra Heilbron's *Remembering Lucy Maud Montgomery* (2001) offered readers a collaborative, intimate portrait of the author in the form of thirty-two interviews with people who'd known Montgomery personally, alongside ten articles from 1909 to 1942 that shed light on how the mainstream press had depicted her during her career. Noting that her book offered "one more piece of the puzzle that was Maud," Heilbron suggested in her introduction that "only when we take in *all* the information — her novels, her journals, and the memories of the people who knew her — do we have as true a picture as possible of the real L.M. Montgomery."[24]

My own contributions to Montgomery studies have touched on her book-length fiction, on her shorter works, on screen adaptations, and even on tourism, and a good many of them have involved unearthing rare and ephemeral print sources as a way to round out our collective understanding of her life and her work. My first large-scale Montgomery project consisted of a restored edition of her rediscovered final book, *The Blythes Are Quoted*, which had formed the basis for *The Road to Yesterday* and which I undertook as my master's thesis at the University of Guelph. A few years after the published edition of *Blythes* appeared in 2009, I published a three-volume critical anthology entitled *The L.M. Montgomery Reader*, which reprinted rarely seen essays by Montgomery, interviews with her, scholarship on her work, commentary in middlebrow periodicals and daily newspapers, and reviews of her books. More recently, I've begun the task of reprinting in book form Montgomery's extensive shorter works alongside commentary that links these items to her books and to her life. Four volumes in The L.M. Montgomery Library have appeared so far: *A Name for Herself: Selected Writings, 1891–1917*, *A World of Songs: Selected Poems, 1894–1921*, *Twice upon a Time: Selected Stories, 1898–1939*, and *Schooled with Briars: Collected Serials, 1903–1913*. My hope is that making this material available more widely will help expand even more our collective understanding of Montgomery's life and work, similar to how the journals did so starting in 1985.

— 4 —

My interest in Montgomery's work started long before I began my graduate studies at the University of Guelph in 1999.

Although I don't remember watching Sullivan Films' first *Anne of Green Gables* miniseries when it aired in 1985, I must have been sufficiently interested in the sequel, which aired on the CBC in December 1987, because not only did I watch it (despite the fact that each of the two instalments ended past my bedtime), but also, I clipped the articles about it from that week's TV listings supplement that appeared in our daily newspaper, the Montreal *Gazette*. At some point, my parents purchased copies of some of the Anne books for my older sister, but somehow, I wasn't terribly keen to read them at first.

My interest in Montgomery's broader body of work began in earnest with the premiere, in January 1990, of *Road to Avonlea*, a weekly series that consisted of a loose adaptation of two pairs of unrelated Montgomery texts — her novel *The Story Girl*; its sequel, *The Golden Road*; and two collections of linked short stories, *Chronicles of Avonlea* and *Further Chronicles of Avonlea* — that served as a spin-off of sorts of the two Anne miniseries.

Because my bilingual family lived in a part of Québec that was predominantly French speaking, my opportunities to purchase reading material in English were limited to occasional shopping trips to Montreal or, in a few cases, funerals for American relatives. It was during such occasions that I bought my first copies of the four Montgomery titles that had formed the basis for *Road to Avonlea*, and perhaps a year after that, I ordered my own copies of all eight Anne books from a catalogue we'd received in the mail — possibly Barnes and Noble.

Around this time, I discovered a bookstore in Québec's Eastern Townships that had a 1-800 number and that was willing to ship books in the mail for a reasonable fee. Because this was before the days of online shopping, customers needed to know exactly what they wanted to order — there was no way to browse. And so, necessity ended up feeding what has remained an organizing principle in my life as a consumer: If I like books by an author or a particular television series, I'll buy everything else by that author or connected to that series. This is why I spent several years reading monthly volumes in The Hardy Boys Casefiles and The Nancy Drew Files, two book series for teenagers that lasted for over a decade, and it also prompted me to take the plunge and order all the remaining Montgomery titles that were advertised in my Bantam Seal editions. That soon came to include trade collections of Montgomery's short stories edited by Catherine McLay and Rea Wilmshurst, and eventually, I purchased Montgomery's journals, letters, and poems, as well as volumes of literary criticism about her work. During the summer of 1995, I discovered this newfangled thing called "the internet," which led me to newsletters such as *The Avonlea Traditions Chronicle* and *Kindred Spirits* (both of which published annual catalogues of books, VHS tapes, and collectibles) and to a Kindred Spirits listserv hosted by the L.M. Montgomery Institute at the University of Prince Edward Island. The following year, at the age of nineteen, I boarded a train by myself and travelled to Charlottetown, where I attended an international conference called L.M. Montgomery and Canadian Culture.

It occurs to me now that this description of my younger self buying and reading forms of academic scholarship and attending an international conference before I'd even started my undergraduate degree makes me seem rather precocious, but I don't see myself that way, and I don't think I did then, either. There was something about Montgomery's work that fascinated me, and these books were all endeavours to satisfy that fascination. What's kept me going all these years is the fact that, even now, there's still more about Montgomery's life, work, and legacy that's left to discover.

Over the years, I've met hundreds of people — almost all of them women — who share my fascination with texts by Montgomery or with adaptations of her work. In some cases, these Montgomery friends were drawn to Anne or Emily as characters in whom they recognized themselves or whom they wanted to emulate. In other cases, they began reading Montgomery's books because they were exceptionally strong readers who were bored by what was more obviously available to readers of their age.

My experience differs from theirs. I had some things in common with the characters in *Road to Avonlea* — I, too, lived a kilometre away from a large body of water, although in my case it was the St. Lawrence River and not the Atlantic Ocean — but beyond that, I enjoyed the television series partly because the characters were so unlike anyone I knew in reality. At some point it dawned on me that *Road to Avonlea* aired as part of CBC Family Hour — an anthology series of programs designed for young people and parents to watch together — and yet the central focus of that series, at least initially, was on the relationships between a semi-orphaned girl and her two single aunts. Because the television series was so different from the two pairs of books it was adapted from, I soon grew accustomed to the existence of multiple, competing Montgomery universes. That experience has allowed me to be more flexible in appreciating stage or screen adaptations of her work as legitimate forms of storytelling in their own right.

At any rate, within a year of the premiere of *Road to Avonlea*, I also began watching *Twin Peaks* and *Saturday Night Live* while continuing to enjoy Saturday morning cartoons, which I think goes to show that, even at thirteen, I wasn't particularly bothered by what stories were supposedly "for" me and what stories were not. And while devoting so much of my professional life to Montgomery's work and legacy proved unwise in terms of a competitive academic job market, I've been able to nurture relationships with fellow Montgomery researchers and readers, and I like to think I've at least come closer to figuring out what her work means and how those meanings have changed across places and over time.

— 5 —

In the twenty-odd years since my grad school days, the preservation of books and periodicals has changed immeasurably, and so has people's access to these kinds of materials.

When I started my master's degree at the University of Guelph in 1999, library card catalogues had been replaced with searchable online databases, but besides that, libraries continued for the most part to acquire books and periodicals in print form. Journals and magazines were often bound together in annual volumes, so lugging a stack of them from the shelf to a desk could be a considerable workout. Over the years, I've spent countless hours in libraries flipping through pages of periodicals such as *The Canadian Magazine*, *The Atlantic Advocate*, *Canadian Home Journal*, *Everywoman's World*, and the *Family Herald and Weekly Star* in search of Montgomery-related content.

And if older items weren't available in print, the most likely alternative in those days was microfilm, consisting of reels of film that researchers have to unwind and read page by page using a specialized machine. But this technology had its challenges, since in those days monitors tended to be on the small side and printouts were often illegible. At some point during my time at Guelph, I decided to go through Montgomery's scrapbook of reviews and other clippings, which was available to researchers on microfilm, but the limitations of this technology — coupled with the fact that I had to pay for each printout — made me give up on this idea almost immediately after I started. A dozen years later, when I was putting together *The L.M. Montgomery Reader*, advances in technology meant I could export an image of each scrapbook page from the microfilm as a PDF that I could bring home on my USB flash drive. Now, more and more print resources have been digitized using an overhead scanner that can take digital photographs of artifacts without damaging them, and the quality of these scans is immeasurably better than what was available before.

Another advantage of digitization is that scanned documents can be made machine searchable through a process known as optical character recognition. This is automated rather than done by humans, so it's not always accurate, but it means that a user no longer needs to sift through pages of a magazine in hard copy or of a newspaper on microfilm for mentions of Montgomery hiding somewhere. A keyword search for Montgomery's name can generate hundreds of search results in a matter of seconds — including results that pertain to *other people* named L.M. Montgomery! This is a tremendous time saver. Once, while visiting a friend in the United Kingdom, I stopped by a public library to search for reviews of Montgomery's books in *The Scotsman*, following a lead in one of her scrapbooks. A keyword search for Montgomery's name generated a dozen PDFs that I was able to email to myself before the librarian heard my North American accent and clued in to the fact that I probably didn't have a library card.

Today, users can access more and more of these digital files, either through library-licensed searchable databases, through open-access platforms such as the Internet Archive, the HathiTrust Digital Library, Canadiana, and the Library of Congress, or through subscription-based websites such as Newspapers.com. This means I'm less restricted to what a certain library has in its collection, and it cuts down on the number of times I need to order microfilm reels from elsewhere (which I have done!). Most of the time, I don't even need to *go* to the library to access this wealth of material. All that's required is an internet browser, a good Wi-Fi connection, and in some cases my university login credentials.

In order to consider how the digitization of print sources has changed what's known or appreciated about an author like L.M. Montgomery, it helps to think first in terms of the kinds of sources that digitization has helped make available more widely.

For several reasons, books have far more authority than magazines or newspapers, especially in the long run. In terms of paper stock and binding alone, most books have literally more shelf life than most periodicals. But the paradox is that many magazines and newspapers reach a far larger number of readers than most books: *Everywoman's World* had a circulation of 130,000 copies when it published Montgomery's "The Alpine Path" in 1917, and on the day the *Toronto Daily Star* used a photo of Montgomery on its front page to advertise her appearance at the 1928 Canadian Book Week, it boasted that its daily circulation the preceding month had been nearly 172,000 copies.[25] But because each issue of a periodical will be replaced by the next one in a month, a week, or even a day, copies are less likely to be preserved than books are, which means that the contents of periodicals are likely to be forgotten over time.

To put it differently, most people view book burning as a shameful practice that promotes censorship and oppression, whereas few people would think twice about using an old newspaper to start a campfire.

Books have also traditionally held more prestige than periodicals. My parents proudly lined our living room bookshelves with a fifty-four-volume hardcover set called Great Books from the Western World, published by Encyclopaedia Britannica — mainly as decorations, since I can't recall any of us ever reading them. After my mother downsized a second time, I took them home with me and put them in a closet, since even though I don't want to display them, I can't bring myself to give them away. But if my parents had hung on to every issue of *Time* and *Scientific American* they'd ever received over the decades, my siblings and I would have called them hoarders. (Of course, they did keep issues of *National Geographic*, but then again, those were square bound in a way that resembled books.)

Another reality, of course, is that the periodicals Montgomery published in — many of them aimed at women, children, or people in rural communities — weren't always deemed sufficiently important to be housed in university libraries, and even when some of them were, the poor paper stock or binding would cause them eventually to disintegrate. There are still several of Montgomery's magazine items that we can't access because it appears that not a single library on earth has a copy. If a single copy of something has survived, it can now be preserved through digitization and shared with the world. But if zero copies survive, it simply can't.

Including periodical sources in the conversation about Montgomery's work quickly gets tricky because of the sheer volume of items, most of which are relatively short, which means a much wider range of voices and perspectives is involved — even in cases when contributors aren't identified. It's also important to keep in mind what function periodical items served at the time of their publication when we look at them differently today. For a periodical's initial readers, a book review acts as a way to advertise and recommend that book to interested consumers, but looking at multiple reviews of Montgomery's books a century later indicates trends in how reviewers — most of them anonymous, which was common practice at the time — perceived her work. Combing through ads for Montgomery's books can reveal a lot about how publishers and bookstores attempted to pique the interest of consumers. Profiles and interviews shed light on Montgomery's life and writing process, and although her spontaneous answers to reporters' questions should be taken with a grain of salt because she wasn't always quoted accurately, looking at several of these together can help trace how she presented herself in public. It was far more common during her lifetime than it is today for magazines and even daily newspapers to publish creative writing alongside news items and advertisements. In Montgomery's case, this included serializations of her novels as well as her short stories and poems, some of which were reprinted so often and so widely that I doubt she was aware of it. Moreover, many periodicals had regular columns devoted to books and invited their readers to write about what they'd read, similar to an online forum today.

In short, if we confine ourselves to the twenty-four books Montgomery published during her lifetime and to the few book-length studies that commented on her writing during that period, then the body of work in question is finite. But once we widen the field of view to include items by or about her that appeared in periodicals, as well as to unpublished documents or to artifacts in institutional or personal collections, the number of texts grows exponentially, leading to fascinating discoveries and to further mysteries.

## — 6 —

Most Montgomery readers will recognize the title of this book, *The Glory and the Dream*, as the title of chapter 36 of *Anne of Green Gables*, in which Anne wins an Avery scholarship that will allow her to pursue undergraduate studies at Redmond College. And to readers who are familiar with nineteenth-century poetry, this title should bring to mind William Wordsworth's poem "Ode: Intimations of Immortality from Recollections of Early Childhood," from which the phrase originated. But Montgomery used that quoted phrase again, as one of the epigraphs in this volume shows, in the last of four nature essays that she published in 1911. While the phrase on its own sounds like a celebration of ambitions achieved, it's important to emphasize that Wordsworth's poem uses it as a kind of lament:

> But there's a tree, of many, one,
> A single field which I have looked upon,
> Both of them speak of something that is gone:
> The pansy at my feet
> Doth the same tale repeat:
> Whither is fled the visionary gleam?
> Where is it now, the glory and the dream?[26]

Montgomery's use of that phrase in *Anne of Green Gables* and in "The Woods in Winter" doesn't capture this lament, but it comes across in chapter 29 of *Anne of the Island* (1915), depicting the occasion of Diana Barry's wedding: "Anne laughed and sighed. She felt very old and mature and wise — which showed how young she was. She told herself that she longed greatly to go back to those dear merry days when life was seen through a rosy mist of hope and illusion, and possessed an indefinable something that had passed away forever. Where was it now — the glory and the dream?"[27]

Throughout her career as a novelist, Montgomery experienced a tremendous amount of critical acclaim, adulation from fans, honours from Canadian and U.K. dignitaries, financial stability, public visibility, and opportunities to express herself in traditionally male public spaces. But with each benefit came a drawback: pressure to undertake projects that didn't align with her evolving creative interests, unfair contract terms, multiple lawsuits, requests for financial assistance from family members who rarely paid her back, invasions of her privacy, and occasional put-downs from (mainly male) critics who saw popular writing about women and young people as beneath their notice in their quest for a more robust Canadian *literature*. Even before *Anne of Green Gables* appeared in 1908, Montgomery sensed that the reality of publishing a book would differ from her ambition: as she noted in a journal entry dated August 16, 1907, in which she announced that her manuscript had been accepted for publication and that her dream of publishing a book was finally about to come true, "The realization is sweet — almost as sweet as the dream!"[28]

For readers who know little about the author of *Anne of Green Gables*, this book is a gateway into the larger world of L.M. Montgomery. But because I bring to these discussions rarely seen periodical and archival items (most of which I haven't mentioned in my previous publications), this book will also add considerably to the understanding of readers who already have extensive familiarity with her fiction and her life writing.

The chapters in this book, organized somewhat chronologically, consist of some of my thinking about aspects of Montgomery's writing life — the creative choices she made, the pressures she faced, the ways her work was commented on, and the ways she engaged with publishers, fans, and critics — as it has evolved over time as a result of engaging with ephemeral print sources that digitization has made more accessible. Still, this book can't cover every aspect of Montgomery's career, nor does it claim to offer any final answers about her experience as a writer. After all, because more and more older print materials get digitized all the time, there will always be new databases to discover, new search items to try, and new search results to sift through and consider. I've learned over the years how important it is to avoid using terms like "first," "last," "never," "only," or "always" — you never know what you'll find next or how it'll trouble or at least add to what you knew before. In other words, as new information is unearthed, the story of Montgomery's writing life will continue to evolve, as will our collective fascination with all aspects of her life, her work, and her legacy.

# 1

# Things Readers Want to Know

## — 1 —

When Montgomery died in Toronto on April 24, 1942, in the midst of the Second World War, multiple iterations of two or three detailed obituaries, as well as numerous shorter notices, circulated in daily newspapers across North America starting the following day. Whether the headlines used the verbs "dies," "passes," "succumbs," or even "expires" to refer to her death, these obituaries offered readers details about the life — and the career — that had just ended.[1] Consider the version of the Canadian Press obituary that appeared under the headline "Author of Anne of Green Gables Taken by Death" in the *Hamilton Spectator*:

> Author of Anne of Green Gables, one of the world's best-selling and best-loved novels, Lucy Maude Montgomery, in private life Mrs. Ewan Macdonald, died at her home here yesterday. She was 67 years old.

Born at Clifton, P.E.I., Miss Montgomery's series of stories about her naive heroine brought fame to their author and to her island province, in which the girl Anne's story was set. The vogue enjoyed by this first novel and its successors became legendary in Miss Montgomery's lifetime as translations into Polish, French, Swedish, Dutch and Spanish were published and two versions of the classic girls' book found their way to the motion picture screen.

**Work Uninterrupted**

The publication of her best-known book was not the beginning of her literary career, however. It dated back to school days when she was a famous character among her classmates as "that girl who writes stories for magazines — and gets paid for them." Her work continued uninterrupted in spite of the busy career of a Presbyterian minister's wife after her marriage to Rev. Ewan Macdonald.

The home of her grandparents at Cavendish, P.E.I., the original Green Gables in which she spent most of her childhood, became a land-mark for tourists and devotees of the simple style and fresh imagination of the girl who lived and wrote there. In later years she described the farm as "12 miles from a railroad station, 24 miles from the nearest town, but only half a mile from the sea."

**On Honours List**

After her marriage the couple moved to Leaksdale, Ont., where their two children, Chester and Stuart, were born. Mrs. MacDonald's fame, which earned her a place on the honours list of King George V's silver jubilee in 1935 and the degree of Fellow of the Royal Society of Arts, made no change in her life.

The old farm at Cavendish was made a part of Prince Edward Island's national park in 1939, and spots made

> famous by her writings, such as Lover's Lane and The Lake of Shining Waters, were preserved as they were described in the "Anne" books.
>
> The esteem of fellow artists is notably the lot of few, but one of the surest fruits of lasting success — Mark Twain described her Anne of Green Gables as "the sweetest creation of child life yet written," and Bliss Carman, the Canadian poet, said Anne "must always remain one of the immortal children of fiction."[2]

This obituary mentions several milestones in Montgomery's life and career, but inaccuracies abound. Montgomery's middle name was Maud (*without* an e); her married surname was indeed Macdonald (how it appears the first two times) and not MacDonald (how it appears the third time); a neighbouring house and not her grandparents' was the original for "Green Gables"; Montgomery did publish her work in periodicals, but she did not get paid for this until her twenties; after her marriage, she and her family lived in Leaskdale, not Leaksdale, but the family moved to Norval, Ontario, in 1926, and then to Toronto in 1935; and while she commented frequently on the geographical isolation of Cavendish, the distances she named between it and the nearest town, railway, or store varied from one telling to another. As for Mark Twain, what he actually wrote about her first book — "In 'Anne of Green Gables' you will find the dearest and most moving and delightful child since the immortal Alice" — was misquoted almost as soon as her first publisher used it as a form of marketing.[3] I also point out that this notice refers to only one of her books by name.

A second obituary that originated in the *Globe and Mail* provided some additional details about Montgomery's life, including the year she'd spent in Saskatchewan during her adolescence, her experience as a schoolteacher, and her two semesters of undergraduate studies at Dalhousie University in Halifax. Not only did it offer a comprehensive list of her books (albeit with several mistakes in terms of publication dates), but also, it offered a tantalizing clue about her creative work: "For the past two years she had been in ill health, but during the past winter Mrs. Macdonald compiled a collection of magazine stories she had written many years ago, and these were placed in the hands of a publishing firm only yesterday." And while it was one of only a few obituaries that described her death using the word "suddenly," it fell in line with all the others by offering no details about the cause of her death.[4]

— 2 —

In addition to several reports about plans for Montgomery's funeral and burial that appeared in the week that followed,[5] her death occasioned the publication of several tributes — most of them unsigned — in a slew of periodicals. Tributes published so soon after an author's death act more like public eulogies than detailed evaluations of their work, but those published about Montgomery offer us a sense of how commentators viewed her and her writing at the time of her death. They also became a source for perceptions — and misperceptions — of her work that recirculated for decades afterwards as part of a posthumous mythology about L.M. Montgomery.

Consider the following paragraphs, which appeared in the *Windsor Daily Star*:

> When L.M. Montgomery (Mrs. Ewan Macdonald) died in Toronto at the age of 67, a literary career that was built upon an appreciation of the simpler things of Canadian life was brought to a close. No cold realist, no pseudo-sophisticate, she wrote of life as she knew and lived it in her girlhood in Prince Edward Island, and the homely truth and honesty of those works brought her international renown.
>
> Fame, however, did not come to her without effort. Long before she established her reputation with "Anne of Green Gables," a work that has been translated into many languages and reproduced on the screen in both silent and sound versions, she was a writer, mastering her craft in the school of experience.
>
> It was not only a flair for plot and facility of expression that made Mrs. Macdonald a great writer. Her

> understanding of human nature was deep and thorough, and her interest in the loves, joys and sorrows of every-day folk transcended professional curiosity. It was from all these gifts that she wove her stories, and it was from them that her novels drew their wide-ranging appeal.

This piece mentions "those works" plural, but because *Anne of Green Gables* is once again the only one of her books referred to by name, I can't help but wonder to what extent this assessment of her writing was made on the basis of a single book. The same question could be asked about another item in the same issue of this newspaper, W.L. Clark's "As We See It" column, which predicts that Montgomery "will continue to live through 'Anne of Green Gables'" and which acts as a reminder that her death occurred during the Second World War: "People were beginning to discover the delights of Cavendish and other parts of Prince Edward Island. The war and the consequent curtailment of travel have meant many journeys to the island will have to be postponed. But, after the war has been won, people will be going in ever-increasing numbers to Prince Edward Island, a province which Lucy Maud Montgomery helped to make famous."[6]

Whereas a tribute in the *Charlottetown Guardian* focused on Montgomery's "contribution to her native Province" and noted that her death "will be felt as a personal loss by every Prince Edward Islander," a similar item in the *Ontario Intelligencer*, a paper published out of Belleville, omitted any reference to her books' recurring setting in P.E.I. or to the fact that she'd spent her entire married life in Ontario (not too far from Belleville, in fact). Instead, its unidentified author considered Montgomery's legacy in decidedly nationalist terms, as the title, "Dealt with Life in Canada," makes clear.

> At this time many thousands of Canadians everywhere are saddened by the thought that the author of "Anne of Green Gables," Lucy Maude Montgomery (Mrs. Ewan Macdonald) has passed away. Gifted with literary power and the talent of portraying character she wisely chose the

> Canadian scene with which she was familiar. Today her books are read by children and grown-ups who delight in the beauties of her work and the lives she has portrayed.
>
> What is important is that she saw in the life of Canada as it is and has been that about which to write. The lives of those whom she drew in her pages in the simple and delightful style of writing she could handle so deftly and which she portrayed with such feeling and freshness of imagination, have been a lesson to all our people to seek the riches in the lives of people in our own country. Life in Canada inspires us. More of our authors should deal with this theme....
>
> L.M. Montgomery reaped a harvest of fame, some other writers do not so succeed and fail to secure a large reading public. Those who portray the true picture of the people who in their quiet way play their role in the nation deserve recognition. They enrich the life and spirit of the people by what they see in life around them.
>
> L.M. Montgomery touched nothing in her story of Canadian life which she did not adorn not only by imagination but also her sane and noble outlook on life. Nothing unworthy is in her works. Through these people knew the noble woman herself.[7]

A second Montgomery-related item appeared in this newspaper four days later. This one started by anchoring Montgomery in Prince Edward Island but quickly widened the scope to consider her value through a Canada-wide lens once again.

> At Cavendish, Prince Edward Island, one of Canada's great writers was laid to rest on Wednesday, Mrs. Ewan Macdonald (L.M. Montgomery). There she received the inspiration which came to her in childhood and which made her great.

> Communities little know what inspiration they may give to some child as Cavendish gave to Lucy Maud Montgomery. Many communities cannot be chronicled as she chronicled childhood scenes in works of art that will live for their fidelity to nature, but they can and do mould lives whose "echoes roll from soul to soul," though it is the rare community that has so finely attuned a spirit as she to record its life....
>
> To be born in a setting where one's forbears have been for many generations warms life! In an age which shows a great shifting of population, fewer children have the privilege of being born in the scenes of their ancestors. Yet it may take generations for the spirit of a scene to become part of the family personality and for the growth of communion between man and nature.[8]

Additional periodical items published in the aftermath of Montgomery's death reveal recurring assumptions about how people at the time understood her work and her readership. J.J. Kerr, writing in the *Vancouver Daily Province*, likewise considered the appeal of Montgomery's books in nationalist terms but did so by focusing on the fact that they'd been translated into five languages by that point. "It is a pleasant thought," Kerr observed, "to realize that thousands of people in these countries have had Canada made beautiful to them through the writing of one of our fellow citizens from somewhat obscure P.E.I." It might be worthwhile to ask Kerr how Prince Edward Island could remain "somewhat obscure" if Montgomery's books set there had already circulated so widely around the world, but instead, I'll focus on two additional statements made in Kerr's article: first, that Montgomery "never made any real money out of 'Anne,' having sold it outright when she was quite unknown," and second, that "the book is still going strong. Even if few men have read it, everyone knows the title."[9]

When L.C. Page and Company accepted the manuscript of *Anne of Green Gables* for publication, the firm offered Montgomery the choice between a flat fee of five hundred dollars and a royalty that would give her a percentage of revenue from each copy sold. In a 1915 essay entitled "The Way to Make a Book," she made clear her rationale for choosing a royalty: "If a book is anything of a success it will bring you in more on the royalty basis, and publishers seldom offer to buy a book outright unless they are strongly convinced that it will be a success." To be fair, the terms of her royalty weren't up to industry standards, and in 1919 she sold all remaining rights to her first seven books to Page in an attempt to sever all ties with him.[10]

While it's certainly the case that Montgomery didn't earn what she should have for these books, it wouldn't be accurate to claim she hadn't "made any real money out of 'Anne,'" as Kerr supposed, especially since she published more Anne books with her subsequent publishers than with her first one. But the myth that she'd sold all rights to her first book for a flat fee of five hundred dollars kept recirculating after her death, including as part of Clyde Gilmour's remarks during a live musical performance of *Anne of Green Gables* on *CBC Folio* in November 1958.[11] And because of the odd habit commentators had of overlooking any of her books besides her first, the recirculation of this idea sometimes implied that this was the only payment she'd ever received for *any* of her writing, which is patently false.

Kerr's speculation that "few men" had read *Anne of Green Gables* likewise requires some unpacking, given the range of ways that commentators viewed Montgomery's target audience in terms of gender and age. An unsigned article in the *Saskatoon Star-Phœnix* the week after Montgomery's death reported that some of the copies of the Anne books available at the local library "are battered and worn, indicating the extensive reading they have been given, and the demand for them is so insistent that they are steadily replaced." This article predicted — rightly, as time has shown — that Montgomery's death would "increase interest in her works," but it seemed to take for granted that her readership consisted exclusively of young girls. Freda Laight of Regina's *Leader-Post* ended her tribute to Montgomery with a statement that was just as nationalistic as the one made by the *Ontario Intelligencer* commentator: "We Canadians, who are said to cherish a kind of inferiority complex about Canadian literature, can be proud indeed to claim as our own the late L.M. Montgomery." But Laight's praise for Montgomery's books also reveals an assumption that was implied rather than stated directly about what *kind* of Canadian literature her work falls under: "Childhood was immeasurably enriched by [Montgomery's] happy stories — so wholesome and yet never dulled by any goody-goody atmosphere or any moralizing. Those books were re-read many times, nor did they lose their appeal as years passed. So warm and human are they, and so delightfully written, that there is enjoyment in them for adults as well as for young people."[12]

*Anne of Green Gables* has always been Montgomery's best-known book, but the fact that so many commentators appeared to assume that this was the only one she'd ever written has implications in terms of target audience as well. It may be reasonable to assume that a novel centred on a child character is intended for child readers, but that assumption doesn't match how the book was published and marketed upon its release, and it certainly doesn't explain why some people presume that *anything* Montgomery wrote must be for a child audience as well. Commentators sometimes refer to her later novels *The Blue Castle* (1926) and *A Tangled Web* (1931) as her "adult" books, but the reality is that the majority of her books, including most of the sequels to *Anne of Green Gables*, focus on characters who are adults or split the focus between adult and younger characters. *Anne's House of Dreams* (1917), for instance, which depicts the first few years of Anne and Gilbert's married life, contains only two lines of dialogue spoken by characters who are under eighteen — and one of them is quoted by an adult. And yet, most editions of Montgomery's novels available today reflect, in terms of cover art and where bookstores and libraries shelve them, the same assumption that the target readership for anything she ever wrote must be kids.

Even so, while several comments and reviews throughout Montgomery's lifetime praised her books as straightforward fiction for girl readers, for the most part commentators either said nothing about target audience or made the point that even her books about child characters were suitable for readers of all ages or would be enjoyed more by adults than by young people. Writing about *Anne of Green Gables* in *The Catholic Record* less than a year after its release, J.O. Trainor noted of this "delightful book in every sense of the word" that "to read it is to revive one's school days — to live over again the joys, sorrows, hopes and disappointments of youth." A review of *Emily of New Moon* in *The Congregationalist* noted that the novel "should hardly be called a juvenile, for while young girls will enjoy it, the story will be most appreciated by older readers. It is quite as truly a story for aunts and uncles as for girls." And in a *New York Times* review of *Anne of Ingleside*, the last book Montgomery published during her lifetime, Jane Spence Southron noted that, despite its shared focus on an adult Anne and her young children, this book wasn't for child readers at all.

> Personally one would style it, in the main, an anti-quack, anti-nostrum, wholesomely corrective study-drama based on the theme of the carelessly natural way of bringing up nice children — badly enough needed in these days of excessive regimentation and heartless, unleisured efficiency. But let not the shocked modern be deterred. There is the purely literary side as a village gossip book and as an album of queer village personalities spicily reminiscent of Jane Austen's provincial England and of "Cranford," but with a tang to it unmistakably North American.[13]

Still, the assumption that Montgomery's books had been intended for girl readers or appealed solely to girl readers wasn't shared by all commentators who paid tribute to her after her death. An unsigned editorial in the Montreal *Gazette* praised her creative talents without naming a target audience: "Possessed of a mind of rare imaginative capacity, Lucy Maud Montgomery had a fine gift of expression and her descriptive powers went into her books to the extraordinary benefit of her beloved Prince Edward Island." In an article appearing in *The Maritime Advocate and Busy East*, Aida B. McAnn praised Montgomery's writing for its "cheerful, wholesome, happy, healthful way of life that seems well-nigh Utopian to our present war-plagued generation." And when an actual young person wrote a tribute to Montgomery — specifically, Mildred Jean Jackson of class 9B at North Little Rock Junior High in Arkansas — the scope was likewise not limited to any specific audience: "I fear the literary world has suffered a great loss in the passing of this author."[14]

— 3 —

In order to publish an obituary in a timely fashion after the death of someone famous, some newspapers kept updated files that they could access as soon as someone died. Those files could also come in handy when a reader, searching for information long before the days of Google searches, wrote to their local newspaper's information column — with titles such as "Questions and Answers," "Look for Your Answer Here," or "Things Readers Want to Know" — to ask about a living person. And so, on April 4, 1923, the *Winnipeg Evening Tribune* published a query from a reader named "J.V." — "Please give me a full account of the life of L.M. Montgomery. What is her real name?" — followed by its response.

> Lucy Maud Montgomery (Mrs. Ewen MacDonald), the Canadian author, was born at Clifton, Prince Edward Island, in 1877, the daughter of the late Hugh John Montgomery and Clara Woolner McNeill. She was educated at the Cavendish District School, the Prince of Wales College, Charlottetown, P.E.I., and at Dalhousie University, Halifax, N.S. For a short time she was a school teacher. In July, 1911, she married the Rev. Ewen MacDonald, of Leaskdale, Ont.; she has two sons. She belongs to the Canadian Women's Press Club and to the Authors' League of America.[15]

Typical of this kind of newspaper response, this one misspells the names "Macneill" and "Ewan Macdonald," keeps the focus on basic biographical information such as date and place of birth (albeit with the wrong date), schooling, work, marriage, and offspring, and goes on to provide a list of her books published to that point — really, the same information that would appear in her obituaries. But judging by some of the reader queries I've come across in newspapers during her lifetime, Montgomery's life story was sometimes of less interest than basic questions of identity. Consider the question and the response printed in the *Middletown Times Herald* of New York in January 1935: "Is the author L.M. Montgomery a man?" "No, her real name is Lucy Maud Montgomery Macdonald." This curiosity about Montgomery's gender had already made it all the way to New Zealand, as an item in the *Auckland Star* reveals: "[Is] L.M. Montgomery … a man or a woman?" "L.M. Montgomery is one of America's foremost lady writers."[16]

It's important to understand that editions of Montgomery's books published during her lifetime typically didn't include a biographical statement or an author photo; for most readers, then, "L.M. Montgomery" was more a name than a person. And so, it's hardly surprising to find examples of readers writing to their local newspapers for basic information about the person behind the name. In some cases, questions from one reader informed answers to subsequent questions, as shown in a sequence of responses about Montgomery's life published in the *Cleveland Plain Dealer* across a fifteen-year period. In 1927, "H.A.B." of East Liverpool, Ohio, asked for "a brief sketch of the life of the author, L.M. Montgomery," as well as a specific question: "Are any of her books taken from her own life?" In addition to providing basic biographical information, this newspaper replied, "None of her books are strictly autobiographical, although she has put into them a good many experiences of her own and others which have passed under her eyes." When "D.H." of Chardon, Ohio, wrote for some information about Montgomery in 1932, adding that "she writes so much of Prince Edward Island that I am interested in knowing more about her," the response concluded with the following: "She has put into her books a good many experiences of her own and others which have passed under her eyes, though they are not strictly autobiographical." And when "E.R." of Cleveland Heights wrote in August 1943 to ask for information about Montgomery, including whether or not she was still living, the response switched, at least in part, to past tense: "She put into her books a good many experiences of her own and others which passed under her eyes, though they are not strictly autobiographical."[17]

I always assumed that newspapers had access to a central database of basic information about famous people, but apparently that wasn't always the case. In the 1920s, *The Rural New-Yorker* published a "Boys and Girls" column, run by Edward M. Tuttle, which contained a number of interactive components, including a monthly puzzle. But after young readers submitted a description of *Anne of Green Gables* in 1924 and Tuttle invited fellow readers to write in with "anything you can about [the book or the author] that will be interesting to our readers," Tuttle noticed an odd trend in terms of the disconnect between the popularity of Montgomery's books and the amount of information widely known about the author. "More readers sent this answer to last month's Book Puzzle than have come for any we have had in a long time," he wrote, noting as a point of comparison that he'd received "very few answers" to the preceding book puzzle, whose answer was *Pollyanna*. Still, "a curious fact is that we seem to know so little about the author. One reader refers to her as Mrs. Montgomery, another says the initials L.M. stand for Lucy Maud, another says that she is now dead. Your editor has searched in encyclopedias and everything else within reach but can find nothing." In the end, Tuttle invited readers to submit what details they knew and published the results — which likewise sounded like an obituary for a living person — the following month.[18]

But at least Tuttle went the extra mile. When someone asked for a sketch of Montgomery's life from Kathleen Kaye's "The Heartitorium" column in the *Salt Lake Telegram* in 1918, the only detail Kaye could provide was Montgomery's year of birth. "Since she has not yet become sufficiently famous to be eulogized in the encyclopedias, I can give you no further information — except that she is an American." Kaye repeated this non-answer when someone else asked for this information in 1922. In addition to being mistaken about Montgomery's nationality, Kaye evidently was unaware that Montgomery and the Page Company had parted ways and by this point were in the midst of a years-long series of lawsuits against each other. Otherwise, she may not have suggested that the author write to the Page Company, whom she promised would "gladly provide you with a biography."[19]

## — 4 —

Despite Kaye's perception of Montgomery as not "sufficiently famous," Montgomery had several experiences of seeing biographical information about her published from dubious sources — or from no sources at all. As part of an "anecdote competition" in late 1921, the *Toronto Star Weekly* published an item entitled "Why She Refused to Offer Her Opinions," subtitled "Miss L.M. Montgomery Wanted to Remain Friends":

> Miss L.M. Montgomery, now Mrs. MacDonald, the well-known Canadian author of the Anne books, was once sitting in an editor's office when a young novelist entered.
>
> "Miss Montgomery," said the novelist eagerly, "I value your opinion very much. Now, I want you to tell me candidly what you think of my new book."
>
> Miss Montgomery smiled.
>
> "No, no," she hurriedly replied; "let us remain friends."

The problem? "I was never guilty of this *bon mot*!" Montgomery protested in a journal entry dated a few weeks later, after someone had sent her a clipping of this item in a western newspaper. She was willing to shrug this incident off as evidence of her fame, but she was decidedly less pleased three years later when this paper published an item entitled "Emotional Actress Lost When She Became Author," subtitled "Witness Early Episode in Life of L.M. Montgomery":

> When L.M. Montgomery, author of "Anne of Green Gables," lived as a child at Prince Albert, Saskatchewan, she had not then decided whether to be a great writer or a great actress....
>
> One day a citizen heard the most bloodcurdling screams coming from little Miss Montgomery's father's woodshed. Now the Canadian woodshed had long enjoyed a prominent place in the correction of children's misdemeanors,

> so that such sounds from such a place were not unusual. But so awful were the shrieks of terror the man was sure no childish crime required such punishment. Hurrying, bent on interfering, you can imagine his surprise at seeing a little girl of twelve alone in the shed.
>
> The villain had dragged the ragged heroine to the precipice and was about to cast her over so that he could inherit the Montmorenci millions. So intent and wrapped up in the part was the maiden that she never noticed the intruder. He retired, amused instead of horrified, but ever since has felt that even if literature gained a successful author, the stage lost a wonderful emotional actress.

Montgomery set the record straight in a journal entry dated March 16, 1924, pointing out that every detail in this anecdote had no connection to the reality of her time spent in Prince Albert as an adolescent. "It annoys me to have misleading things like that published about me," she concluded.[20]

What all this shows is that the appetite for information about Montgomery's life persisted throughout her career, and when those details didn't come from her, there appeared to be plenty of people — like the unidentified former neighbour in Prince Albert — who were happy to provide details, even if they were untrue.

Still, it's worth noting that when Montgomery transcribed these two news stories in her journal, she declined to identify the source of either clipping as part of her commentary, which tended to be her habit. In making that choice, she may have thought she'd reduce the ability of a future reader of her journal text to find the clippings in question. But the digitization of print sources has, alas, made it a lot easier to track down these items — and many more besides.

— 5 —

Kerr's tribute to Montgomery in the *Vancouver Daily Province* ends with a statement that hints at another recurring pattern in discussions of

Montgomery's work — a significant distinction between critical acclaim and popular appeal. "The highbrow critic might be impatient of such literature," Kerr observed, "but this author at least knew quite a secret that is not vouchsafed to many critics: the way direct into the hearts of ordinary people, who are, after all, the majority of the race." What's odd is that Kerr's language echoes similar pronouncements made in three more tributes to Montgomery — all of them unsigned — that appeared in the aftermath of her death. "Stern critics may be dismayed that what is probably the best-known book to come out of Canada should be such a simple and sentimental work," declared an editorial writer in the *Peterborough Examiner* who added that "*Anne* never set the world on fire, and launched no crusade, but she gave a great deal of happiness of an inoffensive sort." Compare this to a tribute in the *Ottawa Journal* that predicted that "if *Anne of Green Gables* were published today hard-boiled book reviewers would give it little space," which is why "when we try to value [Montgomery's books] as literature we should do so by first coming to an understanding of the simpler world in which they had their origin." An editor of *Saturday Night* magazine made a largely similar point in a headnote accompanying a poem that Montgomery had submitted three weeks before her death: "The exalted critics of this day and age look down the nose at her work, because it dealt with surfaces, instead of psycho-analytic depths; because it was interesting instead of being a boring essay in abnormal psychology."[21]

All four commentators distinguished between the tastes of critics and those of "ordinary people." But where does this contrast come from? And who were these "highbrow," "hard-boiled," "stern," and "exalted" critics who supposedly held these negative views about Montgomery's books and from whom all of these commentators were seemingly so keen to distance themselves?

We'll get to that later. For now, let's turn to Montgomery's depiction of her formative years and her earliest attempts at writing in a set of retrospective autobiographical essays published throughout her career as a best-selling novelist — as well as aspects of her early writing career that she opted *not* to write about, either because she didn't deem them sufficiently important, because they conflicted with the image of herself she wanted to circulate publicly, or because they happened outside of her awareness.

# 2

# The Visionary Gleam

— 1 —

In the immediate aftermath of the spectacular success of *Anne of Green Gables*, L.M. Montgomery started receiving questions about the genesis of her novel and about the identity of its author. At first, she responded by providing lots of engaging behind-the-scenes tidbits about what had inspired her to write the book and revealing next to nothing about herself. This includes a letter published in the *Boston Journal*, whose editors clearly hadn't picked up on the fact that "L.M. Montgomery" was a woman, judging by the fact that the article appeared under the headline "Author Tells How He Wrote His Story."[1]

She became more comfortable over time with this kind of media attention, but even so, she tended to be strategic about what she revealed about her life and her environment in these kinds of autobiographical pieces. Here's how she introduced herself in "How I Became a Writer," published in the *Manitoba Free Press* in 1921:

> I was born — praise to the gods! — in Prince Edward Island, that colorful little land of ruby and emerald and

sapphire. I come of Scotch ancestry with a dash of English from several "grands" and "greats." My mother died when I was a baby and I was brought up by my grandparents in the old Macneill homestead at Cavendish — 11 miles from a railway and 24 from a town, but only half a mile from one of the finest sea beaches in the world — the old "north shore."

I went to the "district school" there from 6 to 16. Out of school I lived a simple, wholesome, happy life on the old farm, ranging through fields and woods, climbing over the rocky "capes" at the shore, picking berries in the "barrens" and apples in the big orchards. I am especially thankful that my childhood was spent in a spot where there were many trees — trees with personalities of their own, planted and tended by hands long dead, bound up with everything of joy and sorrow that visited my life — a life that was very simple and quiet. But it never held a dull moment for me. I had, in my imagination, a passport to fairyland. In a twinkling I could whisk myself into regions of wonderful adventure, unhampered by any restrictions of reality.

I was a great reader and devoured every book I could lay hands on no matter what it was. Novels were taboo, but fortunately there was no ban on poetry. I could revel at will in the "music of the immortals" — Longfellow, Tennyson, Whittier, Scott, Byron, Milton, Burns. And one wonderful day, when I was nine years old, I discovered that I could write "poetry" myself!

It was called "Autumn" and I wrote it on the back of an old post office "letter bill" — for writing paper was not too plentiful in that old farmhouse, where nothing was ever written save an occasional letter. I read it aloud to father. Father said it didn't sound much like poetry. "It's blank verse," I cried. "Very blank," said father.

I determined that my next poem should rhyme.[2]

Montgomery, aged ten. "I was in a pensive mood when this was taken," she commented in "The Alpine Path: The Story of My Career."

In "The Alpine Path," by far the most extensive autobiographical account that she published during her lifetime, Montgomery conceptualized her writing life as something that had had no discernible beginning: "I cannot remember the time when I was not writing, or when I did not mean to be an author. To write has always been my central purpose around which every effort and hope and ambition of my life has grouped itself." It's perhaps for this reason that readers who turned to her published journals in search of evidence of this "central purpose" were disappointed or at least perplexed, since in that private account Montgomery discussed her writing ambitions, challenges, and even successes only occasionally. And when she recorded in her journal her retrospective impressions of her childhood, she often highlighted the difficult relationships she'd had, particularly with the maternal grandparents who'd raised her since the death of her mother. In one such retrospective entry, dated January 2, 1905, she commented on her growing realization that her childhood had been so "starved … *emotionally*."[3] Needless to say, these were the kinds of details she tended to leave out of the accounts she published about her life.

More than once in these autobiographical essays, Montgomery told the story — using a version in her journals as a starting point — of her attempt in childhood to find out from a supposedly impartial critic whether her writing had any promise. In a version published in the Toronto *Globe* in 1911, this anecdote reads as follows:

> I remember — who could ever forget it? — the first commendation my writings received. I was about twelve, and I had a stack of poems written out, and hidden jealously from all eyes — for I was very sensitive about my scribblings, and could not bear the thought of having them seen by those who would probably laugh at them. Nevertheless, I wanted to know what others would think of them — not from vanity, but from a strong desire to find out if an impartial judge would see any merit in them. So I employed a ruse to find out. It seems very funny, and a little pitiful, to me now; but then it seemed to me that I was at the bar of judgment for all time. It would be too much to say that, had the verdict been unfavorable, I would have forever surrendered my dreams. But they would certainly have been frosted for a time!
>
> A school teacher was boarding with us then. She was a rather sweet singer, and one evening I timidly asked her if she had ever heard a song called "Evening Dreams."
>
> The said "Evening Dreams" was no less than a long poem of my own, which I then considered my masterpiece. It is not now extant, and I can recall only the first two verses. I suppose they were indelibly imprinted on my

memory by the fact that the teacher asked me if I knew any of the words of the "song." Whereupon I, in a trembling voice, repeated the two opening verses: —

> "When the evening sun is setting
> Quietly in the west,
> In a halo of rainbow glory,
> I sit me down to rest.
>
> "I forget the present and future;
> I live over the past once more,
> For I see before me crowding
> The beautiful days of yore."

Strikingly original! Also, a child of twelve would have a long "past" to live over!

I finished up with a positive gasp, but the teacher was busy sewing, and did not notice my pallor and general shakiness. For I was pale — it was a moment of awful import to me. She placidly responded that she had never heard the song, but that "the words were very pretty."

The fact that she was sincere must certainly detract from her reputation for literary discrimination. But to me it was the sweetest morsel of commendation that had ever fallen to my lot — or that ever has fallen since, for that matter. Nothing has ever surpassed that delicious moment. I went out of the house — it wasn't big enough to contain my joy; I must have all outdoors for that — as if I trod on the amber air of the clear summer evening, and danced down the lane under the birches in a frenzy of delight, hugging to my heart the remembrance of those words.[4]

Of course, in order to make this anecdote from her experience suitable for publication, Montgomery took out several details from the version in her journal: mainly that the teacher in question, Izzie Robinson, quarrelled regularly with Montgomery's grandfather and took revenge on her. Montgomery evidently concluded that identifying this person as a schoolteacher who'd boarded with her was too specific, because when she told this anecdote again in almost identical form in "The Alpine Path," she fudged those details: "A lady was visiting us who was something of a singer."[5]

But her attempts to mythologize a painful interaction in her young life proved too successful, because in 1927, a reporter for the *Toronto Star Weekly* tracked down and interviewed this former teacher, now Mrs. Warren, who evidently had decided to recast herself as one of young Montgomery's earliest supporters:

> I remember her when she was a girl of perhaps twelve; we older people were playing parcheesi round the table at Green Gables, and Lucy Maud sat scribbling at something, unregarded, all that evening. The next day a relative said: "See what she wrote last night!" The child had been lost to our little world, far away from the Island, in some romantic setting in Germany. It was so real that we seemed to be there, too, as we read. She always had such an imagination. And no adverse circumstances could ever have held her back, opposition [would] only have encouraged her.... What a stir her first book made in Cavendish! We are very proud of her and always have been.

Montgomery was decidedly unimpressed with Mrs. Warren's selective memory. And no doubt she was equally displeased with the article's mention of Mrs. Warren recalling the day that "little Lucy" had been "perched on a desk flapping her wings and crowing lustily in imitation of a rooster." In a letter to her pen pal G.B. MacMillan dated February 6, 1928, she claimed to remember "the 'rooster' incident very well — also the merciless calling down I received from her because of my 'unladylike conduct'" and stated categorically that she'd always been known by her middle name, Maud.[6] Mrs. Warren evidently hadn't read any more of Montgomery's books, because she might have seen herself in Emily Starr's teacher from hell in *Emily of New Moon*, published four years prior to this article. And she certainly couldn't have anticipated how she'd be depicted in Montgomery's journals — and how she's now known to Montgomery readers worldwide — as a tyrant and a hypocrite.

— 2 —

Not surprisingly since she wrote these accounts of her writing career in retrospect, from her vantage point as an internationally bestselling writer, Montgomery framed her apprenticeship in terms of eventual success, glossing over struggle and discouragement in order to emphasize her determination to succeed. "Whatever gifts the gods denied me," she wrote in an essay published in 1921, "they had at least given me stick-to-it-iveness." She then described her first publication, just days before her sixteenth birthday, as "indisputably the greatest moment of my life":

> I had sent a yard — just about — of rhyme, written on one of the tragic legends of the old north shore, to the Charlottetown *Patriot*. And the *Patriot* — may its shadow never grow less! — published it. Never, before or since, have I felt as happy and triumphant and uplifted as I felt when I opened that paper and saw my poem in it. It does not at all diminish my feelings of gratitude towards the *Patriot* to remember that there were some fearful printers' mistakes and omissions in it, such as made the flesh creep on my bones. I was as a mother, gazing adoringly at her first-born and finding it all lovely, even if some of its fingers and a piece of its nose have been snipped off![7]

In these autobiographical accounts, Montgomery tended to jump from here to her next big milestone — the first time she was *paid* for her writing — before moving on to the process of writing and submitting the manuscript of her first published novel. But this is one instance where the public record departs from the private one. In several published accounts of her apprentice years, she indicated that receiving a five-dollar cheque for a short story had prompted her to purchase "leather-bound dollar editions of Milton, Byron, Wordsworth, Longfellow and Tennyson" as a tangible reminder of this milestone in her writing career (although in "The Alpine Path," her list omits Tennyson in favour of Whittier). Yet in a journal entry dated February 20, 1896, in which she reported this five-dollar payment — for her second published short story, "Our Charivari," in *Golden Days for Boys and Girls* of Philadelphia — she added that she'd purchased volumes of the work of Tennyson, Longfellow, Whittier, and Byron with the money she'd received for winning first prize in a writing competition sponsored by the Halifax *Evening Mail* on the question "Which Has the Most Patience Under the Ordinary Cares and Trials of Life — Man or Woman?"[8]

Understandably given the relative brevity of most of these published accounts, Montgomery focused on key milestones in the beginnings of her writing career and offered broad summaries of everything else — "I wrote literally thousands of poems and stories," she declared in one version.[9] But a closer look at her published periodical work reveals aspects of her writing life that she decided not to touch on in these retrospective pieces.

From her earliest publications, Montgomery proved to be highly strategic in terms of her subject matter. Her first published poem — the 156-line "On Cape Le Force," dubbed "a legend of the early days of Prince Edward Island" — narrates a legend involving a quarrel between the captain of a ship and his first mate that led to a duel at sunrise and ended tragically. And although the Cape Le Force story was apparently a mainstay of her maternal grandfather's oral storytelling repertoire, she made this story her own by placing herself at the centre of her written narrative.

> One evening, when the sun was low,
>     I stood upon the wave-kissed strand,
> And watched the white-sailed boats glide by,
>     Their sails by evening breezes fanned.
> . . . . . . . . . . . . . . . . . . . . . . . . . . . . . . .

I stood upon that lovely cliff
  And called to mind the legend dread
Which made it an accursed spot —
  One shunned by superstitious tread.

And by the time this poem appeared in the Charlottetown *Daily Patriot*, she'd already submitted an essay on this subject to an essay-writing contest sponsored by the *Montreal Witness*. The text of that essay doesn't survive, so how it compares to the poem or to the account of this event in "The Alpine Path" is impossible to determine, but one of her scrapbooks includes a clipping from the judge's comments that, although quite vague, she apparently recognized as pertaining to her own work: "A legend graphically told of a tragedy said to have occurred about the time of the establishment of British rule in the island on a spot which has perpetuated the memory of one of the principal actors in the occurrence by deriving from him its name."[10]

For her second submission to the *Witness* competition the following year, Montgomery wrote an essay about the story of the wreck of the *Marco Polo*, an event that had occurred on the shores of Cavendish beach the summer after her eighth birthday. The *Witness* published her essay in March 1891, and she published a long poem about this event in 1892.[11] Despite its unique appearance in some of her earliest publications, the story of the *Marco Polo* became a staple of her public appearances throughout her career as a world-famous author. For instance, in 1928, *The Canadian Bookman* reported on "a most entertaining address" she'd given entitled "The Story of a Vanishing World": "Her stirring recital of events in the mackerel-fishing days on the north shore of Prince Edward Island and particularly the incidents in connection with the wreck of the 'Marco Polo,' the Canadian-built sailing vessel with a speed record which had never since been equalled, gave rise to a desire to see these tales put into book form as a real contribution to Canadian literature."[12]

Montgomery made no mention of these *Witness* submissions in her retrospective biographical sketches, nor did she record any information about the fact that, according to the editorial remarks accompanying the publication of her essay, she'd "won a special school prize" for it. Despite this silence, this essay eventually had meaning for her, because it appears to have originated the urban legend, repeated in her *Globe and Mail* obituary, that she'd "won a story-writing contest sponsored by the *Montreal Star*" at the age of twelve. Except she didn't — or, at least, this isn't it. According to the report of the judges for the entries submitted in 1890, Montgomery's essay received third place in her county, and her schoolmate Nathan J. Lockhart, with whom she had a kind of flirty friendship, took second place. But even though Lockhart's essay ranked higher than hers, her essay was one of many submissions from across the country that appeared in the *Witness*, whereas I haven't found any indication so far that Lockhart's essay did. The published piece was signed "Lucy Maud Montgomery / Cavendish, Queen's County, P.E.I.," even though when it appeared Montgomery was living with her father and her stepmother in Prince Albert (in what is now Saskatchewan), but a sketch drawing of the author appearing alongside the essay identifies her as "Miss L.M. Montgomery."[13]

*A Name for Herself*, my volume of Montgomery's selected writings that appeared in 2018, opens with the full text of this essay, followed by two more non-fiction pieces she published as an adolescent: "A Western Eden," an essay about Prince Albert that appeared in the *Prince Albert Times and Saskatchewan Review* in June 1891 (and again in the *Manitoba Daily Free Press* in early July), and "From Prince Albert to P.E. Island," a travel essay about her return trip home to Prince Edward Island that appeared in the Charlottetown *Daily Patriot* that October and was the first of these non-fiction pieces to be signed "L.M. Montgomery." Next are several non-fiction pieces that Montgomery published in student publications at Prince of Wales College (where she completed her teacher training in 1894) and Dalhousie University (where she spent two terms taking courses in English literature in 1895–1896).[14]

One of the highlights in Montgomery's student publications is her essay entitled "A Girl's Place at Dalhousie College," which she published in the *Halifax Herald* as part of a multi-page segment entitled "The Thirty Sweet Girl Graduates of Dalhousie University." In this essay, Montgomery applauded the fact that social and institutional forces that barred women from attaining higher education had been lifted, to the point that "the 'higher education of

Montgomery in late adolescence, around the time she began to publish her work.

women' has passed into a common place phrase.... The way is made easy before her feet; there is no struggle to render her less sweet and womanly, and the society of to-day is proud of its 'sweet girl-graduates.'" The St. John *Progress*, which called Montgomery's piece "perhaps the most interesting article in the supplement," noted that "Miss Montgomery has just completed her first year at Dalhousie and has already shown great literary ability." But on the very day this issue of the *Halifax Herald* was released, Montgomery left Halifax to return to Prince Edward Island. Despite what she'd written about the relative lack of barriers that prevented women from obtaining higher education, her lack of financial support from her family made her unable to continue her undergraduate studies beyond her first year.[15]

Montgomery went back to Halifax five years later, this time as a reporter, editor, and proofreader for the *Halifax Daily Echo* and its sister paper, the *Morning Chronicle*. Part of her responsibilities involved writing "Around the Table," a weekly column signed Cynthia, who lived in a boarding house with roommates Polly, Ted, and Theodosia. These four people of ambiguous age did fun things like start an anti-slang society, play April's Fool jokes on each other, and discuss the most fashionable ways to dress hats. Through these characters, Montgomery parodied some of the grievances she had with modern life. "Polly has been reading a recently published volume of somebody's love-letters — I forget whose, but it doesn't matter," Cynthia writes in the column published on October 5, 1901. "As a result she has burned all hers — a very wise precaution. Nowadays, when we are bombarded with such literature, the people who preserve love-letters are only one degree less foolish than the people who write them." Cynthia concludes this column by writing wistfully about the lack of "time nowadays to inscribe our thoughts in friendly correspondence. Mostly we haven't time to even think the thoughts." Although I haven't come across any supplementary items in those papers that would indicate how the column was presented to readers, let alone received by them, the column itself occasionally shows one or more of the fictional characters breaking the fourth wall. In the instalment on February 3, 1902, Theodosia argues against the doctrine that being cheerful adds more cheerfulness into the world. "No, I shall never pretend to be cheerful when I don't really feel so. I have the right to indulge in a luxury of the dismal dumps now and then. Now, Cynthia, don't you go and put this in the *Echo* next week."[16]

— 3 —

At the same time that Montgomery published these non-fiction pieces, she also began finding success in the two literary forms that would become staples of her literary career: short fiction and poetry. She left no record, in her retrospective essays or in her journals, of her choice to experiment with several *noms de plume* — including Maud Eglinton, Maud Cavendish, and Joyce Cavendish — for some of her shorter publications, but her ultimate choice of "L.M. Montgomery" as her consistent signature gave her unusual freedom to publish for a wide range of gendered and age-based readerships. While as a novelist she would become internationally famous for her literary work centred on female characters, she contributed a significant amount of boy-oriented material to periodicals such as *Golden Days for Boys and Girls* of Philadelphia, the *Springfield Republican* of Massachusetts, *The Children's Visitor* of Nashville, *The Boys' World* of Chicago, and *The American Boy* of San Francisco. Many of these were formulaic stories about boys who learn some sort of lesson and are rewarded for their honesty, their sturdiness, and their commitment to a steadfast code of idealized boy behaviour with a promising job or are sent to college by rich bachelor uncles, and so they're fascinating as examples of a particular type of lesson-based short story that was popular in Montgomery's time. Several of her poems consisted of directive versions of the dominant values that were important for her boy characters to learn, including the emphatically entitled "Don't" (August 1907), which begins as follows:

> My lad, don't be one of the grumblers …
> The world doesn't like them, you see,
> And the boy who aspires to win it
> Bright, cheerful, and manly must be.[17]

Such didactic poems aren't typical of her overall literary output or even of her publications for children specifically. Still, it's worth noting that Montgomery didn't elect to publish material for children under a name separate from her publications for adults. In spite of her initial decision to publish under multiple names during the early years of her career, "L.M. Montgomery" soon became her consistent signature across multiple markets.

Although these poems for children promote a narrow ideal for boys and girls, it's in her poems published in periodicals for adults that her gender-neutral author identity allows for the greatest possibilities, such as in two poems published within four years of each other in *Munsey's Magazine* of

New York. In "If Love Should Come" (December 1897), the speaker tries to reconcile the gap between ambition and the potential for love, ultimately seeing each as incompatible with the other:

If love should come,
Against him would I dare to bar the door,
And, unregretful, bid him come no more?
Would stern ambition whisper to my heart,
"Love is a weakness — bid him hence depart,
For he and I can have no common home,"
If love should come?

And in "Comparisons" (April 1901), the speaker finds the object of desire's beauty even more enchanting than the allure of the natural world:

But your low laughter, 'longshore lass,
Is like a sea harp's melody,
And the vibrant tones of your tender voice
Are sweeter far to me![18]

Given that the object of desire in "If Love Should Come" has he/him pronouns and the object of desire in "Companions" is referred to as "lass," a heterosexual reading of these poems would presume that the speaker of the former poem is female and that the speaker of the latter poem is male. And yet, the fact that "If Love Should Come" was signed "L.M. Montgomery" was evidently a point of confusion for an unsigned commentator who published a response to this poem in the *Arizona Republican*: "The poet considers the probability of the admission of love against ambition and the result, when ambition should no longer stir the blood. He sang of an earthly love." In other words, a gender-ambiguous signature could open up the possibility of a queer or at least multi-faceted reading of these kinds of love poems.[19]

I haven't come across too many examples of published responses to Montgomery's poems or stories, but whenever I do, I'm fascinated by these early forms of literary criticism, especially when they occurred prior to her receiving a lot of media responses to her books. On June 26, 1906, the "Books and Reading" column of the New York *Evening Post* commented on a two-stanza poem of hers that appeared in the July issue of *Outing Magazine*: "It is rather a curious fact that midsummer as portrayed in prose is commonly a season of oppressive heat, when the animal man forgets his soul in attempt to keep cool, whereas in verse this is the season of abundant life and expansion." To illustrate this point, the article proceeded to quote the entire poem, which was called "Midsummer":

> The world is in its splendor of a lavish, fair outflowering,
> And in the idle valleys the dreams are thick and sweet,
> While every wind from golden west and purple south is showering
> The petals of the roses all about our gypsy feet.
>
> In every glen and dingle, in every poppied meadow,
> Is upgathered all the ripeness and the sweetness of the year;
> All the hills are drunk with sunshine, all the woodways
> pranked with shadow.
> Oh, the best that ever artist limned or poet sung is here![20]

Montgomery published an estimated five hundred poems across a fifty-year period, so locating copies, not to mention keeping track of them all, can be a daunting proposition. What's made this task even more challenging is that the digitization of newspapers has revealed just how frequently individual items were reprinted — sometimes anonymously. Her 1898 poem "Irrevocable," for instance, appeared in *The Congregationalist* (Boston) before being reprinted in well over a dozen newspapers between 1899 and 1901, including once without Montgomery's signature and under the title "Beyond Recall," in the *Brown County World* of Hiawatha, Kansas. Another burst of appearances of this poem as "Beyond Recall" starts in 1905, except that these versions are either unsigned or are attributed to Ewing Herbert, who owned the *Brown County World*.[21]

Meanwhile, her poem "An Old-Fashioned Woman," first published in that same magazine (by then known as *The Congregationalist and Christian*

Montgomery in 1909, shortly after the publication of *Anne of Green Gables*.

*World*) in August 1901, reappeared more than 150 times in daily newspapers all over the world, under a variety of titles, with or without her signature. This poem, which refers to home as a woman's "kingdom" and praises "her divinest motherhood," apparently struck a chord with newspaper editors, who at this time would most likely have been men. This is demonstrated not only by the sheer frequency with which this poem reappeared but also by occasional editorial comments that accompanied it. "We hear so much about the 20th century woman," declared an unsigned article in the *Lowell*

*Sun* of Massachusetts in March 1903, "that we almost wish for the good old days when women did not essay to rival the men in the various fields in industrial effort." This commentator added by way of introducing the poem, "At such a time the following lines will be refreshing." But when the *Northern Wisconsin Advertiser* reprinted this poem as "The Home-Woman" in November 1901, the poem appeared two columns away from an article entitled "Women Replace Men: They Make Better Tellers in Savings Banks," which appeared with comments from the unnamed head of the savings department at a Chicago bank, who claimed that "the girls do the work more satisfactorily" than the men who'd recently been let go:

> "We do not take the girls because we want to displace the men. Our boys are a good lot of willing workers, but we find that the girls do the work in the savings department better. We have not considered putting any of them in the commercial line.
>
> "They get the same pay the men do and are satisfactory because they keep regular hours, and are willing to work here, and we like to have them.
>
> "There is no flirting. The girls have no time for it, and customers do not try it any more than they try to flirt with the women who sell tickets at the elevated stations."[22]

It's impossible to guess now whether the Boston periodical sold reprint rights to these poems or if it was just common practice for newspapers to reprint material from magazines when they needed a bit more content, and the legality of either scenario is hard to measure. Regardless, Montgomery likely had no knowledge of how widely these pieces recirculated or how they sometimes contributed to public debates about gender, love, and the workplace.

— **4** —

Similar surprises abound when it comes to Montgomery's published short stories. Overall, these items reflect her willingness to conform to the expectations of the periodicals she published in, which isn't surprising given that she wrote to earn a living. But while she published as many as fifty stories some years, she also had a habit of republishing the same story years, if not decades, after its initial publication, with only minor revisions. Several stories are also notable because they consist of early incarnations of well-known characters or situations that would appear in altered form in her novels. Much like the adolescent Montgomery's strategy to narrate local legends as poetry and again as prose, there are innumerable instances of key details from her books that originated in her shorter works, something that's been amply demonstrated in the volumes of The L.M. Montgomery Library released so far. Two more stories that I located recently in *Days of Youth* of Cincinnati also anticipate key scenes in *Anne of Green Gables*.

Published in July 1904, "Marian's Choice" centres on an adolescent orphan who's been raised by her aunt Frances. She'd love to attend "the Academy of Design, in town," but there's no way her aunt can afford to send her. Instead, she's been offered a teaching position at a school nearby, but she seems to be under the impression that teaching would require her to abandon her own ambitions as a visual artist.

> The tears came into Marian's brown eyes. "I don't like the idea of teaching," she said in a trembling voice. "But there! As you say, there is nothing else to do. I must give up all my ambitions and hopes right away. I do wish we weren't so poor! Em Craig's going to the Academy of Design next winter, and her drawings don't begin to be as good as mine."
>
> Miss Frances winced. Marian did not know how deeply her words cut. She was a thoughtless girl, although warm-hearted and generous in the main. Just now she felt herself very ill used and disappointed.

A neighbour named Mrs. Lewis, who "prided herself on her common sense," persuades Frances to reach out to Marian's long-estranged paternal relatives for financial assistance, but Marian's uncle, "a pompous, portly man with 'Railroad President' written all over him," offers instead to adopt Marian as his daughter. Marian's inclined to accept, especially when her uncle offers to pay off the balance of her aunt's mortgage while he's at it, but that night, as Marian sits by her window and ponders her future, the sound of her aunt sobbing in her own room makes her decide not only to decline her uncle's offer but also to give up any idea of going away to study art. "I'm not, and never will be, sorry I refused Uncle Rutherford's offer," she tells her aunt, "but I'm glad he came and made it — because it has opened my eyes to lots of things that it is good for me to understand."[23]

Published four years after "Marian's Choice," *Anne of Green Gables* ends with sixteen-year-old Anne likewise deciding to turn down a scholarship to attend university in order to stay home with the older woman who raised her, but Montgomery made several changes in her novel when she revisited this storyline. While Anne's motivation for getting an undergraduate degree is less goal-oriented than Marian's for going to a design school, she ends up realizing on her own her responsibility toward her guardian due to changing circumstances (Matthew's death and Marilla's declining eyesight) rather than as a result of a tantalizing offer from another character. And although the narrator of *Anne of Green Gables* does a bit of moralizing when mentioning that Anne "had looked her duty courageously in the face and found it a friend — as duty ever is when we meet it frankly," Anne frames her decision to stay home and teach as evidence of being flexible with her plans. "I'm just as ambitious as ever. Only, I've changed the object of my ambitions." Although the idea of a girl giving up the chance to get an education in order to stay home may seem regressive now, the novel frames Anne's decision as one that will allow her to thrive intellectually and, as a teacher, to be the household's primary breadwinner to boot.[24]

Next, in "The Prize Competition," published in September 1907, fourteen-year-old Fred Cairns has painstakingly written an essay for a prize competition on "My Aim in Life." His mother reminds him that "if you have done your best,... your work will bring its own reward whether you win the prize or not," but Fred has a particular reason for wanting to win: the cash award would allow them to pay for an operation that would help his disabled sister, Hetty. Fred is crushed when Arnold Owen wins the prize, "but he was a manly lad," as the narrator remarks, and he joins the others in congratulating the winner. Later, Arnold reads his prize-winning essay aloud at the award ceremony, but although Fred realizes he's read this essay before, he decides to say nothing about it.

A few weeks later, while Fred is home alone, Arnold bursts in with urgent news about his little sister. "'Minnie has the croup,' gasped Arnold. 'She's awful bad, and there's no one home but the servant girl and me.... There's nobody handy — everybody within a mile is away — everybody who would know what to do. Mary is frightened to death — and oh, if Minnie should die!'" Fred saves Minnie's life, but not by administering ipecac like Anne does in the novel. Instead, he risks his own life by sailing across the bay in stormy weather in search of the doctor. In the end, Arnold confesses the truth to Fred about the essay, and Arnold's respect for Fred increases when Fred admits that he recognized the plagiarized essay but said nothing because he's "not a telltale." But when Arnold vows to come clean about what he did, Fred intervenes so that, although the prize money will go to him instead, Arnold won't be disgraced publicly. The story ends as many didactic stories do, with the wrongdoer announcing what lessons have been learned: "I've made a resolution to keep fair and square and straight for ever more in everything. That is going to be my 'aim in life.'"[25]

Besides Montgomery's youth-oriented short stories, she published a good many stories about adult characters. But while many of these depict rocky courtships that nevertheless end in wedding bells, every once in a while she went against the grain in her romance plots. In "Mock Sunshine," published in *The Home Journal* (New York) in February 1900, thirty-year-old Miriam North receives a marriage proposal from Will Harper, a distant cousin who's a decade younger than she is, but she's disinclined to take him seriously: "You foolish boy! Why won't you stop talking such nonsense? I've told you often enough I'm too old for you to marry. It would never do. Why, you're just a boy, Will, and I — I am an old maid." The only compromise she'll agree to is that if he feels the same way once he's returned home from a school year at college and asks her again, she'll give him an answer. But on the night of his return, she dresses with the intention of accepting his proposal, only to discover that during his time away he fell in love with the daughter of his Greek professor.[26]

"Mock Sunshine" ends with Miriam pretending to forgive Will for his past "folly" and then sobbing by herself in her room, and it's unclear what kind of moral, if any, this story points to. But it would be a mistake to assume that Montgomery's fiction for adult readers was never as didactic as her work for youth readers could be.

In "A Passing Confidence," published in *The Ladies' World* (New York) sometime around 1904, Persis Sheraton, the envied wife of a millionaire, confides to a seemingly much happier woman about her decision to leave her husband. "He drinks and gambles and — and — " But that's not all. "This morning — the anniversary of our wedding day — he swore at me. I *despise* him — and yet I love him still. And that seems to humiliate me more than all the rest." To her astonishment, her new friend (whose name is never revealed) admits that she went through something similar with her own husband, but with an important difference in attitude.

> I just kept on loving him and believing in him.... I wouldn't let myself think evil of him. I felt down in my heart that it would all come right sometime if I was a good, true wife to him. So I tried my best to be that.... I felt that the Jim I had supposed him to be was the *real* Jim — and that if it hadn't been possible for him to be that, I would never have believed him to be it. So I thought I must hold fast to that real self of him, and if *he* didn't live up to it *I* would. And after a long time it all came right.

The takeaway message here seems to be that if Persis is miserable in her marriage, it must be *her* fault her husband mistreats her. In the end, Persis blames herself for "the years of recrimination and bickering," then returns home and apologizes to her husband for being "too hard" on him, the fact that he swore at her that morning apparently being forgotten.[27]

Perhaps even more than with her poetry, Montgomery's published short fiction consists of the work of a writer who wrote material that would fulfill the expectations of the marketplace. Many of the plots are formulaic, and the relative brevity of a short story gave her far less space in which to develop complex characters the way she did later in her books. While few readers would consider this body of work to consist of five hundred literary masterpieces, her short stories are nevertheless fascinating in terms of being a resource she drew on frequently and liberally when she developed material for her books, and every once in a while, she found a way to get around formula and archetype and to insert humorous or subversive moments for which she's well known today.

— 5 —

*Anne of Green Gables* was Montgomery's first *published* novel, but in a journal entry dated July 16, 1925, she admitted that it had not been her first attempt at writing one. Prompted by her reading about an author who'd described "a book he had once hoped to write and never would," she described three books she'd planned to write as a teenager: one about two girls who attempt to run a P.E.I. farm by themselves, one about the thwarted love affair between a French Canadian hired man and the daughter of his employer, and one involving a split in a country church after an older minister is replaced by a younger one. She also mentioned a book-length work of fiction that she'd written for the Sunday school market "back I think in '99 or '00": "It was called *A Golden Carol* — a title punned from the name of the heroine, 'Carol Golden,' who was a girl at Halifax Ladies' College when the story opened. Summoned home suddenly by the death of her mother she had to stay there, rebelliously, to keep house for her father and young brother 'Bobbles,' who supplied the comedy relief to Carol's struggles and trials — said struggles of course culminating in a victory over self and a determination to live up to the college distortion of her name and make life 'a golden Carol.'" Montgomery still held the belief that her manuscript had been on par with similar books written for this market, but after failing to find a buyer for it either as a novel or as a seven-chapter fiction serial, she burned all copies of it and vowed that "never again would I try to create a Sunday School heroine." And in the time since, she'd come to see her supposed failure to find a publisher as a blessing in disguise.[28]

What Montgomery overlooked in this journal entry was that in April 1900, she'd published a short story in the Philadelphia *Times* entitled "An Invitation Given on Impulse," which featured a character named Carol Golden. Carol — or "Golden Carol, as her particular friends sometimes called her, partly because of her beautiful voice, and partly because of her wonderful fleece of golden hair" — is a popular girl at Oaklawn seminary who receives a letter from her mother giving her the go-ahead to invite a friend to go home with her for the holidays. Her plan is to invite Maud Russell, "the cleverest and prettiest girl at Oaklawn" and "undoubtedly the richest," but when she learns that sullen, friendless classmate Ruth Mannering has nowhere to go, her conscience nags her until she invites Ruth instead. Soon, Carol is astounded by the change in Ruth, which is described but never shown: "Under the influence of kindness and pleasure Ruth seemed transformed into a different person. Her shyness and reserve melted away in the sunny atmosphere of the Golden home ... and, if she did not make the social sensation that pretty Maud Russell might have made, the Goldens all liked her and Carol was content." In the end, a ringing doorbell reveals the Goldens' family friend Mr. Swift, who's kind and rich and who turns out to be the much older half-brother of Ruth's recently deceased mother.

This story, which anticipates the plot strands involving Katherine Brooke and Lewis Allen in *Anne of Windy Poplars* (1936), doesn't resemble in any way the plot of *A Golden Carol* that Montgomery described in her 1925 journal entry. But the character is certainly here, as is the kind of moralizing that Montgomery claimed to have woven into the book-length manuscript in order to make it conform to the expectations of a Sunday school publication. This is shown in the story's closing paragraph, in which Carol articulates to her mother how fortunate she feels about her own role in this turn of events: "Just think, mother, if I had not asked Ruth to come here, this would not have happened. And I didn't want to! I wanted to ask Maud so much, and I was dreadfully disappointed when I couldn't — for I really couldn't. I could not help remembering the look in Ruth's eyes when she said that she had no home to go to, and so I asked her instead of Maud. How dreadful it would have been if I hadn't."[29]

— 6 —

The number of shorter works that Montgomery wrote during her career is impossible to estimate given that so little of this work survives in manuscript and typescript form, but the number of shorter works that she *published* prior to the start of 1908, the year *Anne of Green Gables* appeared, totalled three hundred poems and at least 340 short stories. As Montgomery described her work as a freelance writer during this period, "Every year new magazines opened their portals to the wayfarer on thorny literary paths. I gradually built up a clientele of editors on whom I could depend for a comfortable livelihood if I wrote just what they wanted and sawed it off into suitable lengths." Still, these requirements meant that her writing still didn't measure up to "the visionary gleam" mentioned in Wordsworth's poem. "It was not all I wanted — not what I had dreamed of … in years agone."[30] Sometime in 1904 or 1905 — the dates vary from one retrospective account to another — Montgomery began a new project that, as she narrated it in "The Alpine Path," "really all just 'happened.'"

> I had always kept a notebook in which I jotted down, as they occurred to me, ideas for plots, incidents, characters, and descriptions. In the spring of 1904 I was looking over this notebook in search of some idea for a short serial I wanted to write for a certain Sunday School paper. I found a faded entry, written many years before: "Elderly couple apply to orphan asylum for a boy. By mistake a girl is sent them." I thought this would do. I began to block out the chapters, devise and select incidents and "brood up" my heroine. Anne — she was not so named of malice aforethought, but flashed into my fancy already christened, even to the all-important "e" — began to expand in such a fashion that she soon seemed very real to me and took

> possession of me to an unusual extent. She appealed to me, and I thought it rather a shame to waste her on an ephemeral little serial. Then the thought came, "Write a book. You have the central idea. All you need do is to spread it out over enough chapters to amount to a book."
>
> The result was *Anne of Green Gables*.[31]

And it changed everything.

# 3

# Such Simple Little Tales

— 1 —

When L.M. Montgomery received her first copy of *Anne of Green Gables*, she wrote in a journal entry dated June 20, 1908, of her experience of holding in her hands "the material realization of all the dreams and hopes and ambitions and struggles of my whole conscious existence — my first book! Not a great book at all — but *mine, mine, mine,* — something to which *I* had given birth — something which, but for me, would never have existed."[1] By this point, Montgomery had been publishing short stories, poems, and miscellaneous pieces for almost two decades, so the experience of seeing her name in print was hardly new to her. But publishing a book marked a major benchmark in her career as a writer, not only because her earnings would be in direct proportion to the number of copies sold rather than consist of whatever flat fee editors offered her, but also because it would lead to several aspects of a writer's life that for the most part she'd avoided up to this point: publicity, visibility, criticism, and reviews. While she succeeded in keeping her wits about her in public, she commented in her journal how frequently she was taken aback by the attention she began to receive.

Montgomery couldn't have known, on the day she received her first copy of *Anne of Green Gables*, what her new reality as a writer would look like. But her poem entitled "Let Us Walk with Morning," published coincidentally the same day, begins with an invitation to meet the unknown with curiosity and confidence.

> Come, let us walk with the morning, let us go to meet its glory
> Down through uncharted valleys where haply a thrush may sing,
> For us the young dawn will bloom over seas that in mist are hidden,
> And the wind will pipe in the pines, like a joyous unfettered thing.[2]

Even though Montgomery felt the need to undercut the quality of her writing even at this momentous occasion, the response from the reading public far exceeded everyone's expectations. On June 27, the *Boston Herald* reported that Montgomery's publisher, L.C. Page and Company, had ordered a second printing of the book, the first printing having run out after ten days. It's impossible to guess just how many copies were in that first printing, but the fact that it sold out so quickly proves that Page had seriously underestimated the sales potential of this book. That same newspaper reported on the book's third printing in mid-August, and two weeks later, it announced the fourth printing of "that winsome story by L.M. Montgomery" that "has been so constantly in demand by readers that it has been difficult to keep pace with orders."[3]

Moreover, ads and celebrity endorsements praised the book to the skies, as did most reviews. But given how frequently Montgomery's books are now found in the children's section of bookstores and libraries, what may be surprising was that most of the initial media coverage for the book predicted how enjoyable the book would be for readers of any age or took for granted that this book about an eleven-year-old orphan was aimed at adult readers or at an all-ages readership. In doing so, this coverage took its cues from the official publisher's description:

> Every one, young or old, who reads the story of "Anne of Green Gables," will fall in love with her, and tell their friends of her irresistible charm. In her creation of the young heroine of this delightful tale Miss Montgomery will receive praise for her fine sympathy with and delicate appreciation of sensitive and imaginative girlhood.
>
> The story would take rank for the character of Anne alone; but in the delineation of the characters of the old farmer, and his crabbed, dried-up spinster sister who adopt her, the author has shown an insight and descriptive power which add much to the fascination of the book.[4]

Accordingly, then, praise for the book appeared in some unexpected places. "To those who like the simple and appealing, the clean and wholesome, the cheerful and inspiring in literature, this book will be a delight, and Canadians should be proud of an author who can arouse these finer feelings," declared the September 1908 issue of *The Busy Man's Magazine* of Toronto. The following month, this magazine referred to Montgomery's "charming story" that "has been so well received in many quarters" as evidence of their contention that her Boston publishers had "made a notable name for themselves as patrons of Canadian literature."[5]

To be fair, Montgomery herself seemed remarkably inconsistent about her book's intended audience. In a journal entry dated October 15, 1908, less than four months after the book's release, she reported incredulously that her novel had become a bestseller: "I *can't* believe that such a simple little tale, written in and of a simple P.E.I. farming settlement, with a juvenile audience in view, can really have scored out in the busy world." Yet, in a journal entry dated March 1, 1930, she took the opportunity to set the record straight concerning several misconceptions about her and her work: "One review said I had 'written *Anne of Green Gables* for children and *Anne of Avonlea* for adults and was mistaken in both.' I was not. I did not write *Green Gables* for children. And *Avonlea* was not written for anybody or any class but merely to carry on Anne's adventures for anybody who was interested in them."[6]

It may seem heretical to question the idea that *Anne of Green Gables* is a book for children, given that it's about a child, that most bookstores and libraries today shelve their copies in the children's section, and that many readers have fond memories of reading it when they were the same age as the character. And if *Anne of Green Gables* is *for* children, then that would make Anne a role model that the text invites real child readers to emulate, which seems ideal given how appealing she is as a character—at least until she grows up, according to some commentators. But that is not how the novel

Cover of the original edition of *Anne of Green Gables*, which depicts Anne as looking far older than the sixteen-year-old character at the end of the book. Cover illustration by George Gibbs.

was interpreted and talked about in the media when it was first published and that's not the only way to understand the book.

Despite Marilla's determination to transform Anne into a "model little girl of demure manners and prim deportment," arguably it's Marilla who evolves throughout the book, more than Anne. In chapter 7, entitled "Anne Says Her Prayers," Marilla is appalled to learn that Anne has only minimal understanding of their faith tradition, and she views the fact that praying isn't part of Anne's bedtime routine as "a terrible wicked thing" that's evidence of Anne being "a very bad little girl." Read one way, this chapter depicts Marilla's attempts to teach Anne about the basics of prayer according to how she understands it, coaching Anne about what to say and instructing her to kneel, and when this backfires, she vows to begin Anne's religious education the next day. But read another way, this chapter suggests that Marilla is the one with insufficient understanding. Marilla's been so well socialized into the dogmatic values of Avonlea Presbyterianism that she concludes that if Anne doesn't conform to those values already, she must be "wicked" and "bad." Her narrow view of what a prayer should consist of makes her miss what is authentic, spontaneous, and refreshing in what Anne does say, including the girl's fantasy of going alone into nature in order to "look up into the sky" and "just *feel* a prayer." Or, as M.G. Hesse put it in the introduction to a 1979 fiction anthology entitled *Childhood and Youth in Canadian Literature*, which reprints "Anne Says Her Prayers," this chapter suggests that "a young person's values may be superior to the unquestioning conformity of adults." But if that's the case, it's a lesson that's offered to *adult* readers, not to child readers.[7]

And later, when Anne shares her thoughts about her first experience of Sunday school — which begins with "I didn't like it a bit. It was horrid" and goes downhill from there — what surprises Marilla and ultimately prevents her from responding is that she realizes that Anne is *right*: "Marilla felt helplessly that all this should be sternly reproved, but she was hampered by the undeniable fact that some of the things Anne had said, especially about the minister's sermons and Mr. Bell's prayers, were what she herself had really thought deep down in her heart for years, but had never given expression to. It almost seemed to her that those secret, unuttered, critical thoughts had suddenly taken visible and accusing shape and form in the person of this outspoken morsel of neglected humanity."[8] Although for the most part the narrator follows Anne's perspective throughout the novel, at moments like these the narrator relates Marilla's point of view instead, giving readers access to what she *doesn't* say in response to Anne's speeches — and inviting readers to sympathize with Marilla's changing perspective.

One of Montgomery's tricks as a writer is to follow potentially subversive comments either by a more conventional response or an abrupt change of topic. In chapter 30 of *Anne of Green Gables*, for instance, Marilla brings up the fact that Anne's teacher just paid her a visit, to which Anne responds with a stream-of-consciousness monologue that veers from one topic to another without stopping for two pages. "Mrs. Lynde says Myrtle Bell is a blighted being. I asked Ruby Gillis why Myrtle was blighted, and Ruby said she guessed it was because her young man had gone back on her." There is no other mention anywhere of Myrtle Bell, so why this might be significant enough for Anne to repeat to Marilla is anyone's guess. And the very next chapter shows that even though Anne has matured considerably since her arrival at Green Gables, she continues to stir the pot with her questions.

> Why can't women be ministers, Marilla? I asked Mrs. Lynde that and she was shocked and said it would be a scandalous thing. She said there might be female ministers in the States and she believed there was, but thank goodness we hadn't got to that stage in Canada yet and she hoped we never would. But I don't see why. I think women would make splendid ministers. When there is a social to be got up or a church tea or anything else to raise money the women have to turn to and do the work. I'm sure Mrs. Lynde can pray every bit as well as Superintendent Bell and I've no doubt she could preach too with a little practice.[9]

Given that there's no response from Marilla about either Myrtle Bell or why the ministry is barred to women at this time and place and in their Protestant denomination, the novel leaves it up to readers to decide whether to carry on with the rest of Anne's speeches or to pause and reflect on the social norms she questions.

— 2 —

Despite Montgomery's willingness to discuss the origins of her book in public and in private, her attempts to do so ended up revealing little about how she'd written her work. "I revised and re-wrote and altered words until I nearly bewildered myself," she told her correspondent Ephraim Weber in a letter dated September 10, 1908, but given the absence of details, the best way to see what her process of writing and revision actually looked like would be to study her handwritten manuscripts. Fortunately, those for sixteen of Montgomery's books have survived, and interested readers now have access to editions of three books that transcribe her handwritten manuscripts. These consist of *Readying Rilla: L.M. Montgomery's Reworking of "Rilla of Ingleside"* (2016), edited by Elizabeth Waterston and Kate Waterston, followed by *Anne of Green Gables: The Original Manuscript* (2019) and *The Blue Castle: The Original Manuscript* (2024), both edited by Carolyn Strom Collins. These editions recreate Montgomery's experience of drafting and revising, which included her use of an alphanumerical system of notes for materials she added later. They also reveal some fascinating surprises in terms of characters' names: Montgomery initially named Anne's prospective best friend Laura, then Gertrude, before settling on Diana, whereas Valancy, the protagonist of *The Blue Castle*, was named Miranda until quite late in the revision process. And in *Rilla of Ingleside*, Sophia Crawford and Kenneth Ford began life as Caroline and Selwyn, respectively, whereas Dog Monday — whose name alludes to Man Friday, a character in Daniel Defoe's *Robinson Crusoe* — was initially called Jink, Jack, and Rags.[10]

Reading these editions reveals some fascinating discrepancies with the published texts, but in Montgomery's case, the two intermediate stages of a book's creation — the author's typescript and the publisher's page proofs, sent back to the author for correction and approval — ended up back in the publisher's hands and were subsequently discarded. And, of course, reading these editions can't replicate the experience of handling the original manuscripts, which allows readers to trace shifts in Montgomery's mood based on the legibility of her handwriting or examining what's on the other side of the sheets of paper she wrote on. Fortunately, interested readers can now do just that, at least on their screens, thanks to Emily Woster's curated digital humanities website, The Anne of Green Gables Manuscript: L.M. Montgomery and the Creation of Anne, available at annemanuscript.ca.

But while the handwritten manuscript of *Anne of Green Gables* offers a record of *how* she wrote her manuscript, it can't account for *why* she made the creative choices she did. The ending of the novel, which depicts Anne declining a scholarship to Redmond College in order to stay home with Marilla and agreeing to be friends with Gilbert, is disappointing to a lot of readers, either those who don't like the idea of Anne sacrificing her future for a life of domesticity or those who yearned for a more definitive romantic resolution. But even though the ending appears to offer the promise that either part of Anne's story will develop along more satisfactory lines later on, Montgomery made it clear to Weber that she'd ended this novel with no thought of a sequel. "If I had known I was to be asked to write a second Anne book I wouldn't have 'ended' it at all but just 'stopped.' However, I didn't know and so finished it up as best I could."[11] And so, much like in her short story "Marian's Choice," in which Marian realizes that staying at home with the person who raised her is more important than any professional ambition, Montgomery evidently meant to end Anne's development with a form of self-sacrifice that was entirely on her own terms.

Montgomery's chosen resolution for *Anne of Green Gables* may lead to mixed reactions from readers, but it's important to view it as a response to its author's own circumstances. When she decided, a decade earlier, to return to Cavendish in order to care for her grandmother and to write full-time after her grandfather's death, she did so with full knowledge of the fact that this arrangement wouldn't be permanent. Her grandfather's will bequeathed the house to one of his sons, who lived nearby, but added the provision that his widow could remain in the house for the rest of her life. If anything, Montgomery's willingness to stay with her grandmother led to some animosity from that uncle and some of his family members, who saw her as blocking their attempts to take the house sooner on the pretext that her grandmother couldn't manage on her own. And so, the resolution of *Anne of Green Gables* — in which two single women had the freedom to continue living together without interference from any man — was not, as it may seem in some ways today, a way to reinforce the status quo about women and domesticity. Given that Montgomery was living with the certainty that she'd be out of a home as soon as her grandmother died, in a kind of community in which unmarried women had few to no options for living independently, her novel's ending was, in fact, revolutionary.

— 3 —

In the last volume of my three-volume critical anthology *The L.M. Montgomery Reader*, subtitled *A Legacy in Review*, I included the full text of twenty-two reviews of *Anne of Green Gables*, almost all of them overwhelmingly positive. One of the outliers was the *New York Times*, which called Anne "one of the most extraordinary girls that ever came out of an ink pot," but not in a particularly positive way. "The author undoubtedly meant her to be queer, but she is altogether too queer." (In 1996, this newspaper included its 1908 review of *Anne of Green Gables* as one of several past reviews that had trashed books that turned out to be classics, in a segment entitled "Oops!")[12] Besides being full of praise, most reviews followed a recurring pattern in their treatment of Montgomery's novel, describing it as intended for adult readers but suitable for readers of all ages.

And when the novel appeared in a U.K. edition early in 1909, commentators followed the precedent set by their counterparts in North America in declining to limit the book's target audience by age or gender. Just as the first known mention of *Anne of Green Gables* in the North American press — a listing in the February 29, 1908, issue of *The Publishers' Weekly* — referred to the novel simply as "a story of character," London's *The Athenaeum* included the novel in its list of new books under "fiction," not "juvenile books," and called it "the story of an imaginative, talkative, and perplexing child." Of course, the fact that Montgomery's novel had appeared first in the United States led some English commentators to assume it was set there — *The Bookseller* of London referred to "this very remarkable portrait study of a young American girl" — but even so, it predicted that Anne "is sure to make as many friends in England as she has in America. It is a book to be read, and when read will not be very soon forgotten."[13]

In a sense, this shared assumption in England shouldn't be surprising, since it followed the English publisher's description, which likewise gave no indication that this novel was intended for readers of any age or any gender:

> The story of an imaginative child, growing up among the most prosaic people, to whom she was at once a delight and a puzzle, is here told by Miss Montgomery. In it there is a blend of pathos and humour. The plot is of the simplest; the setting is of the homeliest. As a picture of the life of everyday folk in a district of Canada it is convincing, but it all might happen in any country, for the only conditions that are required are the development of an imaginative girl, and the ever increasing affection for her on the part of her bewildered foster-parents and neighbours.[14]

And so, several English reviews, like those in North American periodicals, endorsed the book not only for its ability to appeal to readers of all ages but also for its superior literary quality. The *Daily Telegraph* of London "heartily recommend[ed] this book to old and young, feeling sure that they will revel in it, and recognise in it a piece of work which is quite uncommonly good, as well as thoroughly interesting from the first page to the last." The *London World* suggested that the novel was "destined to live as long as 'Alice in Wonderland' and 'Little Women' and one or two other delightful studies of girlhood," adding that "it is better to have written one such book as this than to have produced a dozen novels of the ordinary type." And the London *Spectator*, which Montgomery viewed as "the biggest of all the 'big' literary reviews," praised the book to the skies, particularly the ending: "It needed considerable restraint on her part to leave off where she did without developing the romantic interest hinted at in the last chapter, but the result is so excellent that we trust she will refrain from running the greater risk of writing a sequel. Having sown her wild oats, 'the Anne-girl' could never be so attractive as the little witch, half imp, half angel, whose mental and spiritual growth is vividly set forth in these genial pages."[15]

It would be easy to assume that it was the spectacular success — critical *and* commercial — of *Anne of Green Gables* after its publication in June 1908 that led to the creation of several sequels. But as Montgomery's journals and letters reveal, the request for a sequel occurred in tandem with her signing her contract for the first book. Montgomery finished drafting the second book in early August 1908 and completed the revision and the typewriting by late October. But as it happens, her attempts to finish the sequel quickly in order to capitalize on the sales success of *Anne of Green Gables* proved unnecessary, for the simple fact that the high sales of the first book remained steady far longer than expected. A full-page ad on the cover of the December 26, 1908, issue of *The Publishers' Weekly* provided an explanation of what would happen next for Anne:

> Thousands of readers have been made happy by an acquaintance with the delightful ANNE OF GREEN GABLES. And each of these will in turn recommend or present the book to another friend. "You really must read it," passed from one friend to another accounts for ANNE'S tremendous popularity....
>
> No new book by Miss Montgomery will be published until ANNE AT AVONLEA, which will not appear until the Fall of 1909, and ANNE OF GREEN GABLES is bound to continue one of the best sellers of the Winter and Spring.[16]

Ultimately published as *Anne of Avonlea*, this second book begins only a few weeks after the ending of *Anne of Green Gables*, with sixteen-year-old Anne about to start teaching in the one-room schoolhouse she attended throughout the first book. But despite being only slightly older, the Anne of the second book is not quite as interesting or spontaneous as her younger self was, much as the *Spectator* feared, and Montgomery acknowledged that the process of writing and revising this second book hadn't been as organic as it had been for the first one, especially given the time constraints under which she'd written it. She also drew a fair bit on some of her periodical pieces: A lot of material about teaching, including the humorously wrong answers offered by Anne's students, first appeared in her 1894 sketch "Crooked Answers" and her 1901 sketch "Half an Hour with Canadian Mothers," whereas the early plot thread involving the mistaken identity of a Jersey cow originated in a short story she'd published a decade earlier entitled "Miss Marietta's Jersey," except in that version the Anne character ends up marrying the farmer in question.[17]

Illustration by George Gibbs of Anne Shirley, appearing as the frontispiece in the first edition of *Anne of Avonlea*.

Given that Page had requested a sequel of *Anne of Green Gables* as a matter of course at the contract signing stage, I have no doubt that as a result of the sheer popularity of the book, the prospect of a third title about Anne was soon on Page and Montgomery's radar. Perhaps this accounts for the fact that *Anne of Avonlea*, which for the most part sidelines Anne's evolving friendship with Gilbert, ends not with their romance but with the wedding between two middle-aged characters who reunite thanks to Anne's involvement after a quarrel thirty years earlier.

> "Yes, it's beautiful," said Gilbert, looking steadily down into Anne's uplifted face, "but wouldn't it have been more beautiful still, Anne, if there had been *no* separation or misunderstanding … if they had come hand in hand all the way through life, with no memories behind them but those which belonged to each other?"
>
> For a moment Anne's heart fluttered queerly and for the first time her eyes faltered under Gilbert's gaze and a rosy flush stained the paleness of her face. It was as if a veil that had hung before her inner consciousness had been lifted, giving to her view a revelation of unsuspected feelings and realities. Perhaps, after all, romance did not come into one's life with pomp and blare, like a gay knight riding down; perhaps it crept to one's side like an old friend through quiet ways; perhaps it revealed itself in seeming prose, until some sudden shaft of illumination flung athwart its pages betrayed the rhythm and the music; perhaps … perhaps … love unfolded naturally out of a beautiful friendship, as a golden-hearted rose slipping from its green sheath.
>
> Then the veil dropped again; but the Anne who walked up the dark lane was not quite the same Anne who had driven gaily down it the evening before. The page of girlhood had been turned, as by an unseen finger, and the page of womanhood was before her with all its charm and mystery, its pain and gladness.

In short, by ending *Anne of Avonlea* with just a momentary realization about Anne's love for Gilbert, Montgomery almost guaranteed that readers would express a desire for more. Unfortunately for them, by the time *Anne of Avonlea* appeared in September 1909, she'd just begun work on a new novel — to be called *The Story Girl*.[18]

— 4 —

Overall, reviews of *Anne of Avonlea* were as strong as those of *Green Gables* had been, although a recurring refrain was that the second book wasn't *quite* as interesting as the one that had preceded it. Moreover, the steady — and, if anything, growing — audience for the Anne books in some ways set Montgomery up to write anything she wanted. After all, as an ad for her third book in *The Bookseller, Newsdealer and Stationer* proclaimed, "The popularity of the author's previous stories … will insure for her new story a wide interest." As it happened, though, her work on *The Story Girl* progressed more slowly than her publisher wanted, so Page persuaded her to expand a nine-chapter fiction serial entitled "Una of the Garden," which had appeared in a magazine in late 1908 and into 1909. *Kilmeny of the Orchard*, the result of this endeavour, has proven to be one of Montgomery's least reprinted books, and there are several factors that account for this. First, despite Kilmeny's name appearing in the title, the book's protagonist is Eric Marshall, a twenty-four-year-old man of privilege who agrees to substitute for a school-teaching friend in a rural P.E.I. settlement. As such, it's through his perspective that the narrator depicts Kilmeny — beautiful, a talented musician, and mute — as well as the hot-tempered Italian boy who acts as the story's villain. And while the repeated use of the word "dumb" to refer to Kilmeny's inability to speak is certainly cringeworthy now, a study of several dictionaries from the half-century leading up to the book's publication shows that this word was widely understood as a neutral word for "mute," not as a word denoting lesser intelligence, and so it would have been less likely to offend. Still, Montgomery worried about how readers would react to the shift from a protagonist who talked too much to one who couldn't talk at all, not to mention that doubling the word count led to what she saw as a tremendous amount of filler. But the reviews were mostly positive — although not nearly as plentiful as those of her first two books — even if they sometimes disagreed with each other about its target readership. A pair of reviews from far-away New Zealand ably demonstrates this. Whereas *The Press* of Canterbury proclaimed that "there is a fresh wholesomeness about the book that is extremely pleasant, and that should win for 'Kilmeny' a host of admirers among the younger generation of novel readers," the *Otago Daily Times* saw things differently: "'Kilmeny' is one of the books that will not be appreciated by very young people. They crave action and life, fighting and adventure. They are themselves too young to know the charm of youth. It is only those who have passed it by who are able to appreciate what they have lost. It is those who tire in the noonday heat who love to dwell on the freshness of dawn; and we think that Eric Marshall, at 24, is too young to appreciate the rare charms of the orchard nymph."[19]

*The Story Girl,* which appeared in May 1911, seems at first glance to be an idealized story for young people, given that its eight child characters are between the ages of eleven and fourteen. And unlike *Anne of Green Gables,* which depicted Anne maturing from eleven to sixteen, this novel takes place over a single summer. This book also departs from the expectations created by the first three in terms of its use of a first-person narrator who not only is male but also is looking back on this childhood summer from the vantage point of middle age. These are all factors that contribute to making *The Story Girl* echo the notion put forth by the *Otago Daily Times* that Montgomery's books would be best appreciated by readers who were no longer young. Narrator Beverley King suggests as much when he recalls the Story Girl, otherwise known as Sara Stanley, persisting in her belief in fairies:

> There is such a place as fairyland — but only children can find the way to it. And they do not know that it is fairyland until they have grown so old that they forget the way. One bitter day, when they seek it and cannot find it, they realize what they have lost; and that is the tragedy of life. On that day the gates of Eden are shut behind them and the age of gold is over. Henceforth they must dwell in the common

> light of common day. Only a few, who remain children at heart, can ever find that fair, lost path again; and blessed are they above mortals. They, and only they, can bring us tidings from that dear country where we once sojourned and from which we must evermore be exiles. The world calls them its singers and poets and artists and story-tellers; but they are just people who have never forgotten the way to fairyland.[20]

*The Story Girl* is the first of Montgomery's novels I ever read, and I did so at fourteen, the same age as the title character. And while I don't recall my first impression of what this excerpt seemed to suggest about the differences between childhood and adulthood, I sometimes wonder how far this book contributed to ruining the surprise.

When Montgomery finished writing *The Story Girl*, she deemed it far superior to *Anne of Green Gables* in terms of its literary quality, something that the Canada Drug and Book Company echoed in an ad, published in the *Daily News* of Nelson, B.C.: "The previous books by this author have all been good but this is the best." In making this statement, this ad echoed a prediction made in *The Youth's Companion* a few months earlier, namely that Kilmeny Gordon would "prove as dear to the hearts of old and young readers alike as did her predecessor, Anne Shirley." And by this point, Montgomery had achieved such an admirable track record that it led to a delayed publication date, as the *Montreal Daily Star* noted in its "Book Chat and Anecdote" column, due to "the size of an unusually large first edition, to be simultaneously published in the United States, Canada, Great Britain and Australia."[21]

Still, Montgomery sensed that *The Story Girl* wouldn't equal her first book in terms of its popularity, and in this respect she was right. When the Page Company published *Anne of the Island* in 1915, its advertising included sales figures of Montgomery's "previous successes," measured in units of one thousand copies: 310th thousand for *Anne of Green Gables*, 109th thousand for *Anne of Avonlea*, 33rd thousand for *Chronicles of Avonlea*, 45th thousand for *Kilmeny of the Orchard* and for *The Story Girl*, and 27th thousand for

*The Golden Road.* While the discrepancies in these figures can be accounted for in part by the fact that *Anne of Green Gables* had been published seven years earlier, these early numbers make it clear that back then, as now, Montgomery's first novel remained by far her strongest seller.[22]

— 5 —

By the time *The Story Girl* was released to the public, Montgomery had other things to worry about than book sales. In March 1911, her maternal grandmother died of pneumonia, an event that set in motion a whirlwind of changes that left Montgomery with barely any time to write journal entries, let alone creative work: She packed up her belongings, said good-bye to Cavendish, and headed to nearby Park Corner to await the beginning of the next chapter of her life — as a Presbyterian minister's wife who would no longer call Prince Edward Island home. Only after she'd settled in her new home in Ontario did she have the chance to resume work on the project she'd started before her grandmother's death, again at her publisher's suggestion: rewriting some of her short stories to fit the general setting of Avonlea. One aspect of her task that she was less thrilled about was her publisher's pressure to weave in Anne at every possible opportunity.

In the end, Anne appears only briefly in *Chronicles of Avonlea*, most prominently in the opening short story, "The Hurrying of Ludovic," published in its original incarnation in 1905. But while the Anne who appears in the stories is in her early twenties, several more stories make reference to her as a child who's just as innocently disruptive as she appears in *Anne of Green Gables*. In "The Quarantine at Alexander Abraham's," Miss Peter MacPherson opts to teach a Sunday school of boys because the girls' class has Anne among its pupils, and Anne is "the one living human being that I was afraid of" due to her "habit of asking weird, unexpected questions, which a Philadelphia lawyer couldn't answer." In "Each in His Own Tongue," the experience of listening to child prodigy Felix Moore play the violin reminds Abel Blair of Anne, "a little girl" who "lived with the Cuthberts down at Avonlea":

> We got into a conversation at Blair's store. She could talk a blue streak to anyone, that girl could. I happened to say about something that it didn't matter to a battered old hulk of sixty odd like me. She looked at me with her big, innocent eyes, a little reproachful like, as if I'd said something awful heretical. "Don't you think, Mr. Blair," she says, "that the older we get the more things ought to matter to us?" — as grave as if she'd been a hundred instead of eleven. "Things matter *so* much to me now," she says, clasping her hands thisaway, "and I'm sure that when I'm sixty they'll matter just five times as much to me." Well, the way she looked and the way she spoke made me feel downright ashamed of myself because things had stopped mattering with me.

And the last story, "The End of a Quarrel," depicts Nancy Rogerson returning to Avonlea after working elsewhere for twenty years as a nurse and confiding in her cousin Louisa that although she hates being an old maid, getting married holds no appeal for her either. "Do you remember that story Anne Shirley used to tell long ago of the pupil who wanted to be a widow because 'if you were married your husband bossed you and if you weren't married people called you an old maid?' Well, that is precisely my opinion. I'd like to be a widow. Then I'd have the freedom of the unmarried, with the kudos of the married. I could eat my cake and have it, too. Oh, to be a widow!"[23]

By contrasting Anne in her twenties with the more disruptive child of the past, the collection makes Anne's potentially subversive commentary easier to digest. Although Montgomery had no interest in making Anne even more prominent in the collection than she had already, she did revise far more stories than could reasonably fit into a single volume, leaving her publisher to select and arrange the material. She'd have reason to regret this later on, but given the kudos she received for this book as a collection of linked short stories, it proved to be one of Page's better suggestions.

# 4

# In Lands Afar

— 1 —

In "The Alpine Path," published in six instalments in *Everywoman's World* of Toronto in 1917, L.M. Montgomery made a rather revealing statement about her attachment to her home province. "Prince Edward Island … is really a beautiful Province — the most beautiful place in America, I believe. Elsewhere are more lavish landscapes and grander scenery; but for chaste, restful loveliness it is unsurpassed." She also suggested that this attachment for P.E.I. was part of a collective phenomenon: "Great is our love for it; its tang gets into our blood; its siren call rings ever in our ears; and no matter where we wander in lands afar, the murmur of its waves ever summons us back in our dreams to the homeland." Only in the final paragraphs of this memoir did she mention her own move six years earlier to a "land afar," and her phrasing signals to attentive readers that this departure hadn't been her choice: "As my husband was pastor of an Ontario congregation, I had now to leave Prince Edward Island and move to Ontario."[1]

What's equally remarkable about the end of this memoir is Montgomery's decision not to name her husband, identify the Ontario congregation in question, or say anything at all about her six years in Ontario besides the titles of the books she'd published during that time. Moreover, the twenty photographs and captions that accompanied her text included on the final page snapshots that are captioned "Chester" and "Stuart," but nothing in the text identifies these lads as her sons.[2]

To me, these omissions indicate three aspects of her writing life that were entirely separate from her private life. First, as Montgomery biographer Mary Henley Rubio suggests, "[Montgomery's] love for the Island was undoubtedly intensified by her sense of loss in leaving it." Second, as Montgomery retorted years later to a vacationer to the island who'd written to the Charlottetown *Guardian* to question the accuracy of her depiction of Islanders in her later novel *Magic for Marigold*, "I was born and brought up in the very heart of three of our old 'pioneer' clans, and I know them from A to Z," and this knowledge didn't carry over to the population of Ontario, with its own ethnic, linguistic, religious, and class hierarchies and histories.[3] The third has to do with Montgomery's decision to end her celebrity memoir not with the publication of her first book (as might be expected in a writer's memoir) or with her marriage (as might be expected in a memoir by a woman, especially at this time), but with a travel narrative of her honeymoon in England and Scotland, followed by the announcement of her move to Ontario, which arguably signals to readers that she saw her move to Ontario as an ending of sorts in her writing life. Her phrasing captures none of the loss she felt over leaving her beloved island, but to be fair, Montgomery's mention in her journals of the necessity of moving to Ontario after her marriage is made with a similar lack of fanfare. "I felt badly over the prospect of leaving the Island. But since I had left Cavendish it did not matter so much."[4] If Montgomery ever considered breaking off this engagement in order to stay on Prince Edward Island as a financially independent writer, she did not ponder this in her journal.

And so, rather than consider her move to Ontario as a simple departure, it might be worth thinking about it as a form of expatriation — or, as the *Cleveland Plain Dealer* phrased it in 1932 when it provided a sketch of Montgomery's life in response to a reader's request for that information, Montgomery had "removed to Ontario" after her marriage. After all, intermingled with the beginning of her marriage and a considerable number of new responsibilities as a minister's wife was a sense of tremendous loss, not only of her grandmother but of the house that had been her home for almost as long as she could remember. Even while living with relatives in Park Corner, a mere twenty-two kilometres from Cavendish, between the death of her grandmother in March 1911 and her wedding in July, she recorded in a journal entry dated May 23, 1911, the feeling of being "haunted" by the conviction that she could "never write again."[5]

By the time these events had happened in 1911, she'd already gained a reputation for putting her native province on the literary map. As critic T.G. Marquis exclaimed in his 1913 overview of Canadian literature in English, Montgomery had made "Prince Edward Island, its inhabitants and external nature, known to the world as they never had been before." Even so, the *Toronto Star Weekly* commented on the setting of Montgomery's future books in a news report published merely three days after her wedding: "Here's wishing that Miss Montgomery ... will some day give us an Ontario novel, informed with real knowledge and full of the delicate charm with which she can always invest a tale."[6]

But she did not do this — at least, not for quite a while after her move.

In a journal entry dated January 28, 1912, almost a year after the date of her preceding entry, she recorded that the act of writing "Leaskdale" rather than "Cavendish" at the start of the entry still felt unreal to her. But as she narrated the events of the intervening time in retrospect, using as a basis some entries she'd written in a separate notebook, she recorded in passing one decision she'd made about her literary work: to continue writing as "L.M. Montgomery," which she termed "the name of my father, the name linked with the experiences of a lifetime, the name under which I have won my success." She said little else about her writing in this long retrospective entry, so it's unclear how firmly she'd already decided to continue with P.E.I. as a setting for her future work, a decision made for reasons she revealed in talks given in the 1930s. A 1937 newspaper article in the *Globe and Mail* quotes her as saying that "when I came to Ontario ... I thought it was not safe to lay the scene [of my books] in Ontario lest all my husband's congregation think they were in the book." And in a report of a talk she'd given in

1935, a University of Toronto student paper quoted her as offering a rather curious observation about the two provinces: "After living 24 years here, I still find Ontario drab and dull when I compare it with the colourful land of Prince Edward Island with its red roads, green grasses and blue sky." It's a rather innocuous remark, but someone among the newspaper staff evidently thought this was a major scoop, because the article appeared on the paper's front page under the title "L.M. Montgomery Finds Ontario Drab."[7]

— 2 —

According to that retrospective journal entry dated January 28, 1912, Montgomery had taken up her creative work again just recently. By this point, she was pregnant with her first child and busy with new responsibilities as a minister's wife and social functions with fellow writers in Toronto, and although she felt contented enough in her new home, she reported experiencing "agonizing hours of homesickness." Having her cat, Daffy, with her again helped her stay grounded in her connection to Cavendish, as did having enlarged photographs of the Cavendish landscape, including Lover's

Montgomery's personal library in her home in Leaskdale, Ontario, where she lived between 1911 and 1926.

Lane, on the walls of her library, but the effect was mixed: "I don't know whether [the photographs] delight or pain me most."[8]

Montgomery had difficulty adapting to this new place and these new circumstances — in terms of both her private life and her writing life. *Chronicles of Avonlea*, the first project she completed in her new home, appeared in July 1912, around the time she gave birth to her first son, Chester. Later, she reported that she hadn't enjoyed writing her next book, *The Golden Road*, amid constant interruptions due to competing responsibilities as a minister's wife and as the mother of a newborn. This book reunites the young characters from *The Story Girl*, but while the first book depicted the characters enjoying a golden summer together, the sequel emphasized the inevitability of change, given the way that the group is broken up by *three* fathers taking their children away. On the same day she received her author's copies of that book in September 1913, she recorded that she'd finally given in to the pressure to write another Anne book, about Anne's university career, which would be published in 1915 as *Anne of the Island*. But her enthusiasm for this return to Anne was negligible: in a letter to G.B. MacMillan dated September 13, 1913, she likened the project to "putting on a dress worn years ago, which, no matter how beautiful still, is something I have outgrown and find out of fashion with my later development." Her progress on the manuscript was stalled due to events that happened outside of her writing life: England declared war on Germany on August 5, 1914, and twelve days later, her second son, Hugh, died at birth. With great effort amid her grief, she managed to finish the manuscript in late November of that year.[9]

Because Montgomery tended to mention only her book-length projects in her journals, her comments about *The Golden Road* and *Anne of the Island* give the impression of a writer whose work is driven more by the pressures of deadlines and expectations than anything else. But three poems published during this time period offer a more nuanced picture of her frame of mind.

"The Exile," published in *Zion's Herald* of Boston in early 1913, depicts a speaker who declares that "this land of yours, be it never so fair, cannot be home to me." And while Montgomery's shorter works tended to downplay geographical specificity to make them more universal, this poem contains a number of visual details that bring to mind the landscape of Prince Edward Island:

> Ever my thoughts must be where my hungry heart is,
> Far away on shores that are very lone and gray,
> Where the hoarse waves dash on rocks that are black and rugged,
> And the wild, red sunrise flares over misty headland and bay —
> A harsh, bleak world to you of this golden shore;
> But were I there again, I would roam from it nevermore.[10]

In contrast, two poems published in 1914 focus on the yearning to return home. In "The Summons," the speaker travels from "the turbid city" to "my childhood's home" ("I hear the homeland summons / And I must follow far"). And in "When I Go Home Again," the fantasy of return involves not just a putting aside of "all bitterness of exiled years" but also a reunion with "my mother, with her tender eyes."[11]

But in the same retrospective journal entry in which she recorded her receipt of copies of *The Golden Road* and her decision to start a third Anne book, she also wrote about her own experience of returning to Cavendish — specifically the site of the Macneill homestead — for the first time since her marriage two years earlier. The discovery of her former home in disrepair and the fact that the old lane leading up to it had been replaced by a potato field were far more devastating than what she expressed in those three poems: "To me, the disappearance of that old lane had a symbolism all its own. It was not only that the way to the past was closed — it was altogether gone. Only on the wings of imagination could I revisit it — could I cross the gulf of time and change that yawned between me and the spot I loved."[12]

In short, the path to her beloved Cavendish home was now closed to her — literally and figuratively. And yet, she evidently wanted to continue setting her fiction in Prince Edward Island. What could she do, besides hang paintings of Cavendish scenery in her Leaskdale library, to nurture her imagination in the future?

— 3 —

In the midst of her transition from Prince Edward Island to Ontario in 1911, *The Canadian Magazine* of Toronto published four nature essays that Montgomery had written in mid-1909, each focusing on one of the four seasons in the woods. Elizabeth Rollins Epperly reads these four essays, set in a geographically non-specific location, as "memory pictures of her favourite home in nature, Lover's Lane" — a stretch of woods near her home in Cavendish that she'd made internationally famous by depicting a place with the same name in *Anne of Green Gables*. These essays are fascinating examples of creative non-fiction, the kind that Montgomery could easily have written more of or even developed into a book of essays, and I've often wondered how her literary reputation might have evolved differently had she done so. After all, in *Highways of Canadian Literature*, J.D. Logan and Donald G. French claimed that Montgomery's nature descriptions "reveal at once the author's intimacy with nature and her poetic attitude of mind."[13]

By the time I began preparing the text of these four essays to include in volume 1 of *The L.M. Montgomery Reader*, Epperly had preceded me in pointing out a curious connection between these Lover's Lane–inspired essays and Montgomery's novel *The Blue Castle* (1926), specifically concerning the work of Valancy Stirling's beloved nature writer, John Foster. As Epperly notes, "All six John Foster descriptive passages, together with half a dozen of the narrator's comments, are taken from [these] articles."[14] But as I started to read these essays more carefully, I couldn't manage to shake the feeling of déjà vu. Thanks to the search capabilities that are now possible in the digital age, I figured out that Montgomery repeated phrases, sentences, and often entire paragraphs from these four essays, with only minor changes, in almost all the books she wrote in Ontario — including *The Blue Castle*, which is set there.

Consider the following excerpt from "The Woods in Winter," which is the one of these four essays that contains an allusion to Wordsworth's phrase "the glory and the dream":

The beeches and maples are dignified matrons, even when stripped of their foliage; and the birches … look you at that row of them against the spruce hill, their white limbs gleaming through the fine purple mist of their twigs … are beautiful pagan maidens who have never lost the Eden secret of being naked and unashamed.

But the conebearers, stanch souls that they are, keep their secrets still. The firs and the pines and the spruces never reveal their mystery, never betray their long-guarded lore. See how beautiful is that thickly-growing copse of young firs, lightly powdered with the new-fallen snow, as if a veil of aerial lace had been tricksily flung over austere young druid priestesses forsworn to all such frivolities of vain adornment. Yet they wear it gracefully enough … firs can do anything gracefully, even to wringing their hands in the grip of a storm. The deciduous trees are always anguished and writhen and piteous in storms; but there is something in the conebearers akin to the storm spirit … something that leaps out to greet it and join with it in a wild, exultant revelry. After the first snowfall, however, the woods are at peace in their white loveliness. Today I paused at the entrance of a narrow path between upright ranks of beeches, and looked long adown it before I could commit what seemed the desecration of walking through it … so taintless and wonderful it seemed, like a street of pearl in the New Jerusalem. Every twig and spray was outlined in snow. The undergrowth along its sides was a little fairy forest cut out of marble. The shadows cast by the honey-tinted winter sunshine were fine and spirit-like. Every step I took revealed new enchantments, as if some ambitious elfin artificer were striving to show just how much could be done with nothing but snow in the hands of somebody who knew how to make use of it. A snowfall such as this is the finest test of beauty. Wherever there is any ugliness

> or distortion it shows mercilessly; but beauty and grace are added unto beauty and grace, even as unto him that hath shall be given abundantly.[15]

The phrase about birches reappears in chapter 10 of *Rilla of Ingleside* (1921). The sentences about firs and pines reappear in chapters 16 and 9 of *Emily Climbs* (1925). The phrase "at peace in their white loveliness" reappears in chapter 7 of *Mistress Pat* (1935). The phrase beginning with "taintless and wonderful" reappears in chapter 4 of *The Golden Road* (1913). The sentences starting with "every twig and spray" reappear in chapter 31 of *The Blue Castle*, in a scene in which Barney suggests to Valancy that they head back the way they came, as does the phrase about "tramping": "We must not commit the desecration of tramping through there." The sentences beginning with "every step I took" reappear in chapter 4 of *Mistress Pat*.[16]

In a few cases, these borrowings from the four nature essays are woven into more than simply description. Consider the following excerpt from "Spring in the Woods":

> Before us is a young poplar, the very embodiment of youth and spring in its litheness and symmetry and grace and aspiration. Its little leaves are hanging tremulously, but are not yet so fully blown as to hide its delicate development of bough and twig, making poetry against the spiritual tints of a spring sunset. It is so beautiful that it hurts us, with the pain inseparable from all perfection. Why is it so? Is it the pain of finality, the realisation that there can be nothing beyond but retrogression? Or is it the prisoned infinite in us calling out to its kindred infinite expressed in that visible perfection?[17]

In chapter 26 of *Anne's House of Dreams* (1917), Owen Ford points to "a slender shapely young aspen" in an attempt to change the subject of a tense conversation. "Isn't it beautiful?" he asks Anne.

> "It's so beautiful that it hurts me," said Anne softly. "Perfect things like that alway[s] did hurt me — I remember I called it 'the queer ache' when I was a child. What is the reason that pain like this seems inseparable from perfection? Is it the pain of finality — when we realise that there can be nothing beyond but retrogression?"
>
> "Perhaps," said Owen dreamily, "it is the prisoned infinite in us calling out to its kindred infinite as expressed in that visible perfection."

Yes — perhaps. But quite possibly Montgomery had second thoughts about transforming this excerpt into a believable exchange between two people, because she made her man-hating character Miss Cornelia interrupt the scene with a decidedly more prosaic remark, despite the fact that her sentences rhyme: "You seem to have a cold in the head," she tells Owen. "Better rub some tallow on your nose when you go to bed."[18]

— 4 —

What does this reveal about Montgomery's writing process? Quite a bit.

As a well-read author who peppered her writing with allusions to the creative work of major and minor authors, the Bible, and even popular songs and speeches, Montgomery inserted hidden meanings into her work for readers who could not only identify the source of the allusion but also understand the context of the quotation. But here, what Montgomery alluded to in these and several other instances is not the work of British or American authors that she enjoyed reading and rereading throughout her lifetime. It was to her own work, and readers would be unlikely to identify their sources because, after these four essays appeared in *The Canadian Magazine* in 1911, they were soon forgotten.

In my comments on these essays in volume 1 of *The L.M. Montgomery Reader*, I suggested that "these borrowings reveal an attempt on [Montgomery's] part to recapture a delightful 'spot' that lived on in her memory,"[19] but now I'd like to take this a step further. In spite of the ambivalence she expressed to her correspondent Ephraim Weber about the literary quality of these essays, she must have seen them as authoritative depictions of Prince Edward Island scenery in order to turn to them again and again for several of the nature descriptions that appeared in most of her novels written in Ontario — including one set in Ontario and not in P.E.I. These essays, then, acted as a bridge between the Montgomery of Lover's Lane and the Montgomery of Ontario who never recovered fully from leaving her beloved island behind. Montgomery didn't abandon P.E.I. due to political turmoil, but given that she did, in fact, cross a national border on her 1911 journey from P.E.I. to Ontario when she and her husband embarked on their honeymoon in England and Scotland, perhaps there's a way

Montgomery in front of a white blossom tree, circa 1927.

to view Montgomery as a kind of migrant author living in exile, as the title of one of her 1913 poems suggests.

Not surprisingly, there's another complication here. Copies of these four essays are found in one of her twelve scrapbooks that house the majority of her shorter works, but even though I haven't yet found an instance in which she reused the same extract twice, the copies in her scrapbook are free of markings that would indicate her keeping track of which excerpts she'd used already. What this shows is the careful way in which Montgomery repurposed some of her work and ultimately left no evidence of it, creating yet another puzzle for later literary detectives to piece together.

— 5 —

In *Anne's House of Dreams*, whose publication coincided with the serial publication of "The Alpine Path," the natural landscape of Prince Edward Island takes on a remarkably different quality, in terms of not only Montgomery's language but also Anne's sensory experience of nature:

> There was a certain tang of romance and adventure in the atmosphere of their new home which Anne had never found in Avonlea. There, although she had lived in sight of the sea, it had not entered intimately into her life. In Four Winds it surrounded her and called to her constantly. From every window of her new home she saw some varying aspect of it. Its haunting murmur was ever in her ears.... There was always a certain sense of things going to happen — of adventures and farings-forth. The ways of Four Winds were less staid and settled and grooved than those of Avonlea; winds of change blew over them; the sea called ever to the dwellers on shore, and even those who might not answer its call felt the thrill and unrest and mystery and possibilities of it.[20]

This description of the Prince Edward Island seascape sounds more like Montgomery's description of the P.E.I. scenery in "The Alpine Path" than like the nature descriptions in her earlier books, which were more tame and less clearly anchored in specific locations, to the point that while many reviewers and early critics celebrated her as a P.E.I. author, others had difficulty remembering where her work was set. Here, in two works published in 1917, six years since her exodus to Ontario, Montgomery appeared to renew her commitment to being a P.E.I. author, keeping the location of the Anne books but shifting the setting to a different part of the island, in order to introduce not only new characters but also a new kind of P.E.I. landscape.

Did I say "two works published in 1917"? I actually meant three. In chapter seven of *Anne's House of Dreams*, entitled "The Schoolmaster's Bride," Captain Jim Boyd captivates his listeners with the story of schoolmaster John Selwyn, whose fiancée, Persis Leigh, sailed across the ocean to join him on Prince Edward Island, and the ship was detained so long that John Selwyn began to lose his mind in his worry, until finally a supernatural vision reassured him that the ship would soon pull into the harbour safely. As with all instances of oral storytelling in Montgomery's books, the storyteller is interrupted frequently with the questions and commentary of the listeners, as well as their reactions once the story has concluded. In its issue dated July 1917, mere pages away from the second instalment of "The Alpine Path," *Everywoman's World* published Montgomery's short story entitled "The Schoolmaster's Bride." It is almost identical in terms of plot to the corresponding chapter in *Anne's House of Dreams*, except that there is no audience of listeners interrupting the first-person narrator. This is not the first time that Montgomery repurposed a story eventually told in fiction by an oral storyteller — several pieces of the Story Girl's repertoire, for instance, appeared in earlier form as standalone stories — but this is a rare instance in which Montgomery published separate but almost identical versions of the same story in such close proximity to each other. In this story, too, the natural world is personified as moody, willful, unpredictable, and somewhat menacing, as in this description of yet another house: "The old house, for it is an old house now, is still there, looking seaward through its small windows. But no one has lived in it for many years. The winds blow around it mournfully and the gray rain beats upon it, and the white mists come in from the Gulf to enfold it. And the moonlight falls over it and lights up the old paths where John Selwyn walked and planned, that happy, busy summer."[21]

Montgomery moved this section to the end of the novel and reworked it into Anne's departure from her House of Dreams for a larger house in the nearby village of Glen St. Mary. The narrative attempts to focus on the positive side of this bittersweet ending, on the life that will live on in the home that Anne has loved. Yet the final moments of the novel show hints of heartbreak and trauma, for all that.

> She was going away; but the old house would still be there, looking seaward through its quaint windows. The autumn winds would blow around it mournfully, and the gray rain would beat upon it and the white mists would come in from the sea to enfold it; and the moonlight would fall over it and light up the old paths where the schoolmaster and his bride had walked. There on that old harbour shore the charm of story would linger; the wind would still whistle alluringly over the silver sand-dunes; the waves would still call from the red rock-coves.
>
> "But we will be gone," said Anne through her tears.[22]

Montgomery often recorded that she shed tears — or wanted to — when leaving Prince Edward Island, even after years in Ontario. But what never changed was her attachment to the landscape and the people of this place. Her earliest known attempt to express this investment publicly can be found in her 1891 article "From Prince Albert to P.E. Island," written on her first return to the island after a year in Saskatchewan during her adolescence:

> It is rather rough crossing over, but we do not mind that, and, as the fresh breeze comes dancing up the Strait, bringing the echo of the salt seas, we realize, with a happy thrill, that we are very near home. Somebody says, "see, there is

> Prince Edward Island," and we eagerly rush on deck to catch a glimpse of the old sod! Yes; there it is — the long red line of cliffs, sloping to the green uplands with villages nestled here and there — dear P.E.I. at last! Never, Canada over, have we seen a lovelier, fairer spot than this! We feel like the old Scotch Islander in Winnipeg did. He said he was from "the Island!" What Island? queried a listener. "*What Island*," repeated our honest countryman, in amazement. "Why, Prince Edward Island, man? [*sic*] *What other Island is there?*"[23]

Montgomery returned to this notion again in an essay she contributed to *The Spirit of Canada*, published in 1939 by the Canadian Pacific Railway as a souvenir album that would be presented to the king and queen of England during their royal visit to Canada. That same year, *The Canadian Bookman*, an official publication of the Canadian Authors Association, mentioned that Montgomery had sent a note "expressing regret that she was unable to be present, and reaffirming her loyalty to the Maritimes 'after twenty-eight years' absence.'"[24]

Indeed, no matter how much she enjoyed the communities she created in Leaskdale and Norval, no matter the benefits to her career that she gained by her proximity to Toronto, and no matter where she wandered or how long she remained exiled in Ontario, she would always remain anchored in Prince Edward Island. As she claimed in a journal entry dated July 13, 1927, "Yes, this is home — my Island. Only here does my soul feel perfectly at home."[25]

# 5

# The War at Home

— 1 —

In a journal entry dated July 26, 1915, in which she acknowledged receipt of her author's copies of *Anne of the Island*, Montgomery announced that she'd reached the end of the road with her publisher, then known as the Page Company. By this point, she'd heard too many reports from booksellers, sales staff, and fellow authors about Lewis Page's erratic behaviour and shoddy business practices. But more pragmatically, the only terms she'd managed to renegotiate since signing her contract for *Anne of Green Gables* in 1907 involved removing the obligation to submit all future book-length manuscripts to the firm, to be published under the same conditions, for the next five years. All other terms — no royalty for the first thousand copies sold, followed by a percentage of sales that she saw as less than half of what was industry standard — had remained the same.

To be fair, Montgomery specified in this journal entry that she'd never *asked* Page for an increased royalty rate. As she put it, "He never hinted at such a thing — and I knew it was of little use to ask it." It would be easy to conclude that Page's rejection of a manuscript of her poems proved to be the final straw in her decision to look for a new home for her work, but that idea doesn't quite square with the language of her account in her journal. "Page practically refused to bring [my poems] out some years ago declaring that poetry wouldn't pay," she wrote in an entry dated March 21, 1916. She found his position rather galling in light of the fortune his company had made on her books, and she thought he could have afforded to publish a volume of her poems anyway, even if only as a personal favour to her. Since he appeared uninterested in doing so, she figured that he couldn't possibly object if she tried to publish such a volume somewhere else.[1]

In the end, she found a new publishing home in the Toronto firm of McClelland, Goodchild, and Stewart, whom she appointed not only as her Canadian publishers but also as her literary agents. It's unclear whether she'd recently approached Page with a firm proposal for a volume of poems, let alone submitted a full manuscript for his consideration, but John McClelland and his colleagues jumped at the chance to publish it, since doing so meant a two-book deal that also included her next novel — which she didn't describe in the entry in which she announced her move. According to her account, she insisted that McClelland and his colleagues offer Page the U.S. rights to that novel, but Page responded to this olive branch by threatening to sue her if any firm but his published her next book. Although his threats added to the list of things she had to worry about in the midst of the Great War, she doubted he had a leg to stand on, legally speaking. "We have had some correspondence about the literary contents of my next book," she acknowledged in an entry dated April 20, 1916, still without providing any details, "but I feel sure that there was nothing in my letters to bind me." Only in a journal entry dated two months later did Montgomery reveal her chosen title for this next book — *Anne's House of Dreams* — which would continue Anne's story beyond the happily-ever-after ending of *Anne of the Island*.[2]

Published in November 1916, *The Watchman and Other Poems* consists of ninety-four poems, most of which had appeared previously in periodicals, some as early as 1899. It received stellar reviews in the periodical press, but the deflated tone of the journal entry in which Montgomery acknowledged receipt of her copies suggests a lack of enthusiasm on her part: "It is very nicely gotten up. I expect no great things of it." In an unpublished letter to

G.B. MacMillan dated January 18, 1917, Montgomery repeated the line about "expect[ing] no great success for the book" but added that she'd "published it merely for [her] own satisfaction." Still, her response in the next paragraph to MacMillan's question about her interest in "writing scenarios for cinema films" puts her lacklustre attitude about the sales potential for her book of poems in a remarkably different light: "I have made enough out of my books to render me independent and the [screenwriting] work itself is too ephemeral to attract me." She then added another reason she no longer needed to worry about book sales: "I understand that the Page Co. have arranged with a cinema firm to produce *Anne of Green Gables*, so possibly my other books may be also produced in this fashion."[3]

At any rate, the willingness of Montgomery's new publishers to commit to her book of poems proved to be advantageous to everyone in the long run, despite the narrower market for books in this genre. This firm, which became McClelland and Stewart in 1918, would publish all of Montgomery's remaining novels between 1919 and 1939, and although *The Watchman* soon went out of print, the continued sales success of these novels helped keep the company afloat for the rest of the twentieth century — despite the fact that M&S's back catalogue didn't include any of the books that Montgomery had published with Page until *Anne of Green Gables* joined M&S's prestigious New Canadian Library series in 1992, following the New Canadian Library editions of *Emily of New Moon* and its two sequels in 1989.

One way of looking at the discrepancy in tone between the journal entry and the letter to MacMillan is to assume that Montgomery would be more honest in her journal than she would be in a letter to a friend, particularly one who'd long admired her success as a writer. But this letter to MacMillan makes me disinclined to interpret her journal entry as a tacit acknowledgement of her reduced talents as a poet. After all, it was better for her to express low expectations and be pleasantly surprised than to predict a bestseller and be disappointed or embarrassed, especially given the unpredictable nature of book publishing as an industry. And besides, no book of poems could possibly come close to meeting the spectacularly high sales of her preceding books, all of which had appeared on several bestseller lists in Canada and the United States. *The Teachers Monthly*, a Toronto publication, noted in its review of *The Watchman* that the book offered readers "the setting of Anne of Green Gables, the sweet 'Island' atmosphere in which she grew," but added that "nothing of Miss Montgomery's will perhaps quite equal Anne of Green Gables, which is a human story of exquisite charm."[4]

Moreover, an ad for *The Watchman and Other Poems* that appeared in the Toronto *Globe* called the volume "one of the choicest books of the year," making no distinction between poetry and more commercially viable literary genres, and described it as consisting of "beautiful poems of rare quality, delicate, lilting and full of music." The ad also referred to Montgomery's volume as being "a Canadian book through and through," even though the vast majority of the periodicals Montgomery acknowledged in the book as the poems' first homes were American. And while the book's contents make little direct reference to the Great War, except in Montgomery's dedication "to the memory of the gallant Canadian soldiers who have laid down their lives for their country and their empire," there's a subtle connection to the war found in a later unpublished letter to MacMillan dated March 29, 1916, that likewise provides some context for her decision to publish this book for her "own satisfaction" over something that had more obvious potential in terms of commercial success.

> Don't expect to make much out of them of course. But there comes to be a better market now for poetry than has been for many a year. The revival of poetry in the schools is quite remarkable and it has occurred since the war. A prominent book dealer says he sells a hundred volumes of poetry now where before the war he sold only one. That is certainly peculiar, isn't it? But the war has permeated and altered everything so of course the market for poetry will be affected too. I should rather have expected it to be affected adversely though.[5]

The idea that the Great War had increased interest in poetry that had nothing to do with the war may seem unexpected, but *The Watchman* coincided with the release of *Canadian Poets*, an anthology edited by John W. Garvin that included five of Montgomery's poems. An ad in the *Toronto Star Weekly* referred to the anthology as "an epoch-marking book" and proclaimed its cultural value in unambiguous terms:

> The Great War necessarily closes the first era, since the Confederation of the British North American provinces, July 1st, 1867; and this beautiful and notable work, appearing in the fiftieth year, includes the fifty Canadian Poets of the era whose poetry in theme and artistry is most distinctive. There are fifty pages of portraits and critiques, fifty pages of biographical data, and three hundred and sixty pages of the best verse in Canadian literature, including quite a number of superior War-poems.
>
> This valuable book should increase the pride of Canadians in their native talent, and be regarded as a national and a home asset.
>
> This is the work Canadians have desired for years. A veritable library of the choicest work of Canada's poets. It is an artistic and beautiful volume, and has all been made in Canada.[6]

Even if these two volumes couldn't compete with *Anne's House of Dreams* in terms of units sold, it would be overly simplistic to measure success solely in terms of sales revenue. After all, *The Watchman* was republished the following year by the Frederick A. Stokes Company, the New York publisher that would go on to publish all of Montgomery's remaining novels in the United States, and in the United Kingdom by Constable, which published the first U.K. editions of several Montgomery novels. Garvin's anthology was likewise reprinted by Stokes in 1917 (under the title *Canadian Poets and Poetry*) and appeared in a revised edition in 1926. And cementing the link between Canadian poetry and the Great War was Garvin's follow-up anthology, *Canadian Poems of the Great War* (1918), which included Montgomery's poem "Our Women." Anticipating some of the creative choices she'd make in her subsequent books, this poem centres on the losses experienced by women at home during the war, shifting the focus away from male combatants.[7]

— 2 —

Given that the Page Company's marketing campaign for *Anne of the Island* in 1915 included the phrase "completing the 'ANNE' trilogy," it's worth looking at Montgomery's subsequent decision to continue Anne's story past the point of her marriage. She never explained in her journals *why* she'd decided to undertake this project — a fair question to ask given how reluctant she'd been to write *Anne of the Island* — but it would be reasonable to presume that she'd opted to write a new story about Anne in order give her new publishers a book with the strongest sales potential. Her decision to make Anne and Gilbert depart for a new P.E.I. setting after their wedding likewise makes sense if we view it through this lens, since doing so would create some distance between this book and the preceding ones, which would remain available from a competing publisher. But a typewritten memorandum from the Commonwealth of Massachusetts Superior Court concerning a lawsuit between Montgomery and Page — part of a messy, multi-year legal battle that I'll return to later — contains another clue, one that also provides some context about Page's supposed anger toward her for her decision to submit this book somewhere else. According to this document, which summarizes legal testimony from both parties, it was Page who'd "urged [Montgomery] to write the fourth book dealing with Anne's married life."[8]

True, Montgomery hadn't signed a contract with Page for *Anne's House of Dreams*, but there was some precedent for him to view the contract as a formality. After all, although he commissioned a second book about Anne upon acceptance of the first manuscript in March 1907, the contract for *Anne of Avonlea*, now housed at Library and Archives Canada, is dated February 16, 1909 — two months after the *Publishers' Weekly* announcement that this book would appear the following fall. And while I haven't yet come across a notice in a periodical that made a big announcement about Montgomery's switch in publishers, perhaps there should have been:

Cover of the original edition of *Anne's House of Dreams*, in which Anne appears far younger than in her mid-twenties. Cover illustration by M.L. Kirk.

When *The Publishers' Weekly* included *Anne's House of Dreams* in its lists of bestsellers for September and October 1917, it named Page as the book's publisher both times.[9]

Similarly, it's tempting to assume that Montgomery tended to concentrate on one book at a time — that she never thought beyond whatever project she was currently working on. The fact that she rarely used her journals as a forum for recording ideas for possible future projects or for venting her frustrations with how her projects were developing reinforces this idea. But in a letter to Ephraim Weber dated November 25, 1917, a few months after the release of *Anne's House of Dreams*, she mentioned that she'd already started "a book in which Anne's children figure and then I plan to write one in which her sons go to the front."[10] These stated plans help explain the significant time jumps between volumes in this second trilogy of Anne books: Jem Blythe, Anne and Gilbert's oldest son, is a baby at the end of

*Anne's House of Dreams*, thirteen at the beginning of *Rainbow Valley* (1919), and twenty-one at the start of *Rilla of Ingleside* (1921). And if Montgomery was already planning to write about Anne's family during the war — a year before she knew how, when, or even if the war would end — then it stands to reason that she'd include hints of the war in the books she'd written while the war raged on but were set years earlier.

Montgomery's stated longer-term plans for these characters are significant in light of an article by journalist and poet Katherine Hale — whose husband happened to be John W. Garvin — that appeared in the *Toronto Star Weekly* a month after this letter to Weber. Entitled "Canadian Novelists, as a Rule, Apparently Untouched by the War," this article included *Anne's House of Dreams* in its overview of Canadian novels published in 1917. But Hale's praise zeroed in on Montgomery's "love of nature and her deft descriptions of it" rather than on anything having to do with book's plot. "Look where you will, through catalogues, book shops and review pages," Hale declared, "you shall not find echoes of any world-shaking cataclysm disturbing the calm of Canadian story writers," with the exception of a novel by Ralph Connor and a collection of linked short stories by Nellie L. McClung. This creative avoidance was hardly limited to Canadian fiction, as a *Boston Post* article by Alfred S. Clark published earlier that year makes clear. Despite the fact that "we have entered upon the fourth year of war ... the complete upheaval of the world has not inspired as many enduring novels as one might have expected," with the exception of "half a dozen stories with the war as background that have had much more than average merit." Instead, Clark praised *Anne's House of Dreams* for offering "relief from all the horrors of these days," calling it "a pleasant story of Prince Edward Island, of quiet days in a remote village where dwell several lovable characters. It is an attractive romance without great excitement, but wholesome and refreshing."[11]

Montgomery inserted into *Anne's House of Dreams* several reminders that this story was not contemporary. The first of these is the dedication to "Laura" — referring to Laura Pritchard Agnew, a close friend from her year in Saskatchewan as a teenager — "in memory of the olden time." Next is the introduction of telephones in Avonlea, which Anne finds "so preposterously up-to-date and modernish for this darling, leisurely old place." And the most notable is the federal election that leads to victory for the Liberals after eighteen years of Conservative leadership, something that older readers in 1917 would have been likely to remember had happened in 1896. But she also inserted clues that foreshadowed the Great War by alluding to recent war poems. Lines from Rupert Brooke's poem "Song of the Pilgrims" — "Our kin / Have built them temples, and therein / pray to the gods we know; and dwell / in little houses lovable" — which she described in an unpublished letter to MacMillan as "really the most exquisite thing of its class I have ever read" — appear as an epigraph on the book's title page. When Anne spots the woman whom she will later know as Leslie Moore, Anne pays particular attention to "the bunch of blood-red poppies [Leslie] wore at her belt." Poppies, after all, had become a key symbol of the war due partly to the publication, late in 1915, of John McCrae's poem "In Flanders Fields."[12]

I like to imagine that some astute readers of *Anne's House of Dreams* in 1917 who remembered that the Liberal victory had occurred twenty-one years earlier could have pieced together the fact that Anne and Gilbert's eldest son, Jem, born in the preceding chapter, would now be old enough to fight in the war. Of course, the timeline Montgomery established in this novel doesn't quite add up — Jem and Walter are said to be twenty-one and twenty early in *Rilla of Ingleside*, set during the summer of 1914, which would put their births in 1893 and 1894, a few years too early — and at any rate, the book's first commentators were more likely to praise this story for its apparent *avoidance* of reality, as did Hale in the *Toronto Star Weekly* and Clark in the *Boston Post*.[13]

And even though *Rainbow Valley*, published in August 1919, includes several scenes in which adult characters discuss their fear — or disbelief — that mounting unrest in Germany might lead to a war with England that would involve Canada, attempts to market the book continued to minimize any connection between the world of Montgomery's characters and the war that had just ended. An ad in the *New York Times* commended the book for its "common sense and cheerfulness," which "are especially welcome in these unsettled days," whereas an ad in *The Publishers' Weekly* applauded this "simple love story chronicling the everyday events in a community of kindly people whose lives are the counterpart of other lives the country over" and promised booksellers that "there is no hint of the war in it." Canadian critic Austin Bothwell was one of the only commentators who saw what was coming: "It is as plain as a pikestaff that the Blythe boys and the Meredith boys will reach military age in 1914 or thereabouts," and he predicted that "the part they play in the war and their romances will form the substance of a book to come."[14] But while he was right in predicting that a sequel set during the war would follow, he missed the mark in terms of whose story it would tell — or what might happen next in Montgomery's writing life.

— 3 —

Lewis Page responded to Montgomery's decision to move to new publishers in the most baffling way possible: By uttering legal threats one minute and sending her an advance for her next book — something he'd never done before — the next. But when she received a royalty cheque from which a thousand dollars had been deducted due to an apparent overpayment in an earlier royalty report, she joined the Authors League of America and sued *him*. This led to more stress, not only in terms of testifying against Page but also in terms of having to hide the details of her business trip from members of her husband's congregation.[15]

When it looked like Montgomery would win the lawsuit, Page offered as a settlement to buy all remaining rights — including claims to any future royalties and payments for subsidiary rights in perpetuity — to the seven books of hers published by his firm. After much negotiation, Page finally came around to the amount she'd named — eighteen thousand U.S. dollars — which she planned to invest in the hope that the yearly interest would generate roughly what she would have earned in royalties from those books over the long term.[16]

Unfortunately, agreeing to this offer led to two complications.

First, shortly after all parties had finalized the agreement, Page sold the film rights to four of Montgomery's books for forty thousand U.S. dollars, thus denying the author her 50 percent share. Montgomery wrote in a later journal entry that she'd anticipated Page would do this, and an unpublished letter to MacMillan dated April 7, 1918, suggests that Page dragged his feet about film rights as part of his malice over Montgomery's departure from his firm. "As for *Anne* appearing in cinema, that is all off at present, owing to the imbroglio with Page. He refuses to take the necessary steps in the matter and I am powerless."[17]

Second, Page manipulated her into consenting to the publication of a book consisting of the short stories that hadn't been selected for *Chronicles of Avonlea*. Such a project would go against her reasons for letting him buy her out, which were to sever ties with the firm forever. But she agreed due to some gaps in international copyright law that might permit him to publish the volume anyway, in an attempt to ensure that the book wouldn't compete with a book of hers published elsewhere and wouldn't make any reference to Anne. In the end, Page insisted on proceeding with a version of the manuscript that she didn't authorize, and she sued him for publishing this book — called *Further Chronicles of Avonlea* and released in April 1920 — on the grounds that doing so had damaged her literary reputation. The lawsuit was eventually settled in her favour, but only after eight years of courtroom appearances, countersuits, appeals, and stress. And in contrast to the care she went to in 1919 to hide her legal battles from her husband's parishioners, her experience eventually made its way into some of her public appearances, as shown in how she was quoted in an article published in 1937 by an official magazine of the Canadian Authors Association: "I am the only writer … who ever got an injunction against the publication of her own book. That was in the course of a lawsuit with the first publisher of *Anne of Green Gables*. We finally wound up in the United States Supreme Court, where I won."[18]

Montgomery even went to the trouble of annotating at least four copies of the book, enumerating by hand every passage that had motivated her to take Page to court in order to compel him to withdraw the book from the market. But there's one excerpt that she *didn't* highlight: the reference, in the penultimate story "Only a Common Fellow," to the protagonist, whose "heart was in France, in that grave nobody knew of, where the Huns had buried Owen Blair — if they had buried him at all."[19] Given that the published volume consisted of versions of these stories that Montgomery had completed in 1912 for possible inclusion in *Chronicles of Avonlea*, how does this reference to Owen Blair's presumed death during the Great War make any sense?

The first version of this short story, published in the *American Agriculturist* in 1908, refers to the protagonist's heart being "down there in South Africa in that grave nobody knew of, where the Boers buried Owen Graham, if they *did* bury him at all." If Montgomery had decided to alter this reference to the South African War of 1899–1902 to fit the vague timeline of this point in the book series, she would have been more likely to pick an earlier conflict, not a later one. One of the reasons why she didn't want this book to include any references to Anne was no doubt due to the fact that she'd already planned to depict a middle-aged Anne and her family living through the Great War — in a book published by a competing publisher. This reference to the Great War didn't mention Anne directly, but it altered the timeline of the collection by making this story almost contemporaneous with the time of the book's publication. But somehow, in the midst of all of Montgomery's outrage about a book that she referred to semi-jokingly, in a letter to MacMillan dated August 29, 1926, as "that illegitimate offspring which I have never acknowledged" and "that sole stain on an otherwise spotless career," this presumed alteration appears to have escaped her notice.[20]

## — 4 —

In a journal entry dated March 11, 1919, Montgomery announced that she'd begun work on "another 'Anne' story — and I fervently hope the last" — adding that Anne "belongs to the green, untroubled pastures and still waters of the world before the war." While Montgomery's 1917 letter to Weber indicates that she'd planned to write about Anne's sons going to war, *Rilla of Ingleside* depicts the experience of the war through the perspective of Anne's youngest daughter. The novel addresses readers who'd just experienced the war themselves and who thus could draw on their own prior knowledge of the story's historical and cultural contexts — an ability that would obviously decrease with subsequent generations of readers.[21]

A review of *Rilla of Ingleside* in *Saturday Night* of Toronto commented that "in Rilla is reincarnated all the charm of the youthful Anne Shirley," but the novel takes pains to make Rilla her own character. Where she differs from members of her own family stems from the fact that she's the only one of her siblings who has no interest in getting any kind of higher education, a source of worry for the middle-aged Anne: "She has no serious ideals at all — her sole aspiration seems to be to have a good time."[22]

I mentioned in the preceding chapter that Montgomery had written *Anne of the Island* while grieving for the loss of her baby son Hugh, who'd died at birth just nine days after England declared war on Germany. She'd already drawn on her journal's record of that loss to write about Anne's experience of grief, in *Anne's House of Dreams*, after her first daughter, Joy, lives only a day. Writing fiction set during the Great War no doubt meant revisiting that difficult part of her life, and by the time she started writing *Rilla of Ingleside* in March 1919, barely two months had elapsed since the death of her first cousin Frederica Campbell McFarlane, known to readers of Montgomery's journals as "Frede," whom she'd once referred to as "my more than sister." Perhaps not unexpectedly, some of the choices she made in this novel suggest an attempt to avoid drawing too closely on her own experience, arguably as a form of self-protection. An early chapter in the novel depicts Rilla's decision, in the early weeks of the war, to care for an orphaned baby after the death of his mother, a reversal of Montgomery's experience. The novel also touches on Rilla's friendship with Gertrude Oliver, a twenty-eight-year-old schoolteacher who, like Montgomery, has "occasional moods of gloom and cynicism," but while there are parallels between the two friendships in terms of age differences, the novel focuses on the younger of the two women. Montgomery, who had dedicated *The Story Girl* to Frede, dedicated *Rilla of Ingleside* to Frede's memory.[23]

In order to write authentically about the war from the perspective of those who'd worked and waited at home, Montgomery drew extensively on her journal and her correspondence for accurate details about specific war events, the ebbs and flows of victory and defeat, and the experience of waiting between newspapers for updates. Many excerpts from her journal appear with few alterations in the mouths of her characters, particularly Gertrude

Oliver. In one case, she borrowed a statement in a letter from Weber — "It is a commercial war and utterly unworthy of one drop of Canadian blood being spilt for it" — and attributed it to "a stranger from the shore hotel." In private, she argued against Weber's perspective by calling the war "a death-grapple between freedom and tyranny," whereas in the novel this statement doesn't receive any kind of direct response — perhaps because the entire novel reflects her position.[24]

In some cases, though, Montgomery revised her own experience during the war in order to increase suspense for her readers, for whom the war was something that had ended. In an unpublished letter to MacMillan dated March 29, 1916, she described a recent "curious psychological experience," one that she'd written about in her journal already:

> I think I have told you that I have often had very strange dreams which came true or seemed to do so. Well, shortly before the first rumors of the German drive at Verdun I dreamed a peculiar dream. I was in my room and the sun was shining. Suddenly everything became black as night. The sky was covered with an inky cloud, thunder crashed and lightning blazed incessantly while rain and hail came down in torrents. I lost my head with terror and ran down stairs screaming wildly for Ewan. He came running through the hall and as we met the front door flew open and a soldier clad in khaki rushed in, asking shelter from the storm.
>
> At this moment a cry from the baby awakened me. At the moment of waking the conviction flashed into my mind that my dream had reference to some impending event of the war and I felt keen regret that I had not been able to "dream it out" and see how it ended. I got up, attended to the baby, returned to bed, and fell asleep. Then I did what I do not think I ever did before in my life. I *finished* the dream. I was standing out on the lawn. The storm had passed and the sky was clear and blue. The sun was shining

> on the wet world. I was dressed in white, I was crowned with flowers and I was *dancing*, with the most wonderful feeling of joy and happiness in my heart. When I awakened again I felt a strange assurance that something would soon happen in the war, but that it would come out right in the end.
>
> You may smile, but in the terrible weeks of the Verdun offensive that dream was really my only comfort.[25]

Montgomery shared her propensity for prophetic dreams with the character of Gertrude Oliver. But in chapter 19 of the novel, she altered some of the details and changed the dreamer's interpretation of the dream's meaning in order to highlight the terrifying uncertainty that she'd lived through during those four years of war.

> "I was standing again on the veranda steps — just as I stood in that dream on the night before the lighthouse dance, and in the sky a huge black, menacing thunder cloud rolled up from the east. I could see its shadow racing before it and when it enveloped me I shivered with icy cold. Then the storm broke — and it was a dreadful storm — blinding flash after flash and deafening peal after peal, driving torrents of rain. I turned in panic and tried to run for shelter, and as I did so a man — a soldier in the uniform of a French army officer — dashed up the steps and stood beside me on the threshold of the door. His clothes were soaked with blood from a wound in his breast, he seemed spent and exhausted; but his white face was set and his eyes blazed in his hollow face. 'They shall not pass,' he said, in low, passionate tones which I heard distinctly amid all the turmoil of the storm. Then I awakened. Rilla, I'm frightened — the spring will not bring the Big Push we've all been hoping for — instead it is going to bring some dreadful blow to France. I am sure of it. The Germans will try to smash through somewhere."

> "But he told you that they would not pass," said Rilla, seriously. She never laughed at Gertrude's dreams as the doctor did.
>
> "I do not know if that was prophecy or desperation. Rilla, the horror of that dream holds me yet in an icy grip. We shall need all our courage before long."
>
> Dr. Blythe *did* laugh at the breakfast table — but he never laughed at Miss Oliver's dreams again; for that day brought news of the opening of the Verdun offensive, and thereafter through all the beautiful weeks of spring the Ingleside family, one and all, lived in a trance of dread. There were days when they waited in despair for the end as foot by foot the Germans crept nearer and nearer to the grim barrier of desperate France.[26]

Despite this shared experience of dreaming prophetic dreams, Montgomery mentioned in a journal entry dated August 27, 1919, that she'd come across a clipping in an old scrapbook of a response she'd written to the editor of an unidentified newspaper about her views on Canadian literature. The article in question, part of a round table called "Canadian Writers on Canadian Literature" that appeared in the Toronto *Globe* on January 1, 1910, includes the following statement: "I do not think that, so far, our Canadian literature is an expression of our national life as a whole.... Canada is only just finding herself. She has not yet fused her varying elements into a harmonious whole. Perhaps she will not do so until they are welded together by some great crisis of storm and stress. That is when real national literature will be born." As she remarked in this journal entry, "When I wrote that I had no premonition of the Great War. But if I had known what was coming I could hardly have described it better."[27] Perhaps not, but her reflection after the fact indicates her awareness of the potential in the postwar world for creative writers to create "real national literature."

In a journal entry dated August 24, 1920, in which she mentioned writing the last chapter of *Rilla of Ingleside*, she recorded her "dark and deadly vow" that she was done with the Anne characters. A year later, in anticipation of the book's release, she even made this declaration publicly, judging by a profile in the *Evening Times and Star* of St. John, New Brunswick, entitled "No More of 'Anne' Books, Says Author," which quotes Montgomery as saying, "Positively the last of the 'Anne' books." But even though, as I noted earlier, fiction writers had for the most part avoided mentioning the war by the end of 1917, the situation had apparently changed so significantly in the four years that followed that she now worried about the book's sales potential: "The public are said to be sick of anything connected with the war," she noted in an entry dated September 3, 1921. Perhaps this explains the rather baffling way that the war is almost completely absent from the marketing campaign for this novel, including an ad that appeared in the *Boston Herald* and elsewhere that referred to *Rilla* simply as "a wholesome novel of youth and of love which doesn't always run smooth."[28]

Even so, some of the comments about this book that did mention the war setting did so in such a way to suggest that this book's value wasn't simply in terms of being a worthwhile read. It was also a book that had — or would have — historical value. A review in the *Manitoba Free Press*, for instance, predicted that "a hundred years hence, *Rilla of Ingleside* will be useful to historians for a picture of Canadian home life during the Great War." And a review in the *Rochester Democrat and Chronicle* argued against a recent article about how "Canada has not developed anything in the way of literature" by drawing attention to Montgomery's work.

> More wholesome and readable romances have seldom been written in any country. They are of a type of literature of which any Canadian critic might well be proud, and if they do not arrive at a permanent place in a strictly Canadian literature, then it will be the fault and the loss of Canada. It might be said, ought to be said, in passing that no writer has before so grasped the spirit of the world war, so sensed its influence on the life of the quiet country villages and country sides from which came many of the men who fought to victory in the war, as has Mrs. Montgomery, and no one has written a more graphic recital of the subtle

> change wrought by the war in these centers of rural life than has Mrs. Montgomery. "Rilla of Ingleside" may not be the great book of the war, but it undoubtedly is the best portrayal of the effects of the war on the average home that has yet appeared.[29]

By the time this supposedly final Anne book appeared in the fall of 1921, Montgomery had already begun work, with renewed enthusiasm, on a new book about a new protagonist — a writer-in-embryo named Emily. In writing Emily's story, she returned to what had accounted for the popularity of *Anne of Green Gables* by focusing on the development of a child protagonist before the pressures of mixed-gender romance, but she would keep as a major focus something she'd end up downplaying in the Anne books — Emily's ambition as a writer.

# 6

# With Hamlet Left Out

— 1 —

L.M. Montgomery's scrapbooks and her ledger of earnings are among the surviving artifacts that she organized with care as comprehensive records of her writing life. Twelve scrapbooks house the vast majority of more than one thousand shorter works — short stories, poems, and miscellaneous pieces — that she published in periodicals between 1890 and 1942, consisting either of pasted clippings or of entire periodical pages sewn together. Several more scrapbooks contain reviews of her books and additional appearances in the periodical press, as well as news items and visual materials she wished to keep for posterity. Her ledger of earnings contains tallies of the sums of money she received — in the form of royalties in the case of her books and one-time payments in the case of her shorter works — throughout her writing life. Rea Wilmshurst, whose work from the late 1970s to the mid-1990s has contributed enormously to our understanding of Montgomery's shorter works, created a cross-reference between the scrapbooks and the ledger, and in doing so, she identified items that were missing from her scrapbooks, several of which still haven't been found.

In short, the scrapbooks house the *products* of Montgomery's writing life, whereas the ledger contains a record of the financial *effects* of her writing. These artifacts are inconsistent in terms of recording *where* and *when* specific items appeared, which accounts for some mysteries that still remain to be solved, and while Montgomery preserved the handwritten manuscripts of most of her books, only a few manuscripts and typescripts of her shorter works survive, as does only a small percentage of her business correspondence.

Around the same time she started publishing shorter works in periodicals, Montgomery launched on another lifelong writing project: a journal. In an entry dated September 21, 1889, fourteen-year-old Maud Montgomery recorded that she'd decided to burn the journal that she'd kept since the age of nine and that apparently consisted mostly of weather reports, in order to start anew. "Life is beginning to get interesting for me — I will soon be fifteen — the last day of November. And in *this* journal I am never going to tell what kind of a day it is — unless the weather has something to do worth while. *And* — last but *not* least — I am going to keep this book locked up!!" The Montgomery in this first entry sounds remarkably like young Anne, and the mention a few paragraphs later of "a matronly old geranium called 'Bonny'" that "blooms as if it *meant* it" anticipates two early moments in *Anne of Green Gables*: Anne comments that the cherry tree outside her window "blooms as if it meant it," and when Marilla balks at Anne's request to name a geranium on a window sill "Bonny," Anne replies that "I like things to have handles even if they are only geraniums," a line lifted directly from this journal entry.[1]

Even in her earliest journal entries, Montgomery recorded forms of adversity that she tended not to broach in her fiction — unless, of course, her characters could overcome them. Within a year of starting this new diary, she left her grandparents' home in Cavendish, Prince Edward Island, to join her father and his second family in Prince Albert (in what is now Saskatchewan). While she was overjoyed to be reunited with her beloved father, she clashed with her stepmother, who expected her to stay home from school and provide free household help and child care. She returned to Prince Edward Island a year later, where she faced another obstacle in her

Montgomery, aged fourteen, the same year she destroyed her childhood diaries and began a new journal that she would maintain until the end of her life.

desire for more education: the opposition of her grandparents, who agreed with great reluctance to let her return to school so she could prepare for the entrance exam that would allow her to study for a teacher's licence.[2]

Curiously for a journal that was supposedly started when Montgomery was a teenager, even some of her early entries show a penchant for revelling in the past — something that would only increase as she got older. In an entry dated August 1, 1892, when she was seventeen, she mentioned a visit from two orphan brothers who'd boarded with her and her grandparents a decade earlier. After commenting on the boys' changed appearance, she wrote paragraph after paragraph about "our lang-syne playdays," much of which she'd reuse with little revision in "The Alpine Path." She mentioned nothing about what the brothers were doing (except that one of them "talks of going out west"), where they'd been living all this time, or why they'd returned to Cavendish for a visit.[3]

And in some cases, Montgomery wrote openly about the fact that what she revealed in her journal included parts of her life that she didn't want circulating in public. In a journal entry dated January 5, 1917, for instance, she mentioned that the editor of *Everywoman's World* had asked her to add another thousand words to the text of "The Alpine Path" about her "love affairs." But while she claimed to have informed that editor that she was "not

Montgomery and Ewan Macdonald in Glasgow in summer 1911, while on their honeymoon.

one of those who throw open the portals of sacred shrines to the gaze of the crowd," she then added another two dozen paragraphs with that information in her journal entry, which ended with a remarkably candid assessment of her relationship with her husband, whom, she claimed, she didn't regret marrying even though she'd never been in love with him. "I have been contented in my marriage, and intensely happy in my motherhood. Life has not been — never can be — what I once hoped it would be in my girlhood dreams. But I think, taking one thing with another, that I am as happy as the majority of people in this odd world and happier than a great many of them."[4]

Montgomery and Macdonald proved to be mismatched, and starting in 1919, his symptoms of mental illness gave her something new to worry about for the rest of her life. But while her Ontario journals contain innumerable entries about her marital unhappiness or about her fear of scandal if her husband's struggles became public, they're also noteworthy for how frequently Ewan Macdonald is absent from their pages.

— 2 —

Readers who turn to Montgomery's journals in search of behind-the-scenes tidbits about her writing process are bound to be disappointed, since Montgomery offered little detail about her writing life — certainly not as much as might reasonably be expected given that, in a journal entry dated September 28, 1893, she referred to writing as "my dearest ambition." While she frequently mentioned times her shorter works had been accepted or published, particularly in her early years, she rarely described what she was actively working on or hoped to write in the future. She waited until she'd signed the contract for *Anne of Green Gables* before describing the writing and revision process in retrospect — as she mentioned to her correspondent Ephraim Weber in a letter dated May 2, 1907, "I didn't squeak a word to anyone about it because I feared desperately I wouldn't find a publisher for it" — and so there's a great deal of uncertainty about when, exactly, Montgomery wrote it.[5]

But much like in her first entry, dated September 1889, her journals contain several surprising overlaps with the work she published within her lifetime. "The Alpine Path" consists to a great extent of anecdotes that she transcribed from the pages of her journal — albeit with some strategic changes and deletions, as we saw earlier with Montgomery's account of asking a teacher who hated her for feedback on an early poem. In some cases, the overlaps extend to her fiction as well.

In "The Alpine Path," Montgomery drew on a journal entry dated 1905 (specifically a paragraph in which she recalled that she'd sometimes been "fiercely unhappy" as a child) to describe one of the key facets of her imagination:

> It has always seemed to me, ever since early childhood, that, amid all the commonplaces of life, I was very near to a kingdom of ideal beauty. Between it and me hung only a thin veil. I could never draw it quite aside, but sometimes a wind fluttered it and I caught a glimpse of the enchanting realm beyond — only a glimpse — but those glimpses have always made life worth while.

Montgomery gifted this childhood impression to Emily, writing about it with only minor revisions in chapter 1 of *Emily of New Moon*, published six years after "The Alpine Path":

> It had always seemed to Emily, ever since she could remember, that she was very, very near to a world of wonderful beauty. Between it and herself hung only a thin curtain; she could never draw the curtain aside — but sometimes, just for a moment, a wind fluttered it and then it was as if she caught a glimpse of the enchanting realm beyond — only a glimpse — and heard a note of unearthly music.[6]

In such instances, Montgomery drew on the text of her journal when writing her fiction, sometimes as a way to establish character, sometimes in order to capture authentic emotion. Consider a journal entry dated June 30, 1897, in which twenty-two-year-old Montgomery vowed that "it seems a century since I was light-hearted and gay and ambitious":

> Ambitious! I could laugh! Where is my ambition now? What does the word mean? What is it like to be ambitious? To feel that life is before you, a fair, unwritten white page [where] you may inscribe your name in letters of success? To feel that you have the wish and power to win your crown? To feel that the coming years are crowding to meet you and lay their largesse at your feet? I *once* knew what it was to feel so!

These lines then appear with little change in chapter 6 of *Emily's Quest*, published three decades after the date of the journal entry:

> "Ambition!" wrote Emily bitterly in her diary. "I could laugh! Where is my ambition now? What is it like to be ambitious? To feel that life is before you, a fair, unwritten white page where you may inscribe your name in letters of success? To feel that you have the wish and power to win your crown? To feel that the coming years are crowding to meet you and lay their largess at your feet? I *once* knew what it was to feel so."[7]

It's worth noting that although the phrasing is almost exactly the same, each version of this excerpt has a unique context. Although Emily writes this paragraph in her diary just after receiving another rejection for her first book-length manuscript, these lines appear in Montgomery's journal when she narrated her regret over her decision to accept a marriage proposal from a man named Edwin Simpson. Moreover, the narrator of the novel adds an aside that could very well indicate how Montgomery's view of this episode in her life had changed so many years later: "All of which goes to show how very young Emily still was. But agony is none the less real because in later years when we have learned that everything passes, we wonder what we agonised about."[8]

But even though these journals make fewer mentions of her creative work than many readers might wish for, part of the fascination involves how they depict a highly skilled writer who attempted to record — and reveal — parts of her real self. As editors Mary Rubio and Elizabeth Waterston noted in their introduction to the fifth and final volume of *The Selected Journals of L.M. Montgomery*, published in 2004, "Keeping a diary had been a compulsion, a way to access the sheer pleasure of writing, a workshop for experiments in description, a means to escape from intolerable realities, a place to 'consume the smoke' of her furies, a way to record her triumphs without exposing the pride she had been taught to consider a sin."[9] And that fascination extends as much to what Montgomery chose to record in the journal's pages as it does to what she opted to leave out.

— 3 —

After the first volume of Montgomery's selected journals appeared in 1985, many readers, reviewers, and academics expressed difficulty reconciling the narrator of the journals and what they'd imagined about the author of *Anne of Green Gables*. Or, as James Adams put it in a 2004 article in the *Globe and Mail*, the publication of the journals shifted the view of Montgomery as "a sentimental, dutiful, upbeat, nature-loving Victorian-era holdover" and revealed that she'd also been "a brooding, illness-plagued, mean-spirited, tart-tongued, barbiturate-popping, wine-loving, hissy-fitting snob."[10] Although Montgomery shared many traits with her best-known characters — she revelled in the beauty of the natural world, read widely, enjoyed passionate same-gender friendships, and drew on her imagination in ways that weren't always understood or appreciated by those around her — she also expressed judgments against those who didn't live up to her high standards or whom she perceived as below her, experienced intense sexual feeling as well as intense feelings of despair, and chafed against some of the constraints imposed on her by her culture in terms of gender, race, and class.

In short, she was a flawed and complex human being, rather than a character in a work of fiction.

Of course, it's important to remember that Montgomery's journals weren't a neutral, objective account of her daily life — they consisted, in part, of confessions she couldn't bring herself to share with anyone else.

"Temperaments such as mine *must* have some outlet," she wrote in an entry dated February 11, 1910, less than two years after the publication of *Anne of Green Gables*, "and the only *safe* outlet is in some such record as this." Later in that entry, in which she described her impressions after rereading the entries she'd written since 1889, she referred to this record as "the refuge of my sick spirit in its unbearable agonies" while acknowledging the reality that her "spasms" occurred between periods during which she felt "tolerably happy, hopeful and interested in life."[11]

These apparent discrepancies between Montgomery the diarist and Montgomery the author evidently posed some dilemmas for Rubio and Waterston, whose detailed introduction to the first volume says next to nothing about Montgomery's creative work, and when it does, it keeps the focus firmly on the journal text: as they note, "The journals reveal the same literary qualities, in a relatively artless form, that have endeared Montgomery's fiction to generations of readers." In a 2001 retrospective account of this editorial project, Rubio revealed that "a phrase calling Montgomery an 'artless' writer" had been inserted into the introduction by her in-house editor, William Toye. "I objected," Rubio reported, "but 'artless' stayed."[12]

Moreover, an ad for the first volume appearing in the Ottawa *Citizen* said even less than this about Montgomery's published writing:

> In 1981 the University of Guelph acquired the journals and scrapbooks of Lucy Maud Montgomery. Oxford University Press Canada will publish a generous selection from these journals in three volumes. "Rich and engrossing," "fascinating," "engaging" are just a few of the words that have been used to describe this first volume of a projected three.
>
> It begins when Lucy Maud was fourteen and covers the years 1889 to 1910, the year before her marriage. Apart from allowing us the privilege of viewing closely the life of this remarkable woman, we are also given a fascinating insight into the social history of her time. This book is a tantalizing prelude to the whole.[13]

Given that it would have been the continued popularity of Montgomery's books that would entice trade readers in the 1980s to buy her journals in the first place, the editorial strategy of highlighting her "fascinating" journal writing while minimizing her creative writing — or ignoring its existence — seems odd. But what Rubio, Waterston, and their colleagues at Oxford University Press had to contend with was the dominant thinking at the time that writing by women, popular writing, and literature for children couldn't possibly be worthy of scholarly attention. (These attitudes have changed since then — to a point.) As Rubio noted, she and Waterston were faced with opposition, sometimes with hostility, as they applied for funding and submitted their proposal to prospective publishers. And although Toye, at Oxford, championed the project publicly — an article in the *Burlington Gazette* quotes him as declaring that "I feel when this is completely published in its three volumes, it will be considered one of the great works in Canadian literature" — he requested that Rubio and Waterston cut Montgomery's text in half because he didn't think the reading public would be interested in more. He relaxed that requirement after the sales of the first two volumes far surpassed expectations, and the projected three volumes turned into five.[14]

In addition to receiving rave reviews, the published volumes of Montgomery's journals had an immediate effect on cultural conversations about her life, her work, and her legacy. But in many cases, critics' interest in Montgomery the diarist or in Montgomery the social historian involved generalizing about or ignoring her fiction. Writing in *Saturday Night* upon the release of the second volume of selected journals in fall 1987, Mark Abley painted a rather depressing picture of Montgomery's life that he saw emerging from the journal text: "When she created Anne Shirley, Lucy Maud Montgomery gave her heroine everything her own life lacked — love, joy, and a happy ending." Although he looked at Montgomery's *The Blue Castle* in some detail, his article offered no examples to back up the claim that "her books are full of warnings against the path her own life took" or his assumption that few people remembered the books she'd written after *Anne of Green Gables* due in part to "the fading of her talent and the withering of her spirit after her marriage." In *A History of the Canadian Peoples* (1998),

J.M. Bumsted included an excerpt from Montgomery's journals in which she cast her own vote in 1917, which he replaced in later editions with excerpts that captured her reactions to war news in December 1914. Bumsted's brief comment about her fiction likewise considered it in terms of "a major conflict of the era: the problem of reconciling the bucolic beauty and tranquility of the rural landscape with the need to leave it in order to fulfil one's ambitions." And when she reviewed the fourth volume of selected journals in the *Globe and Mail* in 1998, Carol Shields offered unstinted praise for this multi-volume body of work — "Very few books in recent years have given me the depth of pleasure I've found in these first four volumes" — but the parallels she drew in her review between Montgomery and Anne appeared to stem from her memories of disliking *Anne of Green Gables* as a child.[15]

In a review article entitled "L.M. Montgomery and the Changing Times," published in 1988, Elizabeth R. Epperly viewed the journals' depiction of "what personal sacrifices are involved in writing what the publishers and the public demand from her" as "fascinating for those interested in the social and gender-related complexities of a female artist's career." But crucially, she also predicted that the publication of the journals (alongside that of volumes of letters and collections of shorter works) would soon lead to a re-evaluation of Montgomery's primary work. "She will gain more credibility and be given more generous (and meticulous) criticism as more and more is found out about her and as more of her writing is republished or published for the first time." Epperly's prediction certainly came true, and she helped lead the way with the publication, in 1992, of her book-length study *The Fragrance of Sweet-Grass: L.M. Montgomery's Heroines and the Pursuit of Romance.* And so, by the time the fifth and final volume of selected journals appeared in 2004, editors Rubio and Waterston could account for how, in addition to being fascinating and culturally valuable texts in their own right, the journals had become a lens through which readers and scholars could rediscover Montgomery's primary texts. "The publication of the journals has redirected attention to the novels, rousing new recognition of their subtexts and ironies, their technical skill, and their subtle subversion of the surface romance and optimism that constitute their original charm. The journals enrich the sense of the novels' context in time, place, and personal vision."[16]

## — 4 —

In a journal entry dated September 2, 1919, Montgomery recorded that she'd decided the preceding winter to "copy my whole journal into a set of volumes all the same size." Although she added that this transcription would include illustrating her text with photographs, clippings, and captions, she specified her intention to be "careful to copy [the text] exactly as it is written." By this point, only two years had elapsed since she'd mined her journal so extensively for material to include in "The Alpine Path" — something that in her journal she never mentioned doing. But she made no connection between the journal text and her awareness of her own fame as an internationally acclaimed writer. Instead, her only stated rationale for undertaking this transcription project was that it would be "a satisfaction when done."[17]

There are several reasons to be skeptical of Montgomery's claim that she made no changes to her journal text when she transcribed it, the least of which is that her writing style had obviously matured in the thirty years since her first entry. Even when "The Alpine Path" quotes explicitly from Montgomery's journal, complete with dates, a close comparison reveals several minor discrepancies between the texts in terms of phrasing and punctuation, in addition to excerpts she omitted from the public text. For instance, in her entry dated June 20, 1908, she recorded her delight at receiving her first copy of *Anne of Green Gables* "fresh from the publishers," whereas in "The Alpine Path," the phrase "'spleet-new' from the publishers" appears instead. Since Montgomery presumably drew on the original journal entry from 1908 for both "The Alpine Path" and the journal transcription, it seems reasonable to wonder whether Montgomery added "spleet-new," an archaic term meaning brand new, to her "Alpine Path" text or whether she deleted that term when she transcribed this entry into her ledger. Adding to this mystery is that when Emily Byrd Starr receives copies of *her* first book in chapter 21 of *Emily's Quest*, the narrator uses the phrase "spleet-new from the publishers" — thus echoing "The Alpine Path" rather than the journal text.[18]

These discrepancies are pretty minor, but they open the door to wondering about the authenticity of some of her remaining entries. Did

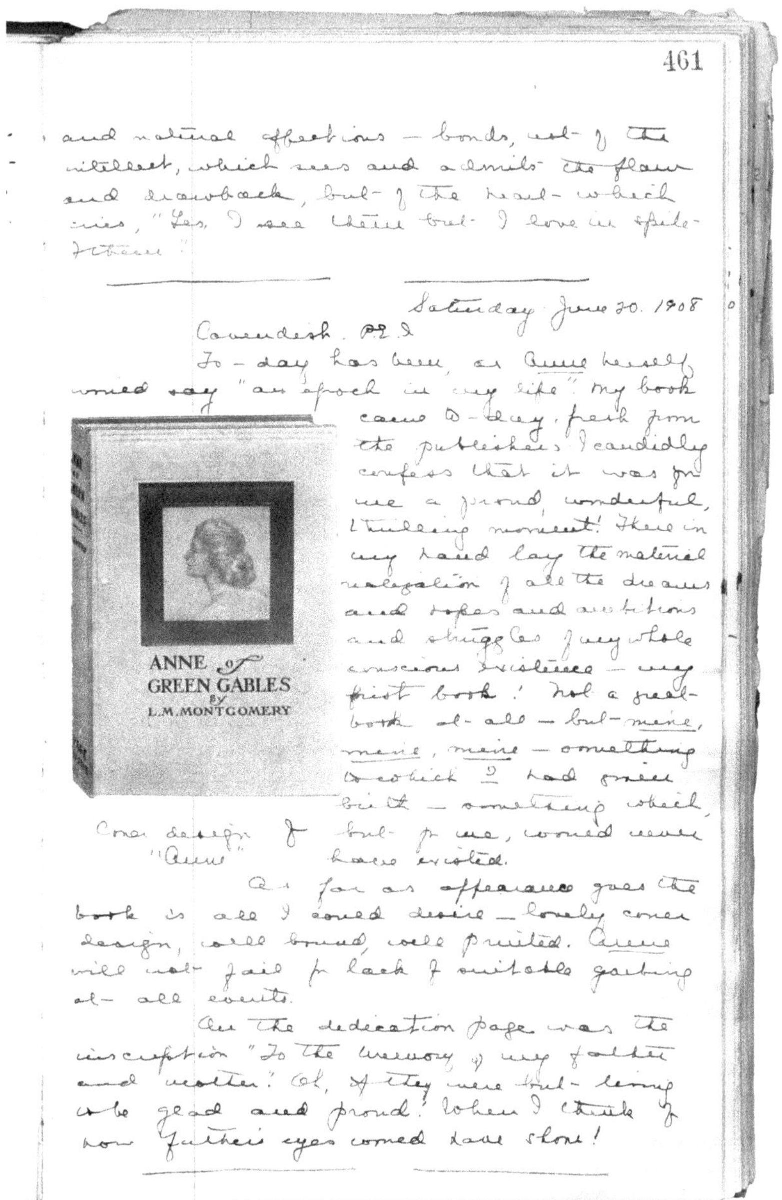

461

and natural affections — bonds, not of the intellect, which sees and admits the flaw and drawback, but of the heart which cries, "Yes, I see them but I love in spite of them."

Saturday June 20. 1908

Cavendish. P.E.I.

To-day has been, as Anne herself would say "an epoch in my life". My book came to-day, fresh from the publishers. I candidly confess that it was for me a proud, wonderful, thrilling moment! There in my hand lay the material realization of all the dreams and hopes and ambitions and struggles of my whole conscious existence — my first book! Not a great book at all — but mine, mine, mine — something which I had created — something which, but for me, would never have existed.

Cover design of "Anne"

As far as appearance goes the book is all I could desire — lovely cover design, well bound, well printed. Anne will not fail for lack of suitable garbing at all events.

On the dedication page was the inscription "To the memory of my father and mother". Oh, if they were but living to be glad and proud! When I think of how father's eyes would have shone!



Montgomery's journal entry dated June 20, 1908, recording her receipt of her author's copy of *Anne of Green Gables.*

Montgomery draw on her first surviving journal entry, dated September 1889, when she wrote about Anne's wish to name a geranium Bonny? Or did she add these elements from her novel when she started "transcribing" her journal entries as a way to introduce a form of retroactive foreshadowing? Researchers who, like editors Rubio and Waterston, work directly with the handwritten journals not only have to decipher Montgomery's difficult handwriting but also have to contend with excerpts that she crossed out in ink, what appear to be later amendments and commentary, and entire pages she razored out and replaced. One notable example of the latter involves "the entry in which she first described her future husband," as Rubio and Waterston noted in their introduction to the first volume — even though the page that was razored out didn't necessarily contain Montgomery's true first impression of him, since the page in question would have held the entry she'd transcribed sometime after 1919.[19]

Besides that, Montgomery had a curious habit of using the beginnings and the endings of the ledger volumes for extensive retrospection and self-analysis. In an entry dated February 7, 1910, in which she reached the end of her second ledger, she reflected on the fact that she'd begun that volume "nearly thirteen years ago." In the next entry, dated four days later, she commented on her experience of rereading entries from her first two volumes and beginning a third. "I turn over its blank pages with a shrinking wonder. *What will be written in them?*" Given that Montgomery had written three decades of entries in an unspecified number of notebooks of varying sizes, her self-awareness of the beginnings and endings of her ledgers likely didn't originate in her original versions of these entries.[20]

You'll notice that just now I wrote "in an entry dated February 7, 1910," rather than the more concise "*on* February 7, 1910," something I've been doing throughout this book. I started using this kind of phrasing years ago because of the number of times when there seemed to be a reasonable doubt that Montgomery actually wrote the entry on the date under which it appears.

After she announced in an entry dated April 16, 1922, that she'd finished her transcription of these thirty years of entries, she left explicit instructions to her heirs about her wishes in terms of both the preservation of the ledgers as material objects and the publication of their contents after her death, either in abridged or unabridged form, "if I do not myself do it before." As part of her instructions, she imagined her journals being of considerable value — both literary and commercial — to her descendants. But she referred to the journal's importance as consisting of "a faithful record of one human being's life" rather than, say, of the unexpectedly candid life record of the world-renowned author of *Anne of Green Gables*, as though she anticipated the marketing strategy that Oxford University Press would adopt more than sixty years later to introduce the journal narrative to the public. But she also made it clear in this entry what value these journals had for *her*. "There is so much of myself in these volumes that I cannot bear the thought of their ever being destroyed. It would seem to me like a sort of murder." It's also noteworthy that she recorded these instructions just two months after she finished writing *Emily of New Moon*, which ends with the title character writing a similar vow that blurs the lines between public and private and between life and afterlife: "I am going to write a diary, that it may be published when I die."[21]

It's impossible to guess at what point during the transcription process Montgomery began to think about posthumous publication — supposing, of course, that this hadn't been her motivation to do this work all along. What Montgomery likewise kept silent about was the fact that she evidently destroyed her original handwritten journals sometime after she transcribed them, just as she'd destroyed the childhood diaries that had preceded her first surviving 1889 entry (an act she later regretted). She likewise destroyed all the notebooks and slips of paper on which she frequently wrote preliminary versions of her journal entries, such as when she travelled or during periods of acute stress. When she died in 1942, she left a total of ten ledgers of handwritten journals that stand as the definitive — which is to say, the only remaining — version of her journal text, and those ten ledgers formed the basis of the three sets of published volumes that have appeared since 1985.

Did I say "only"? Well, not quite.

In the same 1922 entry in which she recorded her wish for her journals to be published after her death, she acknowledged a dilemma she'd have to figure out eventually: to which of her two sons she'd bequeath the handwritten ledgers as well as the responsibility for getting their contents published. The easiest solution to this dilemma — at least for the entries dated 1889 to 1918 — might have been for one son to inherit the original diaries while the other inherited the uniform ledgers. But this solution evidently didn't appeal to her, and in 1930, she embarked on the creation of a typed version of her journal text. As with her September 1919 entry, her first mention of this typescript, in a journal entry dated August 2, 1931, made no mention of possible publication; instead, her stated goal was to have something for whichever son didn't inherit the handwritten ledgers. And this time, she mentioned a curious side effect of using a typewriter for this task. "The slowness of the process allows the details to 'sink in' to such an extent that I seem actually to be *living* them all again."[22]

But in contrast to what she stated — and didn't state — about her goals for this typescript, the surviving documents include several handwritten instructions about stewardship and publication that named each of her sons in turn along with her first grandchild, Luella Macdonald, born in 1934. She evidently kept changing her mind about inheritance, because most of these instructions are crossed out. Those that seem to represent her final intentions — undated, but not crossed out — appear on a sheet of paper that she entitled "Copy of my journal / No. One":

> For Stuart Macdonald or his heirs. To be given to any publisher who may want to publish selections from it after my death in accordance with the terms of my will.
>
> L.M. Montgomery Macdonald.[23]

The phrasing of this note gives the impression that she'd given up on the idea of pursuing publication of these journals herself, and while admittedly there are large gaps in her surviving business correspondence, I don't recall any evidence that suggests she broached this project with her publishers, let alone submitted samples for their consideration. It's also difficult to trace her progress with the typescript, since the few mentions of it suggest a curious approach to chronology. Her August 1931 journal entry refers to her transcription of entries from her time teaching in Lower Bedeque in 1897–1898,

Cavendish 18 April 8, 1908

~~of a pain makes it more bearable.~~

I have grown years older in these past months. Grief and worry and heartbreak have done their work thoroughly. Sometimes I ask myself if the pale, sad-eyed woman I see in my glass can really be the merry girl of olden days or if she be some altogether new creature, born of sorrow and baptized of suffering, who is the sister and companion of regret and hopeless longing.

On March 6, while in Bedeque I received a telegram that Grandfather Macneill had drop-dropped dead the preceding afternoon!

The shock was terrible. In all truthfulness I cannot say that I have ever had a very deep affection for Grandfather Macneill. I have always been afraid of him and in recent years he has been very difficult to live with. Nevertheless, one cannot live all one's life with a person andxxxx not have a certain love for them ... the bond of kin and old association. When death comes this bond is revealed by its being wrenched asunder and we suffer keenly for the time being. Consequently , as I have said, I was shocked and stunned and felt as if

Page 18 of Montgomery's typescript of the second of her ten journal ledgers. The handwritten "1908" is an error — it should be 1898 — and this sheet of paper is a fraction of the length of the two pages that follow.

19

everything in life had fallen blackly xxxxxx together. It seemed impossible that the news could be true. They had all been in good health at home the last letter I had had from grandma.

It was Sunday when I got the telegram and I had to wait until Monday morning when Mr. Leard drove me over the ice to S'Side. There I took the train and reached Kensington at 1:30. John C. Clark came to xxxxxxxx meet me and it was eight o'clock when I finally reached home. xxx Aunt Annie, Aunt Emily and Aunt Mary Lawson were here. It was such a relief to be with them all.

Grandmother was naturally sadly prostrated. Poor grandfather's death had been so terribly sudden. It was presumably caused xxxxxx by heart failure. He had been in good health up to noon on Saturday, then complained of a pain, and in a few minutes dropped from his chair and in a moment passed away.

I went into the parlor with Aunt Annie to look at him. His face was quite unchanged and looked more gentle and tender than in life. I have never, since I learned to feel, stood thus by the coffin of one akin to me and it was a new and bitter experience. But once before I had looked down on a coffined face in that very room —. and that face was the face of my mother.

I was very young at the time — barely twenty two months old — but I remember it perfectly. It is almost my earliest recollection, clear-cut and distinct. My mother was lying there in her coffin. My father was standing by her and holding me in his arms. I remember that I wore a little white dress of embroidered muslin and that father was crying. Women were seated around the room and I recall two in front of me on the sofa who were whispering to each other and looking pityingly at father and me. Behind them, the window was open and green hop vines were trailing across it, while their shadows danced over the ~~floor in a~~ floor in a square of sunshine.

I looked down at the dead face of the mother whose love I was to miss so sorely and so often in after years. It was a sweet face, albeit worn and wasted by months of suffering. My mother had been beautiful and Death, so cruel in all else, had spared the delicate outline ofxxxxxxx feature, the long silken lashes brushing the hollow cheek, and the smooth masses of golden-brown hair.

I did not feel any sorrow for I realized nothing of what it all meant. I was only vaguely troubled. Why was mother so still? And why was father crying? I reached down and laid my baby hand against mother's cheek. Even yet I can feel the peculiar coldness of that touch. The memory of it seems to link me with mother somehow ... the only remembrance I have of actual contact with my mother.

Somebody in the room sobbed and said, "Poor child." I wondered if they meant me — and why? I put my arms about father's neck. He kissed me —. I recall one more glance at the calm, unchanging face —. and that is all. I remember no more of the girlish mother who has slept for twenty two years in the old graveyard, lulled by the murmur of the sea.

~~Grandfather's funeral was very large. I had to return to Bedeque the next day, and there the old heartaches which had been deadened for a time by the newer pain, awoke to gnaw and sting and burn once more.~~

~~Of course my miserable affair with Edwin Simpson was one of these.~~

~~Oh, I know I was guilty of wretched folly in this but have I not expiated this in suffering. For I have suffered ... what no mortal can know. What a curse feeling is! I never really learned to feel before. It takes suffering to teach that and the knowledge is named Marah.~~

~~I wonder if there is anywhere in the future real abiding happin-~~

Page 19 of Montgomery's typescript of the second of her ten journal ledgers. Although the text flows seamlessly between this page, the one that precedes it, and the one that follows it, a different typewriter was used to create it.

20

ess for me. No, I feel sure there is not. Something in my inmost soul tells me so. I could lie dOwn tonight and die, unregretfully, nay, gladly, if I were sure that death indeed meant rest and was not merely the portal to another life ... such a one as this, perhaps, ... Or a better ... but at all events xifx life ... and that means thpught and action and feeling ... perhaps memory as well .... anything but the rest I crave.

"I would not if I might be blest
I ask no paradise but rest."

And I think it is Longfellow in his gxkdxnxkxgxndGOLDEN LEGEND who says,

"Rest, rest, oh, give me rest and peace!
The thpught of life that ne'er shall cease
Hath in it something of despair,
A weight I am too weak to bear.
Sweeter to this afflicted breast
The thpught of never-ending rest,
Sweeter the undisturbed and deep
Tranquillity of endless sleep."

I must stop this wild wondering .....the echo of my confused, troubled thoughts .... and begin my story .... pick up the dropped thread and go on with it .... this miserable life story of mine that can never have a happy ending. I know I am only one of millions who are living just such unhappy lives ... there is no use in protesting against it as if I were the only unhappy atom in the universe. I don't protest now ... I did but that is past. I have sunk into a sort of apathetic resignation. I have grown used to unhappiness ... but oh, I am very tired.

I kept up my correspondence with Edwin Simpson all winter after a fashion and matters dragged on until I cpuld endure it no longer. I had intended ~~to wait until I left~~ Bedeque before confessing to him but there came a day when I felt ~~I cpuld endure it no longer~~ and early in March I wrote him, telling him that I did not and could not love him and could not marry him. I did not try to excuse myself. I admitted in full my weakness and asked him to give me back my freedom in terms that could leave no doubt as to my feelings in the matter. I did not know and could not picture what effect it would have on him. I hoped he would release me quietly, being a proud man ... that he would not stoop to plead or strive to hold but would simply set me free with the scorn I deserved.

I mailed the letter just before I got the news of grandfather's death and for a few days it was almost driven out of my mind. But when I returned to Bedeque and his answer came, I dared not open it that evening. I was too much afraid of its contents, for I knew they would upset me and I needed a night's sleep badly. But the next evening I read it after I came from school.

It was a frantic letter. But it was not at all what I wpuld have expected and infinitely preferred. I had expected accusation and reproach ... contemptuous upbraidings ... and if the letter had contained such it would not have cut me to the heart half as deeply as it did. For it was a heart-broken letter and I felt that the mere reading of it was punishment enough. ~~(Omissions)~~

He went on to say that he could not set me free, ~~in that letter~~. He could not, he declared, give up the hope that all might yet be right.

Page 20 of Montgomery's typescript of the second of her ten journal ledgers. Montgomery corrected typographical errors as she went and made editorial emendations after the fact, judging by the paragraphs at the top of the page, crossed out in green pencil.

whereas in an aside between two entries dated July 1937, she mentioned that she'd recently typed up the entries for the four years that had followed her return from Prince Albert — which *preceded* her time in Lower Bedeque. And in an entry dated June 6, 1938, she referred to "typing a diary record of the year after I came from the west."[24] Then again, given that the pages of the typescript appear to have been created using more than one typewriter, it's entirely possible that Montgomery produced more than one version.

In the end, Montgomery eventually produced a typescript that covered the vast majority of entries from her handwritten ledgers, and the surviving documents are worth looking at as a version of the journal text that she saw as suitable for publication after her death. Rubio and Waterston, who used the handwritten ledgers as the copy-texts for their volumes of published journals but consulted the typescripts when they had difficulty deciphering Montgomery's handwriting, noted that "in this typescript she predictably deleted some of the most interesting and psychologically revealing sections, and toned down criticism of people who were still living." But a closer look reveals two notable exceptions to this pattern. The first is the fact that Montgomery's account of her wedding feast is identical in the typescript and the handwritten ledger, with differences pertaining only to punctuation:

> I had been feeling contented all the morning. I had gone through the ceremony and the congratulations unflustered and unregretful. And now, when it was all over and I found myself sitting there by my husband's side ... *my husband*!... I felt a sudden horrible inrush of *rebellion* and *despair. I wanted to be free*! I felt like a prisoner ... a hopeless prisoner. Something in me ... something wild and free and untamed ... something that Ewan had not tamed ... could never tame ... something that did not acknowledge him as master ... rose up in one frantic protest against the fetters that bound me. At that moment if I could have torn the wedding ring from my finger and so freed myself I would have done it! But it was too late ... and the realization that it was too late fell over me like a black cloud of wretchedness. I sat at that gay bridal feast, in my white veil and orange blossoms, beside the man I had married ... and I was as unhappy as I had ever been in my life.[25]

The second exception involves excerpts that Montgomery referred to in the 1931 entry in which she mentioned the typescript project for the first time. According to that entry, revisiting those entries brought the past back to her so vividly that she felt compelled to leave the house. But her choice of verb — "copying" — to describe her process doesn't begin to capture what's in the typescript text.

— 5 —

In a journal entry dated June 30, 1897, the twenty-two-year-old Montgomery depicted herself as being wholly changed from the writer of the preceding entry. "The girl who wrote on June 3rd is as dead as if the sod were heaped over her — dead past the possibility of any resurrection." Although she added in this initial paragraph that whatever had happened had been "all [her] own fault," her inner storyteller prompted her to unravel the story gradually. But the bottom line was this: She'd agreed to marry Edwin Simpson, despite the fact that he was a Baptist as well as her second cousin (both factors that were frowned upon in her family) and, arguably even more problematic, she didn't love him — "but I thought I *could*." Unfortunately for both of them, Montgomery's lukewarm feelings for Edwin didn't rise in temperature after she accepted his proposal. Quite the contrary: she began to feel "a distinct sense of *physical repulsion*" toward him. But while it quickly became clear to her that nothing on earth could compel her to go through with marrying this man, she found the idea of him — or anyone else — suspecting how she really felt utterly humiliating. A more practical problem consisted of the fact that, according to the customs of her time and her culture, she couldn't, as a woman, end an engagement without the consent of the prospective groom. So she suffered in silence — all winter, in fact. But while she acknowledged in that entry that she might feel better if she wrote about this experience, she evidently came to a different conclusion when it came time to revisit this life chapter decades later, judging by her comments at the beginning and near the end of the entry in her typescript:

> What follows is a condensed account of what happened that spring. The entry in my original diary cannot be written here. I shall present the bare bones of it. I made a terrible mistake and paid the penalty of my folly in intense suffering....
>
> I have condensed into three pages the ten page account in my original journal. The details may never be known to the world unless someone cares enough after I am dead to read them.[26]

In a later entry, dated January 22, 1898, she reported that her feelings of mortification about her misjudged engagement to Edwin Simpson were more or less unchanged — if anything, they'd become even more intense over time. Still, despite her palpable agony, she ended the handwritten version of this entry by hinting that there was more to this story than she'd let on. "It is 'the play of Hamlet with Hamlet left out,'" she declared. "Perhaps some day I may write it over again with Hamlet in — and perhaps I shall never feel that I can!"[27]

And in the handwritten version of the next entry, dated April 8, 1898, Montgomery finally filled in the missing pieces in retrospect, one topic at a time instead of chronologically. First, after months of agony over the situation with Edwin Simpson, she finally bit the bullet and informed him by letter of her wish to end their engagement, a process that took several months of follow-up letters before he accepted the fact that she was serious. Second, after her paternal grandfather died, she decided to leave teaching in order to return to Cavendish and care for her grandmother, which enabled her to turn her full attention to writing while gaining the approval of her extended family and her community for her selflessness. And third, while boarding with the Leard family in Lower Bedeque while she taught school there, she found herself in an intense sexual flirtation with the family's eldest son, Herman. The problem — besides the obvious one that she was engaged to another man at the time — was that she perceived Herman to be beneath her, culturally as well as intellectually. And so, Montgomery saw marriage to Herman as equally unthinkable as marriage to Edwin, if for opposite reasons: as she claimed, "*Ed's* kisses at the best left me cold as ice — *Herman's* sent flame through every vein and fibre of my being."[28]

In her biography, Rubio comments on this account of Montgomery's entanglement with Leard, noting that Montgomery "was an avid consumer of all kinds of literary romance," including the nineteenth-century "'two-suitor' plot" that continues today in innumerable Hallmark movies, "in which a young woman must choose between two men who offer totally different prospects." In the handwritten version of this retrospective journal entry dated April 8, 1898, Montgomery spent pages and pages narrating every development of this romance — from first impression and initial twinge of interest to the frenzied passion, agonizing refusal, tearful departure, and soul-wrenching longing — complete with sensory details and dialogue. But if, as Rubio speculates, Montgomery "probably embellished the story of her entanglement with Herman when she recopied her journals after 1919," a decidedly different frame of mind evidently came into play a decade later when she revisited this entry in the journal typescript, in which she omitted all references to Hamlet being in or out.

> I met a man in Bedeque. I shall in this mangled copy call him X. He was very fascinating. But he had no trace of intellect, culture or education; no interest in anything beyond his farm and the circle of young people in Bedeque. In plain sober truth he was a nice, attractive young animal. And yet he had a mysterious irresistible attraction for me. I determined I would not have anything to do with him. I could not marry such a man, and I knew I was doing a disgraceful thing to accept any attentions from him when I was engaged to another man even though I knew I was never going to marry that man. If I could have kept this resolve I would have saved myself incalculable suffering. For it was not long before I found myself face to face with the burning consciousness that I loved X. with all my heart and soul. I knew it was madness, but I could not conquer it, try as I did — oh, I did! But I might as well have tried to stem the rush of a mountain torrent. My winter in Bedeque was a mingling of brief periods of rapture and hellish unhappiness.
>
> I did not yield to the temptation he more than once put me to — that is all the comfort I have.

Immediately following these paragraphs is one that is crossed out in pencil yet whose text is still legible. This paragraph draws more closely on what appears in the corresponding entry in the handwritten ledger:

Of course all this mental misery, those passion-wrung days and sleepless tearful nights had a destructive effect on my health. I longed for the time to come when I might leave for I hoped that when I was no longer exposed to the power of his fascination I might succeed in forgetting him and find rest. I shall never forget our parting. Since coming home I have spent a wretched week. I miss X. heartbreakingly … I long for him … I cannot, strive as I will, keep him out of my thoughts day or night. He is dearer to me than ever. There are hours when I am frantic for a glimpse of his face … the sound of his voice. But I *will* conquer … I will live it down even if my heart is crushed forever in the struggle.[29]

21

I had not told him in my letter that he was physically repulsive to mmx me. That was somethi[ng] I could not tell him. He asked me a great many questions but he did not ask the one I dreaded ...."Was there another man? " Because, by this time there was another man.... in one sense but not, after all, in the sense such a question or admission would have inferred. I knew I could never marry this other man. And it was just the same about Edwin long before I met him. When I had finished reading that terrible letter I curled myself up on the lounge with my miser[y] and wished again that I had never been born. I knew he loved me truly ... and what a perverse fa[te] it was that I could not return his love. How unutterably happy we might have been if I could onl[y] have loved him as I loved this other man!

But there was only one thing to do and I did it. I wrote again, reiterating all I had said before, asked for a little pity and considerationxxithpx although I deserved none and ended by imploring him to set me free.

His answer came the Friday evening before I left Bedeque.... Alph having returned to take the school again ... but I did not read it until I was on the train next day. I took the train at Freetown station about two o'clock and as soon as I was seated I opened the letter and read it ... and then sat there trembling from head to foot with the violence of repressed emotion while the train swayed on over bleak fields and leafless woods.

He wrote, "Oh Maud, I cannot gixmxymxxx , xxnnxt set you free without sufficient reason."

Sufficient reason! When I had told him that I did not and could not love him! Was not that sufficient reason? He went on;- "Will this do? I will set you free for the next three years ... free to do as you please.... yes, and marry anyone you please. If then you belong to another or are of the same mind as at present you shall be wholly free." Then he proceeded to say that we must still be friends and keep up our correspondence.

I could not agree to this. My haunting humiliation and sense of bondage would never be lessened and would wear my life out. Besides, it would be foolish. I knew I would never change in my feeling towards him. I wrote to him as soon as I arrived home ... such a letter as I ought not to have written. It was harsh and unjust and I am now bitterly sorry for writing such a letter. But I felt like a wild creature, caught in a trap, and biting savagely at its captor's hand. But perhaps it was just as well. It will probably do more than reproachful imploring letters to convince him that I am in earnest and I hope it will go far towards curing [his] love for me and opening his eyes to the fact that he is well rid of me. I have not received his reply yet. I suppose it will come soon.

(There is a great deal omitted in the following pages that is in my original diary. I wrote it all out there to ease my pain .)

Detail from page 21 of Montgomery's typescript of the second of her ten journal ledgers. This page contains excerpts that Montgomery crossed out but that remain legible.

In both versions of this account, Montgomery vowed to push all thoughts of Herman — or X. — out of her mind after her return to Cavendish. She was more successful in this regard in her typescript, in which she compressed a return visit to Lower Bedeque into two paragraphs, both of which end with the parenthetical note "Omission." And when Herman Leard died of complications of influenza in July 1899, Montgomery's grief is just as palpable in her typescript as in her handwritten ledger — perhaps even more so, since in her typescript she continued to refer to him as X.[30]

It's difficult to guess what motivated Montgomery to write about Herman Leard in such detail in a handwritten journal intended for posthumous publication but to censor so much of that experience in a later typescript created with the same goal in mind. The way that she invited interested readers who wanted more details about her feelings concerning Edwin Simpson to consult her "original journal ... after I am dead" suggests that she still considered trying to publish this journal during her own lifetime when she'd created this part of the typescript — although that seems unlikely, since Edwin Simpson was still very much alive when she began to create the journal typescript. To what extent Montgomery was aware that Herman Leard was engaged to a woman named Ettie Schurman at the time of her flirtation with him is likewise impossible to say.[31] It would be understandable if, between the creation of the handwritten ledger and the transcript, she developed second thoughts about revealing this experience to the public, but even if she did, she didn't go back and alter the handwritten journals, as she evidently did with her first mention of the man she later married. In other words, she let both versions of her narrative about Herman Leard stand and presumably wanted both of them to be preserved.

But her typescript contains one slip of the fingers when it came to her attempt to censor Herman Leard's identity — something that could easily have gone unnoticed had the typescript text been the sole version of her journals to survive. It's found at the end of Montgomery's entry dated December 31, 1898, which appears in nearly identical form in both versions:

> And so '98 ends. I am truly thankful. I turn to '99 with a chastened joy and a trembling hope that I may pass out

from the old shadows into the sunshine of its dawning — may throw off the mantle of the past year as an outgrown garment. This night last year I was at the Gardiner's dance and danced the New Year in with Herman. We were dancing together as the clock struck twelve. I took it then as a good omen ... but it was not. Oh, '98, how much I have suffered in you! How much of good and evil you have taught me, stern, cruel, relentless teacher that you were! Yet after all, '98, your harsh discipline has borne good fruit ... and bitter as it was I thank you for it. Thank you and farewell![32]

# 7

# A Fiction Writer on Fiction Writing

— 1 —

In 1923, L.M. Montgomery contributed to a book entitled *Fiction Writers on Fiction Writing: Advice, Opinions and a Statement of Their Own Working Methods by More Than One Hundred Authors*, edited by Arthur Sullivant Hoffman and published by the Bobbs-Merrill Company of Indianapolis — which incidentally was one of the houses that had declined the manuscript of *Anne of Green Gables*, according to Montgomery's journals. Hoffman's book consisted of answers by successful fiction writers to questions about craft, planning, revision, audience, skill development, technique, and realism. In a review of Hoffman's book, published in *The Editor*, T.S. Stribling pointed out that one of the strengths of the volume was that, in capturing the viewpoints of so many authors, it didn't make a consistent set of recommendations but instead offered "a precedent for any course [writers] can possibly pursue." And for Stribling, one of the highlights of the book was Montgomery's admission that "one of her most successful short stories grew out of the fact that she heard an irreproachable lady use a cuss word."[1]

Of the 115 authors who participated in the project, Montgomery is one of only a handful whose work continues to be read today, and her responses offer readers, then as now, a rare window into her writing practice as a best-selling fiction writer. "Sometimes the character suggests the story," she wrote in response to a question about how she developed her fiction. For novels, she explained, "the characters seem to grow in my mind … and when they are fully incubated I arrange a setting for them, choosing incidents and surroundings which will harmonize and develop them." But she reversed this process for short stories, for which "I generally start with an idea — some incident which I elaborate and invent characters to suit." In some cases, her answers shed light on some of her choices as a fiction writer, especially in terms of privileging character and setting over plot. "In the development of [character] and the arrangement of [setting] I find my greatest pleasure and from their letters it is evident that my readers do, too. This, of course, is because my *flair* is for these things." And although most of her books have third-person narrators, she revealed that her preference lay elsewhere: "I prefer writing in the first person, because it then seems easier to *live* my story as I write it.… I often write a story in the first person and then rewrite it, shifting it to the third."[2]

Montgomery offered examples from her own practice as a seasoned professional writer in her answers for Hoffman's volume, as she did in a handful of craft-focused essays and interviews published throughout her career. In an interview with Phoebe Dwight published in the *Boston Traveler* in 1910, for instance, she ruminated on her shifting priorities as a writer over time, from "all kinds of elaborate novels with the most complicated plots" to a firmer appreciation for "the enduring charm of simplicity in writing, as in everything else. Children are refreshing. Stories about them are." And for Owen McGillicuddy's 1920 profile of six Canadian women writers, she shared details about her writing and revision process:

> I select all I think will harmonize with or develop my central idea … and then I build a "skeleton" of my story or

> book, blocking out each chapter fully as regards incidents and development of character, with suitable bits of description and dialogue. When the "skeleton" is finished I begin to write the book and generally do it pretty swiftly. When the story is done I lay it aside for as long as possible, then I read it over, revise, preen, amplify, or correct as may be required. Everything I write receives three such revisions. I work two hours every morning when I am home at actual writing, but collect material all day long by keeping a pencil and note book handy, jotting down everything that occurs to me.[3]

In other instances, she offered more prescriptive advice to fellow writers, such as in a 1915 essay entitled "The Way to Make a Book," in which she urged writers to ensure that they "have something to say — something that *demands* to be said," followed by concrete suggestions about developing a central idea, writing from everyday experience, showing versus telling, and being ruthless in revision. On another occasion, she lamented the difficulties faced by Canadian authors "to make good in Canada," as she termed it during a speech reported on in *Bookseller and Stationer* in 1924, in which she stressed the importance of "our Canadian authors to remain Canadians in atmosphere and in flavor." But she had a practical suggestion for this as well: "Every time you buy, beg, borrow, or steal books, see that one of three is by a Canadian author." And in a speech given in 1935, she encouraged people to turn to writing as a practical way to preserve stories from the past. "Don't let the wonderful tales and legends told you by your grandparents and the old people of today die.... Even if you have no literary ability yourself, write them down and preserve them — they will give color to our native Canadian history and literature."[4]

The publication of Hoffman's book in 1923 coincided with two significant milestones in Montgomery's writing life. In February, she received an invitation to become a fellow of the Royal Society of Arts, the first Canadian woman to be so honoured. As the Toronto *Globe* noted in its report of this invitation, "Ever since 'Anne Shirley' entered the realm of fiction in 1908, the 'Anne' books have taken their place as a permanent addition to the country's imaginative literature, and the charm of Prince Edward Island is now known wherever English is read or spoken." Six weeks later, the *Toronto Star Weekly* included Montgomery in its list of the twelve greatest women in Canada. In her journal, she deflected the first honour by focusing on how little it did to alter the conditions under which she lived and worked. "I wish being a 'Fellow' conferred immunity from smoking furnaces, malicious law-suits, 'flu' and bad 'phone service. But alas, it doesn't." Still, she had no trouble accepting the latter tribute because she interpreted it to mean the twelve "most *widely-known* women in Canada," noting that "I certainly am one and perhaps *the* most widely known."[5] Together, what these two honours show is what continues to be apparent a century later: that Montgomery's writing is culturally important (as measured by positive and frequent commentary by critics and reviewers) *and* popular with readers (as measured by book sales) — two yardsticks of success that even today are often seen as at odds with each other.

— 2 —

All of these strands of the broader public conversation about Montgomery and her writing depict an author who took writing seriously as a craft, who took herself seriously as a practitioner with a substantial body of work to her name, and whose assessment of her value as a writer was shared widely in the press. As such, there's quite a contrast between how she regarded her work in these essays and interviews and how she positioned herself as a writer in "The Alpine Path," which she opened by questioning the very idea of her writing as a career. "Could my long, uphill struggle, through many quiet, uneventful years, be termed a 'career'?" she asked. "It had never occurred to me to call it so" — this despite the fact that *Everywoman's World*, the women's magazine that had commissioned this memoir, had one of the largest circulations in Canada, not to mention that this work appeared with the subtitle "The Story of My Career." Montgomery's apparent modesty — she placed the term "career" within quotation marks three more times throughout the text — would I hope have been understood as somewhat performative, given that a profile by Mary Josephine Trotter, published three years earlier in *Everywoman's World*, had noted that the sales of Montgomery's books up to that point had totalled half a million copies. Even so, the text of "The Alpine Path" reveals less of a concern with Montgomery's writing and revision process or with offering practical writing advice than with describing "the incidents and environment of my childhood, because they had a marked influence on the development of my literary gift." As a way to substantiate the impact of her childhood on her work, she added that "were it not for those Cavendish years, I do not think *Anne of Green Gables* would ever have been written."[6]

But if Montgomery aimed for thinly veiled modesty in "The Alpine Path," she made a curious set of creative choices regarding Anne's own writing career in *Anne's House of Dreams*, released simultaneously. When former pupil and budding poet Paul Irving compliments Anne on her writing ("I've seen a good deal of your work these last three years"), she responds in a way that arguably goes well beyond modesty. "No. I know what I can do. I can write pretty, fanciful little sketches that children love and editors send welcome cheques for. But I can do nothing big. My only chance for earthly immortality is a corner of your Memoirs." Anne's belittling of her own work, especially in terms of her potential for literary fame, stands in stark contrast with the fact that Anne as a literary character was revered around the world by this point, and readers past and present who want to see more emphasis on her writing are no doubt disappointed by the books that depict her married life, by which point her work is described seldomly and in the vaguest terms. In her book-length study of Montgomery's books published in 1992, commenting on how "Anne subjugates her literary talents to a conventional domestic role," Genevieve Wiggins suggests that "the fading of Anne's literary ambition as she adopts the career of wife and mother may reflect Montgomery's own ambiguity about the proper sphere for a woman, or she may simply be conforming to the expectations of her reading public."[7]

In the absence of any concrete statements by Montgomery about why she made these choices regarding Anne's writing, Wiggins's theories seem entirely plausible. But my interpretation differs from hers, due to another writing text that appeared in 1923: Montgomery's *Emily of New Moon*, the first of three novels about the growth of a writer from childhood to adulthood. These books are the only ones that receive their own chapter in Arlene Perly Rae's book *Everybody's Favourites: Canadians Talk About Books That Changed Their Lives* (1997). "So many women — most of them writers — love a particular set of books" about an orphan girl who's "determined to become a writer," according to Rae. "Like her creator, Emily never relinquishes that dream."[8]

I mentioned in a preceding chapter that a 1917 letter Montgomery had written to Ephraim Weber indicated that she'd already begun thinking about the novel that would appear four years later as *Rilla of Ingleside*, which dispelled the supposition that Montgomery only ever thought about one book at a time. Similarly, in a 1923 article she published in *The Editor* five weeks before Stribling's review of Hoffman's volume appeared in this magazine, Montgomery made another revelation that sheds new light on some of her creative decisions: "Very soon after *Green Gables* was published the idea of Emily's character came into my mind — just 'came,' as all my characters do. But I had no time to develop her then because my publishers and public insisted on 'more Anne.' During these years I carried her in the background of my mind and when at last I was free to write of her two years ago, there she was all ready to be transferred to paper."[9]

Granted, Montgomery's revelation arguably oversimplifies her reasons for writing "more Anne," and it doesn't specify whether the character she'd "carried" in her mind long before she began developing the plot for that novel was always going to be a writer. Still, if it is the case that she'd already planned to write a book about the development of a writer, it stands to reason that she wouldn't want to cover similar ground with Anne. It's also possible that she'd decided even sooner than she let on that after *Anne's House of Dreams* she'd shift the focus to Anne's children — including a son who's a poet and a daughter who keeps a diary throughout the war — and the broader Four Winds community.

But even if we take Anne's children and Emily out of the equation, I don't think Montgomery ever meant to develop Anne as a serious writer, judging by several elements of unreality in the depiction of Anne's writing ambition. To explain what I mean, I'll draw on a short story Montgomery published fifteen years before *Anne of the Island*, a television adaptation of that novel that aired seven decades later, and a pattern of suppositions in the press that I suggest would have given her several reasons to create distance between herself and her best-known fictional character.

— 3 —

Published in the Philadelphia *Times* in 1900, "The Adventures of a Story" focuses on Polly and Prue, high school roommates who are studying to become teachers. Prue refers to their shared room as "Poverty Flat," so not surprisingly, they could use some extra money, which is why she decides to try her hand at writing fiction. "Of course, it will be a juvenile story," she explains to Polly. "I won't attempt anything for older readers yet. And I think I'll send it to Sunny Hours. I'm sure I can write as good a story as those I've been reading here."

She even decides — since "Prue Stewart doesn't sound very literary somehow" and "Prudence is worse still" — to submit her work as "P.L. Stewart."

The brevity of this story doesn't allow for a lot of character development, but the narrator offers some pointed contrasts between these two friends. "Polly was a steady, systematic student, and in this respect had the advantage of the more brilliant Prue, who was too much given to day-dreaming, and could be lured from her studies at any time by the fascinations of a storybook or a magazine." Prue's fascinations extend to the juvenile periodical to which she plans to submit her story, which has the "nice and alliterative" title "Marjory's Mistake" but whose plot is never described. After at least six periodicals reject her story, Prue puts it away in her trunk and resolves to put the experience behind her, while Polly looks thoughtful but says nothing.

Readers of the Anne books may sense where this is going.

A month later, Prue is shocked to learn that, thanks to Polly's intervention, "Marjory's Mistake" has won first prize in a writing competition from the Excelsior Baking Powder Company. "I knew it was of no use to ask you to send it after you had forbidden me so tragically ever to mention it to you again," Polly explains. "So I just copied it out, put in a word or a sentence here and there relative to the baking-powder, signed your name and sent it off."

This story contains the origins of Anne's attempt, in *Anne of the Island*, to write, revise, and submit a short story with the similarly alliterative title "Averil's Atonement." Much like how "The Adventures of a Story" never goes into detail about who Marjory is or what mistake she's committed, the novel offers few clues about Averil or what situation she's atoning for. But there are several key differences between the two iterations of this plot, many of them necessitated by Anne as an already established character.

First, similar to Montgomery's stated description of her process of writing a novel, Anne starts by developing the character and then tries to figure out "a suitable plot" — except that, as she confides to Diana, "None of the plots that suggested themselves suited a girl named *Averil*." And even when she overcomes that obstacle, her sense of the character impedes her creativity in unexpected ways. "Averil is such an unmanageable heroine. She *will* do and say things I never meant her to. Then that spoils everything that went before and I have to write it all over again."[10]

Second, Prue writes because she needs the money and attempts to shape her story to fit the expectations of a magazine she enjoys (the name *Sunny Hours* seems reminiscent of *Golden Days for Boys and Girls*, the Philadelphia home of many of Montgomery's earliest publications). In contrast, Anne, although a poor student herself, is motivated more by the "pursuit of fame" than by what the narrator calls "mercenary considerations." Anne enters into the depths of despair after two editors reject "Averil's Atonement," but Prue responds to her string of rejections with a sense of humour and a philosophical attitude. Upon submitting the story to the last periodical on her list ("Youth's Guide," a likely stand-in for *The Youth's Companion*), she vows that "when it comes back again, I shall add the rejection slip to my already extensive collection, and make a scrapbook of them." And where Diana submits the story to a writing contest sponsored by a baking powder company in the hopes of boosting Anne's self-confidence, Polly's rationale for doing so is likewise far more practical: Prue wants to attend "the Summer School of Science at Long Harbor," since apparently "it is such a help to any one that wants to be a teacher," but there's no way she can afford it.[11]

Third, unlike Prue's story, "Averil's Atonement" receives criticism from Diana and especially from neighbour Mr. Harrison, who advises Anne to "cut out all those flowery passages" and who points out that her characters "ain't like real folks anywhere" in terms of how they speak and interact with each other. He recommends that she set her fiction "right here in Avonlea — changing the name, of course, or else Mrs. Rachel Lynde would probably think she was the heroine." Much to Anne's dismay, both of her readers prefer the villain to the hero: "He did bad things," Mr. Harrison acknowledges, "but he *did* them." And although Gilbert manages to smooth down Anne's ruffled feathers by reminding her that the prize money will go a long way toward paying for another year at university, she's far from consoled by the end of the chapter: "The deeper hurt of an outraged ideal remained."[12]

Given that Montgomery had published three earlier books set in Avonlea, including the collection of linked short stories *Chronicles of Avonlea*, there's a certain amount of dramatic irony in Anne's insistence that "Avonlea is the dearest place in the world, but it isn't quite romantic enough for the scene of a story." Montgomery admitted in a journal entry dated January 27, 1911, that "Cavendish is to a large extent *Avonlea*," but she went on to explain for several paragraphs how she'd modified reality to create her setting and her characters. Even so, attempts in the press to create one-to-one links between fiction and reality — including identifying the "originals" to her characters — began almost immediately after the publication of *Anne of Green Gables*, such as in a *Boston Herald* comment that claimed that "many of the incidents in her delightful story are transcripts from her own experience, Avonlea being a picture of Cavendish." Such claims annoyed Montgomery, and rightfully so, because they subtly minimized the process of creation by implying that what she was really writing was thinly veiled autobiography, not fiction. Perhaps that's why when she drew on that 1911 journal entry to write "The Alpine Path," she stated that "Cavendish was 'Avonlea' to a certain extent."[13]

Elizabeth Rollins Epperly views the "Averil's Atonement" sequence in *Anne of the Island* as a sign of Anne's relative immaturity — she still clings to the *idea* of romance and resists the *realities* of romance, something that evolves somewhat throughout the book after Anne receives five marriage proposals. Epperly concludes that Anne "comes to terms with her own true writing voice" by the end of the novel, but the significance of this development becomes more nuanced if we consider how this plot thread unfolds differently in *Anne of Green Gables: The Sequel*, a television miniseries that was written and directed by Kevin Sullivan and released in 1987. This miniseries weaves plot threads from three of Montgomery's Anne books and thus makes major changes to the source material's timeline, but even so, it emphasizes Anne's writing ambition in ways that alter her character development — and her creativity.[14]

When this miniseries opens, Anne (played by Megan Follows) has been teaching in Avonlea for two years and has recently started the process of submitting for publication a short story she's written entitled "Averil's Atonement." But she gives up after receiving a single rejection and, like in the book, feels humiliated when she wins the Rollins Reliable Baking Powder Company writing contest thanks to Diana's intervention. But in this version, it's lovelorn Gilbert (played by Jonathan Crombie) who offers Anne the same criticism that Mr. Harrison did in the novel about the story's characters and language and who urges her to write something that's closer to her own experience. And so, while teaching full-time at a private girls' school in New Brunswick, somehow she finds the time that winter to write a book called *Avonlea Vignettes* that she dedicates to Matthew and Marilla — and Gilbert.

The Anne of this screen adaptation is arguably a more successful writer than Montgomery's Anne, given that by the end of the miniseries she has copies of her first book in her hands. Still, besides the fact that this Gilbert obviously has an ulterior motive when he urges Anne to give up on unrealistic visions of romance and to open her eyes to the reality in front of her, I can't help but notice that Anne's success happens as a result of her writing exactly the book Gilbert told her to write. The only difference is that while Gilbert repeats Mr. Harrison's recommendation that she set her fiction in Avonlea but change the name, Anne disregards the second half of that suggestion, resulting in a book that appears to be a "transcript" of Anne's own life experience, to return to the *Boston Herald*'s word choice, rather than a work of fiction that she created out of the imagination for which she's so famous.

For me, these creative choices in the adaptation shed new light on what happens in *Anne of the Island*. Even though Anne's understanding of romance is relatively more mature by the end of the book than at the beginning, she still doesn't heed Mr. Harrison's advice about writing realistic fiction set in a locale she knows. Later in the novel, she rereads the stories she and her friends wrote as part of the Story Club in *Anne of Green Gables*, including her masterpiece, "a harrowing tale of the wanderings of a Methodist minister's wife" who "buried a child every place she lived in" — the same plot as that of Montgomery's own adolescent literary "masterpiece" described two years later in "The Alpine Path." Then, basking in the nostalgia for "the sunshine and mirth of those olden summers," Anne comes across a story she wrote in chapter 18 of *Anne of Avonlea*.[15]

The problem? This story — "a little dialogue between asters and sweet-peas, wild canaries in the lilac bush, and the guardian spirit of the garden," described in almost identical ways in both books — is even less realistic than "Averil's Atonement." Still, she rewrites this "little sketch," submits it to a magazine called the *Youth's Friend* — a name that likewise brings to mind *The Youth's Companion* — and a fortnight later receives an acceptance letter, a cheque for ten dollars, and an invitation to submit more work in the future.[16]

It's certainly noteworthy that Montgomery's Anne succeeds by disregarding Mr. Harrison's advice and persisting with what *she* wants to write, rather than what a lovelorn Gilbert urges her to write. But the ease and speediness with which she achieves that success is just as unrealistic as it would be seven decades later in *Anne of Green Gables: The Sequel*. And unlike Prue, who decides to write for young people and sees work for older readers as something to try later, Anne arguably goes backward in her development, both as a writer and as a person, by starting off with a short story aimed at adults and finding her success with a work for young readers — one that she wrote four years earlier.

The rest of the novel makes only a passing mention of "the success [Anne's] little sketches were beginning to meet with in certain editorial sanctums," which is all that's offered to reassure readers that Anne will stay true to "her budding literary dreams." And that's more than can be said for Prue, who agrees to accept the prize money only if Polly accompanies her to the summer school — by coincidence, the prize is exactly the amount that two participants would need for tuition, room, and board. But when Polly assumes, as the two friends get ready for bed, that Prue will keep writing stories given this success, Prue surprises her.

> "I've come to the very comfortable conclusion … that I am not a genius after all, and that the editors and the great reading public are not waiting breathlessly for the productions of my pen. When I come back next term I'm going to study hard and systematically and give up day-dreaming. I can be a good student and teacher, if I can't be a great writer."
>
> "Well, I'm glad you wrote one anyhow," said Polly drowsily, "and you know I always believed that story was a good one."[17]

In a journal entry that she quoted in "The Alpine Path," Montgomery complained about the need to ensure that short stories for young people contained some "insidious moral hidden away in it like a pill in a spoonful of jam!"[18] It's unclear what moral "The Adventures of a Story" points to, given that Prue not only fails in her attempt to publish a short story (at least the way she intended to) but also resolves never to try again. Still, in *Anne of the Island*, Anne finds success on her own terms — at least before she bows out of the larger narrative as the focus shifts to her children.

## — 4 —

In chapter 23 of *Anne's House of Dreams*, Anne and her neighbours meet Owen Ford, who has travelled to Four Winds Harbour for his health — and also to work on his "great Canadian novel," which, it turns out, he hasn't even begun yet. "I've never been able to get the right central idea for it," he admits. And when Anne dismisses her own writing as "little things for children" and adds that writing a great Canadian novel "is quite beyond me," Owen ends up joining in the laughter: "I dare say it is beyond me as well." Soon, it occurs to Anne that Owen might have the perfect skill set for a different kind of writing project: breathing life into the "life-book" of Captain Jim, whose considerable powers as an oral storyteller don't extend to the written word.[19]

As Anne asserts to Gilbert earlier in the novel, "To write Captain Jim's life-book as it should be written one should be a master of vigorous yet subtle style, a keen psychologist, a born humourist and a born tragedian." What's crucial is that here, Anne doesn't *diminish* her own abilities, but she acknowledges that her talents lie elsewhere — "the fanciful, the fairylike, the pretty." In short, she sees this project as "not in the power of my gift."[20] Similar to Montgomery in "The Alpine Path," who persisted in placing the term "career" within quotation marks four times but then referred to her "literary gift," Anne seems to be looking for the balance between taking herself seriously as a writer but not taking herself *too* seriously.

Captain Jim proves to be a complex character in his attitude about women. Upon his first meeting with Owen, "a real writing man" whom he looks upon as "a superior being," the narrator adds that he "knew that Anne wrote, but he had never taken that fact very seriously. Captain Jim thought women were delightful creatures, who ought to have the vote, and everything else they wanted, bless their hearts; but he did not believe they could write." His evidence for this damning generalization? A newspaper serial entitled "A Mad Love." "A woman wrote that and jest look at it — one hundred and three chapters when it could all have been told in ten. A writing woman never knows when to stop; that's the trouble. The p'int of good writing is to know when to stop."[21]

Captain Jim's attitude about women as "delightful creatures" and about women writers in particular is reductive and paternalistic. Still, it's important to remember that Montgomery, as a woman, did not get to vote until December 1917 — several months *after* the publication of *Anne's House of Dreams* — so Captain Jim's apparent support of women's suffrage would have been rather forward-thinking in a novel set two decades earlier. And while he may scoff at the literary quality of that newspaper serial, which earlier he claims to read "jest to see how long she can spin it out," it seems to have sustained his interest all the way to the end.[22]

Anne's non-involvement in the creation of *The Life-Book of Captain Jim* might also have been informed by another factor — namely, that for this aspect of the novel Montgomery had drawn on her 1909 short story "The Life-Book of Uncle Jesse," in which Mary and her mother travel to Golden Gate because her mother, like Owen Ford in the novel, needs "sea air and quiet" to rebuild her health. There, they meet a retired sea captain whom they call "Uncle Jesse" as a courtesy. The short story is largely identical to this part of the novel, except that in the story, Mary invites her cousin Robert, who works for a newspaper, to join them at the cottage the following summer in the hopes that Robert might be interested in collaborating with Uncle Jesse. Mary doesn't consider doing this work herself since she isn't a writer, but she provides feedback on a draft of the manuscript and offers a suggestion about the ending, "so that I felt as if I had a share in it too." In the book, both Anne and Leslie Moore "read the manuscript and criticise it," and although it's unexpectedly Leslie, not Anne, who offers the suggestion about "the concluding chapter of the book, which the critics, later on, were pleased to call idyllic," arguably, this change marks the development of Leslie, whose life has up to now been dogged by tragedy.[23]

Owen finishes the manuscript with the conviction that he's written "a book that would *live*" — and, more pragmatically, a book that "would bring him both fame and fortune." And while *The Life-Book of Captain Jim* proves to have a success similar to that of *Anne of Green Gables* — the book "head[s] the lists of the best sellers" and the reviews are "almost all so kindly" — Owen has already disappeared from the story by this point, except to buy the House of Dreams from Anne and Gilbert with plans to keep it for summer vacations. In chapter 2 of *Rainbow Valley*, a conversation between Anne, Susan Baker, and Miss Cornelia reveals that Owen has published several more books in the intervening time, and Miss Cornelia makes a rather baffling revelation: "I make it a point to read every [book] he writes, though I've always held, Anne dearie, that reading novels is a sinful waste of time." But otherwise, there's no room left in the narrative for this writer character as the focus shifts to the broader Glen St. Mary community — particularly Anne and Gilbert's children, including second son Walter, who gave

Rainbow Valley its name and who "had all his mother's vivid imagination and passionate love of beauty."[24]

Although the narrator reveals that twelve-year-old Walter "cherished the ambition to be a poet himself some day," it turns out he's already a working poet, "secretly hard at work on an epic, strikingly resembling [Sir Walter Scott's] 'Marmion' in some things, if not in others." The biggest obstacles in his development as a poet include neighbourhood bully Dan Reese, who taunts Walter for several reasons, including the fact that "your mother writes lies — lies — lies," and housekeeper Susan, who's not a fan of Walter wasting his time "writing silly rhymes" on account of "an uncle who began by being a poet and ended up by being a tramp." Anne seems to find Susan's outrage amusing, but Susan sounds deadly serious about her hope that Walter "will outgrow the tendency. If he does not — we must see what emulsion of cod-liver oil will do." In other words, Susan sees being a poet as a physical ailment that needs to be flushed out of Walter's system. But even though Susan later tells Walter that his agonizing toothache "served [him] right for sitting up in the cold garret yesterday writing poetry trash," her dour view of poetry and poets doesn't appear to sway his determination to keep writing. And later, Walter overcomes his fear of physical pain by fighting Dan Reese, to the astonishment of all the schoolchildren who witness it.[25]

When Walter returns in his early twenties in *Rilla of Ingleside*, neither his ambition to write poetry nor Susan's take on that ambition appears to have evolved: When Walter, after much resistance, finally overcomes his fears and enlists in the war, he tells Rilla that "I've got back my self-respect. I could write poetry," whereas Susan reconciles herself to this development with the reminder that "it may cure him of being a poet, at least ... and that would be something." But as it turns out, Walter's lasting legacy takes the form of "the only poem I've written since I came overseas." While Walter, following in his mother's footsteps, downplays this work as "a little scrap of verse," the narrator goes on to highlight the extent of this poem's reach:

> The poem was a short, poignant little thing. In a month it had carried Walter's name to every corner of the globe. Everywhere it was copied — in metropolitan dailies and

> little village weeklies, in profound reviews and "agony columns," in Red Cross appeals and Government recruiting propaganda. Mothers and sisters wept over it, young lads thrilled to it, the whole great heart of humanity caught it up as an epitome of all the pain and hope and pity and purpose of the mighty conflict, crystallized in three brief immortal verses. A Canadian lad in the Flanders trenches had written the one great poem of the war. "The Piper," by Pte. Walter Blythe, was a classic from its first printing.[26]

The text of Walter's poem is never given in the book. The remaining characters frequently refer to the phrase "keep faith" in quotation marks, but while it's possible that this term appears in the poem, it's equally possible that the quotation refers to Walter's last letter to Rilla, in which he expresses his confidence that she and Una Meredith will "both keep faith," to which Rilla responds aloud: "I will keep faith, Walter." In that same letter, Walter acknowledges that "I'll never write the poems I once dreamed of writing — but I've helped to make Canada safe for the poets of the future," which he sees as coming "not in a year or two, as some foolishly think, but a generation later, when the seed sown now shall have had time to germinate and grow." But the title of the poem evokes a vision that Walter has as a child in *Rainbow Valley* about "the Pied Piper coming down the valley" and that he remembers in the final moments of that novel: "The Piper is coming nearer … he is nearer than he was that evening I saw him before. His long, shadowy cloak is blowing around him. He pipes — he pipes — and we must follow — Jem and Carl and Jerry and I — round and round the world. Listen — listen — can't you hear his wild music?"[27]

Once Montgomery finished *Rilla of Ingleside*, she had no desire to imagine those characters in the postwar world Walter had predicted. Instead, she decided to set her novels about Emily in the years leading up to the war — or, as the narrator of *Emily Climbs* puts it, "the olden years before the world turned upside down."[28]

## — 5 —

In a letter to Ephraim Weber dated October 19, 1921, Montgomery made a revealing comment in the midst of her creative transition from her last book about Anne to her first book about Emily. "People were never right in saying I was 'Anne,'" she wrote, "but, *in some respects*, they will be right if they write me down as *Emily*." But three years later, in a letter dated November 1, 1924, she could hardly contain her annoyance at his suggestion that "*Emily* is another *Anne*." As she put it, "In my mental conception of her there was a big difference between reserved *Emily* with her background of family and tradition and the hail-fellow-well-met little orphan from nowhere."[29]

That may be so, but the marketing strategy for *Emily of New Moon* seemed to hinge on linking Emily to Anne at every opportunity, as shown in ads appearing in three consecutive issues of *The Publishers' Weekly* leading up to the book's publication in late August 1923. "In this novel," an ad in the August 11 issue claims, "L.M. Montgomery creates a delightful new character sure to win the hearts of all lovers of the famous Anne. 'I like this new book better than any I've written since "Green Gables,"' says the author. And certainly the reader will see in Emily all the charm, lovableness, and welcome sense of humor that endeared Anne to young and old." The following week, the quotation from the author stays, preceded by two new sentences: "A new character is created in this story who should win as firm a place in people's hearts as the famous Anne of Green Gables. L.M. Montgomery's stories are known the country over as wholesome, jolly tales, the kind that every member of the family can enjoy." And in the August 25 issue, those two sentences are changed again: "Those who have read this story feel sure that L.M. Montgomery has created a new character as sure of brilliant success as the famous Anne of Green Gables.... A book you can recommend to man, woman or child — and know it's worth recommending."[30]

Despite superficial similarities between the characters of Anne and Emily — they are both orphans, older than their age, with inconsistent experiences in terms of education and religion, and they are misunderstood by well-meaning but narrow-minded adults — the differences between them show a particular care on Montgomery's part in the development of

Emily's character. Whereas Montgomery shared with Anne her aptitude for naming places and plants, her success at school, and her knack for making friends, what she shared with Emily were less externalized parts of her psyche, particularly the need to process hurts, misunderstandings, and forms of injustice by writing about them in a diary. Unlike Montgomery, who claimed to have burned her childhood journals because at fourteen she'd grown to find them too juvenile, Emily impulsively throws her diary into the kitchen stove when Aunt Elizabeth insists on reading its contents. Emily's diary acts as a site of her agency, her self-expression, and her power, and she would rather destroy it than let that record of herself fall into the wrong hands.[31]

Similar to Walter, who endures unkind comments from Susan as well as taunting in the schoolyard because of his ambition to be a poet, Emily faces resistance from her extended family, her first teacher, and many of her peers because of her writing ambition. The difference, of course, is that the adults in Emily's life have more leverage than Susan does in terms of forcing her to give up writing. In *Emily Climbs*, Aunt Elizabeth offers Emily the chance to go to a neighbouring town to attend high school — on the condition that she give up writing completely. A standstill follows, until Cousin Jimmy encourages Emily to meet her aunt halfway: "She doesn't like your writing stories, especially. She thinks they're lies." And so, Emily and Elizabeth agree on a compromise that Emily "won't write anything that isn't *true*," in part because Elizabeth has little understanding of the wide range of options that are left: "air-born fancies in verse — and weird little Jimmy-book sketches of character — and accounts of everyday events — witty — satirical — tragic." Elizabeth ends up relaxing this rule two years in, not because her appreciation of her niece's talent has evolved, but because she's in awe of Emily's ability to earn money from her pen.[32]

What distinguishes Emily's growth as a writer from Anne's and Walter's, of course, is that there is far more of it on the page. *Rilla of Ingleside* consists of several excerpts from Rilla's diary as a way to privilege her perspective, but in these novels, excerpts from Emily's letters to her late father and from her diary show her evolving in her abilities, not only in terms of spelling and the proper use of quotation marks, but also in terms of her powers of observation and her ability to craft a story. These books also show that, unlike in *Anne of the Island*, success requires time and determination and is hardly guaranteed after a first acceptance. The opening chapter of *Emily's Quest* reveals much about the writing life that Montgomery never touched on with Anne: "She knew that a hard struggle was before her; she knew that she must constantly offend Blair Water neighbours who would want her to write obituaries for them and who, if she used an unfamiliar word, would say contemptuously that she was 'talking big'; she knew there would be rejection slips galore; she knew there would be days when she would feel despairingly that she could not write and that it was of no use to try; days when the editorial phrase, 'not necessarily a reflection on its merits,' would get on her nerves." Five of the nine excerpts from Emily's diary that comprise chapter 2 of this last Emily book demonstrate the ups and downs in a writer's life: publication of a poem with an accompanying illustration, acceptance by a prominent magazine after scores of rejections, a night of insomnia after the receipt of four rejections in a row, an accusation from a family member who "thinks I 'put her' into my story *Fools of Habit*," a failed attempt to write a story on commission, and seeing her name listed as "one of the well-known and popular contributors for the coming year" in a magazine called *Girlhood Days*.[33]

But although Aunt Elizabeth learns not simply to tolerate Emily's writing but to accept it — "You seem to be able to earn a living by it in a very ladylike way," she says in this last Emily novel — Emily still has another obstacle in her growth as a writer: the opinion of the increasingly problematic supporting character Dean Priest. As was the case with Gilbert in the 1987 television miniseries *Anne of Green Gables: The Sequel*, Dean's advice is coloured by his romantic feelings for Emily, but where Gilbert encourages Anne to stay true to reality, jealous Dean offers crushing feedback on Emily's book manuscript that destroys what's left of her faith in her abilities: her characters are "only puppets," the story "only cobwebs." But like with Anne and "Averil's Atonement," Emily's next book, *The Moral of the Rose*, happens because someone else intervenes after the author has given up. In this case, Cousin Jimmy crams the manuscript into an old cracker box and mails it to the only publisher he knows of — a house so prominent that Emily didn't even consider submitting to it.[34] And so, while Montgomery drew on her well of experience to create the highs and lows of Emily's writing life, what she changed from her own experience involved forms of help — or hindrance — that came from other people.

In late 1929, two years after the publication of *Emily's Quest*, Montgomery participated in a *Toronto Star Weekly* round table entitled "My Best Piece of Work," which began by pointing out a curious paradox about book publishing: that once it leaves its author's hands and before it reaches readers' hands, a book "lives or dies according to what people say about it," whereas "the only person who says little or nothing about a book is the person who wrote it." The round table sought to correct this convention by inviting authors to write about their own work. While Montgomery's response is hardly boastful, it contains none of the modesty or belittlement that had appeared in "The Alpine Path" or *Anne's House of Dreams*.

> It has come to be a truism that an author is incapable of appraising his or her own work and that the pet book of any writer is likely to be the worst from a literary point of view. Be that as it may, the book I consider my best is "Emily of New Moon." As to explaining the "why" of my preference, that is a cat of a different breed. For one thing, I think it is a more finished piece of work from a literary standpoint than any of my others. For another, I think that the child-psychology of the heroine is superior to that of any other of my book children. It seems to me, in short, that in "Emily of New Moon" I came nearer than in any other book to achieving what I set out to effect.[35]

And despite how *Anne of Green Gables* continues today to overshadow everything else she wrote, many readers in Canada and elsewhere, particularly those who became writers themselves, would agree with Montgomery's assessment of her first novel about Emily.

## — 6 —

Although Montgomery did not attempt, after *Emily's Quest*, to write another novel that centred on a character who was a writer, her later books contain several writers as supporting and bit characters. But somehow, they're consistently depicted through the perspective of judgment, suspicion, or derision. In *Magic for Marigold* (1929), members of Marigold's large family prove to be highly judgmental of tactless Nina, who not only writes poetry but who also, even worse, "peddled it about the country." In *A Tangled Web* (1931), Aunt Becky amuses herself by humiliating several of her relatives at a public gathering, including two writers, but for opposite reasons: Margaret Penhallow for publishing some "rather awful little poems" in a nearby paper and Miller Dark for "talking for years of writing a history of the clan" but never starting. In *Pat of Silver Bush* (1933), Pat writes a letter to her mother in which she mentions, as an aside, a report from her friend Bets about a neighbour who "found out his son was writing poetry and whipped him for it." On top of these examples, Little Sam and Big Sam in *A Tangled Web*, Judy Plum in *Mistress Pat* (1935), Rebecca Dew and Valentine Courtaloe in *Anne of Windy Poplars* (1936), and Penny Snowbeam in *Jane of Lantern Hill* (1937) all express the fear — or the hope — that a writing character will "put them in a book."[36]

In Andrew Stuart, father of Jane, Montgomery depicts with some degree of realism the life of a working writer whose output includes "a little of everything": "stories ... poems ... essays ... articles on all subjects. I even wrote a novel once. But I couldn't find a publisher." His supposedly "dearest dream" — "to write an epic on the life of Methuselah" — becomes a running joke between them because of how little progress he makes on it. In the end, Andrew announces to Jane that he's found a publisher for his novel after all, but it's the offer of an assistant editorship at the (fictional) Toronto magazine *Saturday Evening*, not writing, that allows him to step into his role as provider for a wife and a child. And so, not even Andrew Stuart proves able to achieve any of the financial stability that Montgomery did as a writer.[37]

But besides that, forms of writing end up playing pivotal roles in several of these later novels' plots. In *A Tangled Web*, Aunt Becky sets off a chain reaction among all her relatives in large part because of a fake obituary she writes for herself — it even lights a fire under Miller Dark, who by novel's end has nearly finished his history of the Dark-Penhallow clan. Also in that novel, Gay Penhallow ends up wondering if her fickle fiancé lost interest in her as a result of her not answering a chain letter, whereas Penny Dark is dissuaded from courting Elva Penhallow due to a rumour that "she used to write down in her diary every night the time she had spent in idleness that day, and pray over it," deciding instead to set his cap on Margaret, whom he presumed "would of course give up writing her silly poems when she had a husband." In *Jane of Lantern Hill*, Andrew sets wheels in motion by writing Jane's mother a letter, and by the end of the novel, Jane decides to act after receiving an upsetting letter from one meddling relative and after confronting another meddling relative about a letter that was destroyed. In the endings of *Mistress Pat* and *Anne of Windy Poplars*, Judy Plum and Anne write letters to absent male characters urging them to act in order to bring about someone else's happiness.[38]

As for Montgomery, what remained in her ambition after she finished the Emily books was a new type of novel that she hinted at in letters and journal entries — or as she called it in a letter to Weber dated November 16, 1927, "A book portraying the life among the big 'clan' families of the Maritimes." Although she provided no further clues about this book's plot, her sense of what skills the project would require sounds remarkably like Anne's assessment of what kind of writer would be best suited to flesh out *The Life-Book of Captain Jim*: "The difficulty would be to keep the comedy and tragedy accurately balanced." Hildi Froese Tiessen and Paul Gerard Tiessen, editors of a volume of Montgomery's later letters to Weber, identify this novel as *A Tangled Web*, but their assessment is debatable. At any rate, the stock market crash of 1929 badly affected Montgomery's financial security at just the time that her two sons were ready for university and her husband was near retirement, which made her reconsider taking big risks in her future book projects.[39]

# 8

# A Writer and Her Critics

— 1 —

In November 1928, Montgomery made an appearance at Convocation Hall in Toronto for Canadian Book Week, alongside critic B.K. Sandwell and fellow writers Charles G.D. Roberts and Arthur Stringer. In a journal entry dated the day after the event, she wrote about her experience giving a speech to an audience of two thousand people:

> I had never faced such a big audience before and for a moment I came all out in goose-flesh. But they received me so rapturously that I forgot to be nervous and told my stories of the old north shore as to friends. I wound up by reading a little poem of New Year Wishes [that] seemed to "write itself" and gave me more satisfaction than I have felt for many a year....
>
> After the affair was over I was literally mobbed by hundreds of girls, wanting autographs. One however did not ask for an autograph. She was content with a handclasp. "I

> just wanted to *touch* you, Mrs. Macdonald," she whispered, looking up with adoring eyes. Poor kiddy! Humanity can't get along without some god or goddess to worship. It is well that my young worshippers don't know what a very clay-footed creature their divinity is. Their lives would be poorer if they lost their illusion.[1]

Not surprisingly given the nature of a journal entry, Montgomery's private account of this public appearance centres on her own experience of it, including her tolerant amusement over how some of her younger fans perceived her as a larger-than-life figure. But that's not the only known record of this Canadian Book Week appearance. The Toronto *Globe* also reported on the event featuring these four "writing luminaries," but its news story paid particular attention to "Mrs. Ewan Macdonald, known to millions of her readers as L.M. Montgomery":

> An ovation greeted her. Laughter followed her humorous sallies, and tears were not far away when she told the story of the wreck of the Marco Polo.
>
> Later she stated: "You know, we are all related down in P.E.I. It isn't safe to say a thing against anybody."
>
> Condemning some of the present day stories, which she says she never reads if she can avoid it, she declares: "They never come to an end; they just stop. Nobody is ever happily married or buried or hanged."
>
> The speaker tried to recite a poem in answer to about five minutes of applause when she concluded her speech. She forgot it before she even started. Then good-naturedly conjured up another and gave it. The crowd clamored for another, and she obliged.[2]

Both the journal entry and the *Globe* story mentioned that a large number of people — Montgomery claimed another thousand — had been turned away from the venue due to space restrictions. But it was only a year later that H. Napier Moore, editor of *MacLean's Magazine* (as the title was styled then), speculated about which of the four speakers the oversized crowd of people had gone to see:

> An hour before the time of commencement, the place was packed to the ceiling. Outside, a small army of perspiring policemen were endeavoring to convince hundreds of earnest citizens that, no matter how small they might be, they couldn't squeeze in. And of all the expressions of acute disappointment that heard most frequently was: "I want to see the woman who wrote 'Anne of Green Gables.'" Inside the auditorium, three or four of Canada's most distinguished male poets and authors were given enthusiastic hearing. But it was when L.M. Montgomery (or Mrs. L.M. Macdonald, as she is in private life), stepped to the front of the platform, that one realized who was the main attraction. The creator of Anne could have talked all night had she so desired. Not only because she *had* written a book of phenomenal appeal, but because she *has* an ability to interest, born of a rare understanding of human beings.

Each of these accounts of Montgomery's appearance at the 1928 Canadian Book Week offered its own perspective and served its own function. For Montgomery, writing in her journal was a private act as well as a public one: She reportedly kept her journal ledgers under lock and key throughout her lifetime, but by this point she'd already recorded in writing her wish for her heirs to publish the contents of these journals after her death. In contrast, the *Globe* article turned this experience into a news item for wide circulation, whereas the *MacLean's* editorial, benefiting from almost a year of retrospection, served to introduce Montgomery's short story "A Question of Acquaintance," which appeared in that issue.[3]

Moreover, an important distinction between these versions had to do with control. Montgomery had total freedom to represent herself in her journal according to how she wanted to be remembered — or known — after her death, but she had no say in how the mainstream press depicted her, what it said about her books, what forms of her writing it gave space to, or what direct quotations it attributed to her. And unless she commented on specific news items in her journals or surviving letters or pasted copies of those clippings in her scrapbooks, it's difficult now to determine with certainty which items she was aware of and which had escaped her knowledge.

By the time she took part in the 1928 Canadian Book Week, a new Toronto magazine called *The Chatelaine* had recently published a two-part article that had dubbed her "The Best Known Woman in Prince Edward Island," following similarly high-profile articles about her in *The Canadian Bookman*, *The Canadian Countryman*, and the *Toronto Star Weekly*. In the United States, an article entitled "A Canadian Bookshelf for American Tourists" and appearing in *The Publishers' Weekly* a few months before had declared Anne "the most popular heroine of Canadian fiction."[4] Her international fanbase included none other than Stanley Baldwin, prime minister of the United Kingdom, who in 1927 had requested a meeting with Montgomery during his cross-Canada tour so that he could meet "the author of books which have given me so much pleasure."[5] She had also just won a series of lawsuits and countersuits against her exploitative first publisher over the publication of *Further Chronicles of Avonlea*, and although her last royalty report had indicated that sales of her books had fallen slightly, this had to do in part with the fact that the continued demand for her earliest books was undercutting the sales of her more recent ones.[6]

But even though by 1928 she could point to all these metrics of success, another aspect of the writing life over which she had no control involved how her work got taken up by literary critics — especially university-trained critics who had ideological rather than practical considerations in figuring out what comprised — and counted as — "Canadian literature."

## — 2 —

In *Highways of Canadian Literature* (1924), J.D. Logan and Donald G. French identified the year 1908 as "the real beginning of the Second Renaissance in Canadian fiction" due to the publication of "three novels of the Community type — *Anne of Green Gables*, by L.M. Montgomery; *Duncan Polite*, by Marian Keith; [and] *Sowing Seeds in Danny*, by Nellie L. McClung." Notwithstanding the fact that *Duncan Polite: The Watchman of Glenoro*, the story of a small-town Ontario minister who causes a ruckus in his congregation when he attempts to install an organ in his church, had actually appeared in 1905, Logan and French positioned these three novels as evidence of Canadian authors' growing interest in the "life around them," during a "marked increase in fiction writing in Canada" in the first decade of the twentieth century.[7]

Their high praise is noteworthy not only because all three novelists were women but also because the two titles from 1908 — Montgomery's and McClung's — had been national bestsellers, a type of text that rarely comes to mind when critics attempt to mark a turning point in the development of a national literature. After all, as Mary Vipond observes in her overview of bestselling novels published in English Canada between 1899 and 1918, "Most of the fiction which appears on best seller lists is mediocre as literature. Unlike the serious novel, which challenges the reader and through ambiguity, analogy and archetype exposes him to a deepening and enriching experience, the popular novel thins and dilutes." To put it differently, "Popular novels do not deeply question but rather reinforce the values and attitudes which their readers already hold dear. They verify that which is already known; they fulfil expectations." To be blunt, "their very contemporaneity … makes them so perishable."[8] According to this way of thinking, bestselling novels appear to serve a function similar to that of newspapers and magazines: they help readers pass the time but are not meant to endure.

In contrast to Logan and French, who referred to *Anne of Green Gables* as a novel that "may be confidently labelled a 'Canadian classic,'" with no stated restrictions concerning the book's audience, Vipond discusses *Danny* and *Anne* as examples of books that were "often labelled 'domestic' or 'family' fiction and mainly read by teenaged girls and their mothers." Such books, she adds, "recounted the growing-up and first love experiences of a child or family in a manner notable for its excess of [what James D. Hart calls] 'syrupy pathos, sentiment, and optimism.'"[9] But while both McClung and Montgomery had several works of fiction on the Canadian bestseller lists into the 1920s, McClung is remembered now mainly for her politics and her non-fiction writing, whereas little of her fiction has remained in print.

The sticking point here between high cultural value ("deepening and enriching experience") and high quantity of copies sold ("perishable") depends on the assumption that a text that's enjoyed by a large number of people can't possibly be any good and thus should be beneath the notice of "serious" readers, especially critics and academics. But it raises some thorny questions about Montgomery's books. If bestselling fiction is "mediocre as literature," then how is it that *Anne of Green Gables* alone has been the subject of an ever-expanding body of scholarship, the source text for dozens of stage and screen adaptations, and the basis for booming tourist and commodity industries? If bestselling fiction is "perishable," then how has the popularity of this book persisted after more than a century?

The easy answer to these questions is that *Anne of Green Gables* is an exceptional novel that continues to defy categorization, but the fact that Montgomery's work remains popular even today is obviously something that critics during her lifetime or at the time of her death couldn't have anticipated. Still, it's worth considering to what point negative criticism of Montgomery's work has occurred as a result of this assumption that anything popular can't possibly be any good, rather than a considered evaluation of her actual work.

— 3 —

For someone living at the time of Montgomery's death who wanted to gauge her critical reputation, the most prominent critical sources available would have been five major book-length surveys of Canadian literature that had appeared in the mid-1920s: Logan and French's *Highways of Canadian Literature*, Archibald MacMechan's *Head-Waters of Canadian Literature*, Lionel Stevenson's *Appraisals of Canadian Literature*, William Arthur Deacon's *Poteen: A Pot-Pourri of Canadian Essays*, and Lorne Pierce's *An Outline of Canadian Literature (French and English)*. While Logan and French praised Montgomery's work for "hold[ing] before us the mirror of Canadian country life," MacMechan and Stevenson were somewhat more lukewarm in their assessments ("just misses the kind of success which convinces the critic while it captivates the unreflecting general reader"; "tinged with sentimentalism of a conventional sort dear to numerous readers"), whereas Pierce offered the somewhat backward compliment that *Anne of Green Gables* was "deservedly a classic of its kind, not because of its excellence of style or plot, but because of the altogether charming character, Anne."[10]

Elizabeth Waterston, tracing Montgomery's critical reception in her book *Kindling Spirit: L.M. Montgomery's "Anne of Green Gables"* (1993), sees in MacMechan and Stevenson's half-hearted assessments enough evidence to suggest that "critical respect for the work of L.M. Montgomery [had] dimmed" by the 1920s. Her overview doesn't even mention Deacon, whose comments about Montgomery's "series of girls' sugary stories" were unusually harsh: "Canadian literature was to go no lower; and she is only mentioned to show the dearth of mature novels at the time."[11]

Still, in my view, the fact that these critics mention Montgomery's work at all shows that they consider it to be a force to be reckoned with, similar to how Leslie McGrath detects a "coded endorsement" in the mere act of including *Anne of Green Gables* in the first edition of *Books for Boys and Girls* (1927), a resource prepared by staff at the Toronto Public Library, even though its synopsis for the novel is incredibly broad and contains no evaluation whatsoever: "The setting of this Canadian story is laid in Prince Edward Island." And to my mind, the way that most of these comments held critics to a higher standard than "unreflecting" readers arguably says more about those critics than it does about the work they dismissed. MacMechan, for instance, used his book as a platform to vilify *all* of Canadian literature — not just Montgomery's books — as "conventional, decent, unambitious, *bourgeois*." But even then, MacMechan expressed respect for Montgomery's work as a marketable commodity, if not as *literature*:

> An author naturally desires to repeat a success as soon as possible; and the public created by one pleasing book just as naturally prefers a repetition of the same ideas and sensations to the fatigue of having to readjust its mental

> machinery to new requirements. The author's name becomes a trade-mark, guaranteeing uniform quality in the ware supplied. Miss Montgomery has created her public and she supplies it with what it wants. The conclusion to be drawn from Miss Montgomery's achievement is that the great reading public on this continent and in the British Isles has a great tenderness for children, for decent, and amusing stories, and a great indifference towards the rulings of the critics. Besides, *Anne of Green Gables* and its fellows meet more nearly the common and reasonable requirement of "being true to life" than the Canadian stories of either Gordon [Charles William Gordon, better known as Ralph Connor] or [Gilbert] Parker.[12]

This kind of sustained book-length overview of Canadian literature does not appear to have been attempted again during Montgomery's lifetime, so these five books would have been some of the most logical places to look for a sense of her critical reputation at the time of her death. And so, it would be reasonable to look at these books, particularly Deacon's, and to presume that the decline in that reputation had simply increased since the late 1920s due to continued shifts in what was considered "good" writing.

Still, as the Toronto *Globe* and *MacLean's* stories about Montgomery's 1928 Canadian Book Week appearance make clear, it would be a mistake to assume that these five books were the only forums for critical assessments of Montgomery's work or that these critics (all of them men) were the only arbiters of taste when it came to evaluations of Montgomery's writing.

For that matter, it would also be a mistake to assume that these books offer the sum total of what these specific critics ever had to say about her work.

Several years after I discussed these 1920s CanLit surveys in the introduction to volume 1 of *The L.M. Montgomery Reader*, I stumbled upon an article by Donald G. French that had appeared in the December 1914 issue of *The School*, a Toronto publication. This article contains the bulk of the remarks about Montgomery's books that appeared in Logan and French's *Highways of Canadian Literature* ten years later — including the pronouncement of *Anne of Green Gables* as a Canadian classic — except that it begins and ends with a link between Montgomery and a literary ancestor from across the pond:

> No history of English literature is considered complete unless it gives due place to the work done by Jane Austen in her portrayal of rural English domestic life; and no history of Canadian literature, when such comes to be written, should fail to recognize that L.M. Montgomery has done for Canada what Jane Austen did for England....
>
> In characterizing L.M. Montgomery the Jane Austen of Canada, let it be understood that we are not regardless of the difference in the scope of the work of the two writers. Jane Austen's canvas is immensely broader, yet L.M. Montgomery's portrayal of her fellowmen and fellowwomen shows a much keener personal sympathy; her work has more heart to it.[13]

French revisited this link in two articles published in 1921. In one (signed "D.F.") published in the Toronto *Globe* about *Rilla of Ingleside*, he noted that since the publication of *Anne of Green Gables* "Montgomery has definitely fixed her place as the Jane Austen of Canadian literature and she has gone on employing her wonderful imaginative and creative gifts in portraying the beauty, the humor and the pathos that lies about our daily paths." I use the term "revisited" because this 1921 sentence has a clear precedent in French's 1914 article: "She has the imaginative and creative gifts, but she uses these in enabling us to see the beauty, the humour, and the pathos that lies about our daily paths." And in a short overview of Canadian poetry and fiction published in *The Canadian Magazine* the same month as this *Globe* piece, he repeated these ideas in his discussion of "the community or neighbourhood type of fiction," which he saw as "most strongly developed" in Canadian fiction: "L.M. Montgomery, in her 'Anne' books, pictures the purely Canadian rural community as it may be seen to-day, and it is no mere figure of comparison to say that L.M. Montgomery holds a place in Canadian literature corresponding to that of Jane Austen in English literature. She has rare imaginative and creative gifts and she uses them in enabling us to see the beauty, the humour, the pathos that lies about our daily paths."[14]

And so, except for the mysterious disappearance of Austen and the addition of a paragraph summarizing the preceding ten years of Montgomery's career, the unacknowledged self-plagiarism indicates that not only did French's opinion of Montgomery's work literally not change between 1914 and 1924, but by inserting it wholesale into a co-authored work, he essentially shared his positive assessment with Logan. Fortunately, Logan had his own enthusiasm for Montgomery's work, judging by the fact that, according to an entry in Montgomery's journal dated April 30, 1923, he'd approached her at a social gathering and exclaimed, "Hail, Queen of Canadian Novelists."[15]

French revisited his assessment of Montgomery's writing in a 1926 book entitled *More Famous Canadian Stories: Retold for Boys and Girls* (sequel to Leslie Horner's *Famous Canadian Stories: Re-Told for Children*, for which French was credited as editor), but given the space constraints of his chapter entitled "Stories of Canadian Authors," his comments about Montgomery are limited to one paragraph that offers some biographical details and repeats the mythologized beginnings of *Anne of Green Gables* involving Montgomery searching through her notebook in response to a request for a fiction serial from the editor of an unnamed Sunday school paper. "In more recent books," French added, "she has created an interesting new character Emily and tells the story of her youth." When French assembled an omnibus edition of both volumes in 1945, he added a single sentence about the date and place of her death, and although he made no mention of any of the books she'd published after 1926, in this case the overlap between versions of the same text indicates that French didn't see a decline in the quality of Montgomery's work — at least not enough to bother updating his remarks.[16]

As for MacMechan, Janet E. Baker's 1977 doctoral dissertation — likewise available now as a text-searchable digital file — notes that he discussed Montgomery's books occasionally in his "The Dean's Window" column in the Montreal *Standard*. That newspaper does not appear to have been digitized yet, but fortunately Baker's dissertation offers some clues about what he wrote — as she suggests, "in many places MacMechan notes the strengths of Montgomery's writing." According to Baker, he praised *Rainbow Valley* ("you may call it pretty — you cannot deny its reality"), but his less enthusiastic assessment of *Rilla of Ingleside* ("the elements of a good novel are there, but as you read you wish they could all be raised to a higher power") anticipates the tepid language he used about *Anne of Green Gables* in *Head-Waters of Canadian Literature.* In an appendix, Baker summarizes MacMechan's assessments of *Rainbow Valley* ("considers it successful within the limits it sets itself") and of *Emily of New Moon* ("considers that Montgomery is 'improving steadily in technique'"). So even though his review of *Emily of New Moon*, dated December 1923, appeared prior to the publication of *Head-Waters*, the fact that he saw the more recent *Emily* as an improvement on *Anne* suggests that his opinion of her work did evolve over time — and for the better.[17]

Stevenson's remarks about Montgomery likewise had a first appearance in periodical form, namely in his article "Overseas Literature: From a Canadian Point of View," appearing in late 1924 in *The English Review.* Although some of his specific comments are largely unchanged from article to book, the fact that this periodical was published in London suggests a target audience of readers who were presumed to be unfamiliar with Canadian literature due to geographical distance. And so, when Stevenson claimed in the article that he was "using Canadian literature for illustrative purposes" with the goal of proving "why it is worthy of consideration," he was addressing a predominantly non-Canadian readership. The earlier version of his remarks about Montgomery's work is reduced to a few sentences, and whereas in the book he noted that her works and those of Ralph Connor were "tinged with sentimentalism of a conventional sort dear to numerous readers," that sentence reads as "tinged somewhat with sentimentalism" in the article. Moreover, the backhanded compliment he offered Montgomery in his book — that the "passages of splendid farce" in her novels "give a very strong impression of being events from real life introduced arbitrarily into the narrative" — does not appear in the magazine article. These additions and revisions may suggest a negative evolution in Stevenson's thinking about her work, but, again, his stated goal for both his article and his book was to highlight writing that he saw as "inherently of some distinctive Canadian quality," so even a patronizing mention of Montgomery's work is better than no mention at all.[18]

— 4 —

And then there's William Arthur Deacon.

Several past studies of Montgomery's writing career — including some of mine — have described Deacon as one of its main antagonists, not only for his scathing remarks about her work in *Poteen* (which Mary Henley Rubio terms "an open attack on [her] popularity and reputation") but also because he apparently orchestrated a move to elbow her out of the executive of the Canadian Authors Association in 1938. As Rubio notes, "Deacon's ongoing hostility to her and her writing seemed more personal than professional. He sneered at her books, dismissing them, as if any outright discussion of them was beneath his intellect." And so, as Rubio concludes, "once her critical descent started, Maud's loss of status would continue steadily until her death."[19]

Even Deacon biographers Clara Thomas and John Lennox acknowledged that Deacon had "consistently denigrated" Montgomery and Connor for "their sentimental optimism."[20]

That may be so, but once again, the continued digitization of ephemeral print sources has facilitated the unearthing of materials that might complicate that depiction of him — or at least add some nuance to it.

As is the case with most of the 1920s critics mentioned so far in this chapter, Deacon's first comments about Montgomery appeared in a periodical article that preceded a book-length study — and, like Stevenson's "Overseas Literature" piece, the item in question sought to discuss recent Canadian literature for a non-Canadian readership. In a late 1924 article in *The Saturday Review of Literature* (New York), Deacon took a swipe at the recently published *Head-Waters* and *Highways*, both of which, in his view, "suffer from stylistic defects obvious to any reader," without offering any examples or details. Moreover, one flaw in MacMechan's "sketchy survey" concerned its focus on "treating the last two decades as 'the era of the best-seller,' ignoring writers of consequence in that epoch in favour of extended consideration of Ralph Connor and Lucy M. Montgomery."[21]

Starting around the time the Toronto *Globe* amalgamated with the *Mail and Empire* and became the *Globe and Mail* in 1936, Deacon began a new position as the paper's literary editor, a position he held until his retirement in the early 1960s. In volume 3 of *The L.M. Montgomery Reader*, I included an unsigned review of *Anne of Ingleside* that had appeared in the *Globe and Mail*'s "Saturday Book Review" column, edited by Deacon. Although I acknowledged that it was odd for the reviewer (presumably Deacon) to lend the book to a teenage girl and then quiz her about it rather than read it himself, I also noted that the review appeared alongside a photograph of Montgomery and a caption that pointed out the continued popularity of *Anne of Green Gables*, which "is still finding a widening circle of readers in many countries." At the time, it surprised me that the *Globe and Mail* would review Montgomery's books at all, given that Deacon, as Rubio states, "saw no place for Maud in the Canadian garden of literature he was cultivating."[22]

What I didn't realize until several years later was that Deacon's *Globe and Mail* column "The Fly Leaf," which consisted of a variety of news items about Canadian literature, included several positive — or at least neutral — comments about Montgomery and her work. Some of these were occasioned by mentions of Montgomery elsewhere, such as a 1937 poll of favourite authors held by the *Family Herald and Weekly Star* (Montgomery came in second, behind Charles Dickens); a 1946 radio show in which Roderick Kennedy, editor-in-chief of that magazine and by then president of the Canadian Authors Association, included Montgomery in a list of authors whose work evidenced "the distinctive character of Canadian prose writing"; a 1954 "Reading for New Canadians" list prepared by the Canadian Library Association for the Canadian Citizenship Council that consisted primarily of books published in the preceding ten years, with *Anne of Green Gables* being one of the only older texts to appear; and a speech given by Pierre Berton in 1960 in which "Mr. Berton flatly denied that readers are unkind to books of Canadian origin," using as one example the fact that "L.M.

Montgomery, using a P.E.I. background for Anne of Green Gables, [had] entered the world market."[23]

And on several more occasions, Deacon included short, factual statements about Montgomery and her work, sometimes at the tail end of his column: about the sale of the film rights to *Anne of Windy Poplars* (March 18, 1939), Montgomery becoming "an honorary member of the Canadian Authors' Association" (February 22, 1941), and the fact that Green Gables House in Cavendish had inspired a song entitled "When It's Summer at Green Gables," to which Deacon added, "Thousands of tourists visit this literary shrine annually" (September 20, 1941).

Then, in a column on April 1, 1950, Deacon made an announcement that highlighted the very thing he'd criticized Montgomery's work for a quarter of a century earlier: its popularity. "After 25 years, L.M. Montgomery's Anne of Green Gables had passed the millionth copy and was circulating in 25 countries. It is still finding new readers around the globe." Of course, by then the book had been selling copies around the world for forty-two years, not twenty-five. And in a 1962 column entitled "Japanese Girl Loves Lucy," Deacon shared a letter from a Japanese reader who'd been so touched after reading *Anne of Green Gables* that she hoped to meet correspondents who'd help her learn more about P.E.I. "The influence of Canadian books is sometimes felt in unexpected places in unexpected ways," he claimed, which is quite a leap for a critic who's best remembered now for his steadfast refusal to admit that Montgomery's work could possibly be representative of Canadian literature.[24]

Still, there's one more mention of Montgomery in Deacon's column that I'd like to share with you, with the candid admission that I found it surprisingly moving.

Was it a detailed, heartfelt tribute to Montgomery in the days following her death? No. The closest he got to that was in his column on August 8, 1942: "According to a wish expressed long ago in one of her poems," he wrote, "L.M. Montgomery was buried from Green Gables in the local cemetery in Cavendish, Prince Edward Island." He followed this with a summary of Aida B. McAnn's "interesting obituary article" in *The Maritime Advocate and Busy East*.[25]

The item I'm referring to appeared on September 27, 1941, seven months before her death: "We regret to learn of the continued and serious ill health of L.M. Montgomery (Mrs. MacDonald)."[26]

True, the newspaper misspelled her married surname, and Deacon's acknowledgement of Montgomery's health issues would have done little to repair some of the damage he'd caused to her reputation or to her well-being. Still, given that this is one of the few news reports about Montgomery from the last year of her life that I've come across so far, Deacon's notice — and his use of the term "regret" — offers some nuance in terms of past depictions of him as single-mindedly vindictive toward her.

— 5 —

Earlier in this book, I talked about three tributes that had appeared following Montgomery's death in the *Vancouver Daily Province*, the *Peterborough Examiner*, and *Saturday Night* and that argued against the "highbrow," "stern," and "exalted" critics who supposedly harboured negative views about her work. Montgomery certainly received her fair share of criticism for her work — including the recurring refrain from reviewers that none of her subsequent books could possibly top *Anne of Green Gables* in terms of literary quality and reader appeal — but it's certainly not the case that harsh reviewers such as Deacon set the tone of the conversation about her work.

And despite Deacon's apparent power as a prominent newspaper critic, he wasn't always treated as beyond reproach. The February 18, 1927, issue of *The Ubyssey*, a student paper published at the University of British Columbia, reported on a lecture entitled "Canadian Authors and Canadianism" given by Percy Gomery — who happened to be president of the Canadian Authors Association. The article stated that "Mr. Gomery spoke chiefly on the lack of interest taken by Canadians in Canadian authors and their books, despite the excellent work that has been done by our authors towards producing a national literature." But then the lecture apparently became far more specific. "Mr. Gomery maintained that Canadians tend to belittle their own literature. One Canadian pronounced L.M. Montgomery's novels as having sunk to the lowest level of literature. These books have been accepted all over the world as among the best books written for girls. Mr. Gomery wanted to know why it was necessary for Canadians to belittle their own literature, especially after it has been accepted all over the world."[27]

I haven't yet found any other mention of Gomery's rebuttal to Deacon, and so it seems unlikely that Montgomery had known about it. Which is too bad, because if Gomery's counterargument had gained more traction, it might have contributed to offsetting Deacon's rude remarks in *Poteen* and alleviated the impression that Montgomery's reputation had lessened within the Canadian literary community.

# 9

# The Scarce Hints of Love

— 1 —

"The old graveyard heard the most charming sound in the world … the low yielding laugh of a girl held prisoner by her lover."[1]

I first encountered this final sentence in Montgomery's late novel *Mistress Pat* when, around the age of sixteen, I embarked upon my first binge reading of her books. The novel's overall depressing tone didn't particularly bother me then, since it fit fairly well with my adolescent angst. Still, I remember feeling vaguely troubled and perplexed by this "happy" ending. This was long before I read a review of *Rilla of Ingleside* in the Rochester *Post Express* that declared that "with Miss Montgomery everybody that can marry gets married," but I'd already figured out that this was almost always the case — unless, of course, there was a sequel. Still, something about the final image of Patricia Gardiner yielding and imprisoned in a graveyard has never sat well with me, nor does what former boy next door Hilary Gordon declares to her "triumphantly" a few pages earlier: "I've made you mine forever with that kiss.… You can never belong to anyone else."[2] At the time, I probably rationalized my discomfort with the reminder that, as a boy, I wasn't really a typical Montgomery reader, so perhaps that made me less likely to get swept away by her books' romantic resolutions. But more than thirty years after my initial reading of this book, I'm still wondering if there's more to my wariness about its resolution than I thought back then.

I've mentioned a few times already instances in which Montgomery recycled her own writing, usually from periodical to book or from journal to book, in a way that wouldn't have been apparent to readers of her novels until those shorter works were collected in book form and her journals were published. In this chapter, I'm interested in how repetition dovetails with some of the ways that certain behaviours pertaining to mixed-gender romantic relationships are either presented as natural in her fiction or nurtured into becoming natural, particularly in four novels from across her career whose plots are resolved by the promise of wedding bells: *Anne of the Island* (1915), *Rilla of Ingleside* (1921), *Emily's Quest* (1927), and *Mistress Pat* (1935). While all of these books end with the man and the woman declaring their love for one another, some of the recurring dynamics in Montgomery's courtship plots are rather troublesome in terms of how they restrict the protagonist's growth, well-being, and agency.

All four of these novels include will-they-or-won't-they romantic plots that are driven by two types of complications: Anne and Pat persist in denying their feelings for Gilbert and Hilary (Pat fairly convincingly, Anne less so), whereas Rilla and Emily, although secure in how they feel about the men they love, spend the majority of their narratives plagued with doubts about whether Kenneth and Teddy really love them back. What these four protagonists have in common is that, although they're highly articulate and outspoken in most respects, they somehow cannot compel themselves to speak about their budding relationships with men — whether they're interested in the men in question or not. Rilla writes in her diary about her distress concerning Fred Arnold, who's "been coming here very often lately and though I like him so much it makes me uncomfortable, because I am afraid he is thinking that perhaps I could care something for him." Later, she insists that "I *never* encouraged Fred to think I cared about him," but she still feels "heart-broken and remorseful" after he proposes marriage and only then learns that she's already made a promise of sorts to someone else.

In *Emily Climbs*, after enduring endless visits from her cousin Andrew that she can't get out of, despite how much he bores her, Emily writes a similar diary entry about her relief that Andrew finally proposed to her — relief because she finally had something tangible she could turn down. "I've felt it coming for some time," she adds.[3]

As Montgomery noted in a letter to G.B. MacMillan dated September 3, 1924, that drew on a nearly identical journal entry dated seven months earlier, part of the challenge she faced while writing *Emily Climbs* had to do with pressures to conform to readers' expectations.

> The public and publisher won't allow me to write of a young girl as she really is. One can write of children as they are; so my books about children are always good; but when you come to write of the "miss" you have to depict a sweet insipid young thing — really a child grown older — to whom the basic realities of life and reactions to them are quite unknown. *Love* must scarcely be hinted at — yet young girls often have some very vivid love affairs. A girl of *Emily's* type certainly would. But the public —[4]

Montgomery may have seen herself as being unable to write honestly about her adolescent characters' "love affairs," but Emily's dilemma with her cousin Andrew and Rilla's anxiety concerning Fred Arnold are in keeping with her own real-life experience. Emily's account of Andrew's proposal has several details in common with Montgomery's diary entry dated July 1, 1891, in which the sixteen-year-old diarist wrote about a declaration of interest from a man named Mr. Mustard whom she found repulsive — and who happened to be her teacher. "The only truly descriptive word I know of to apply to the whole interview is *sickening*," she declared. But although this entry is preceded by several more in which the adolescent Montgomery recorded feeling compelled to accept Mr. Mustard's invitations because she didn't know how to decline them, her account of this conversation included some contempt as well: "Any sane man might have taken the hint that I had no use for him long ago." Four years later, almost to the day, an almost identical situation happened with a boy named Lou Dystant during one of her teaching stints. Montgomery insisted in a journal entry dated July 2, 1895, that not only had she never encouraged him, but also, she'd done everything, "in all the indirect ways permissible, to *dis*courage him." But while she sympathized with Lou's broken heart, she also thought "his abandon of feeling was rather disgusting."[5]

Montgomery's accounts of her relationships with men — flirtatious, platonic, or anywhere in between — reveal a complex courtship system that involved a tangled web of silence, hints, innuendo, concerns about family standing, and community gossip. Openly declaring interest or non-interest were among the options that her culture did not deem "permissible." And although men held most of the cards since only they were expected to issue invitations or make proposals, they, too, were bound by strict conventions. As the cases of Mr. Mustard and Lou Dystant show, misinterpreting the signals they received from the women they courted could lead to hurt feelings, embarrassment, and the discovery that a lot of time had been wasted. Montgomery dramatized these problems several times in her fiction. One of Anne's ill-fated marriage proposals comes out of the blue from Charlie Sloane, but while Anne, like Rilla after her with Mark, "felt that she had never given Charlie the slightest encouragement to suppose such a thing possible," she feels anger more than anything else toward Charlie for his presumptuousness.[6] Meanwhile, there's no mention of Andrew or Fred asking permission to call or doing any form of check-in to gauge romantic interest. Like Mr. Mustard, they appear to take for granted that a formal declaration or proposal will be received favourably — perhaps because Emily and Rilla, like the adolescent Montgomery, don't feel comfortable declining such advances too definitively.

To me, these forms of silence within rituals of mixed-gender courtship are particularly distressing given that in Montgomery's fiction, a woman's choice of a husband is the most central decision of her life. And in the case of someone like Susan Baker, housekeeper at Ingleside, the fact that no one has ever proposed to her is something she brings up frequently as her biggest regret. But however common it is for novels to end with the promise of marriage, in Montgomery's case these courtship plots are contrasted with mutually satisfying and nurturing relationships with female friends, older people, and siblings. In *Anne of the Island*, for instance, Anne and her three girlfriends make a home for themselves at Patty's Place, in an arrangement that the narrator refers to as "almost as good as getting married. You had the fun of home-making without the bother of a husband."[7] But by the end of the novel, Anne, like so many of her fellow Montgomery characters, must distance herself from these platonic attachments in order to embrace her destiny as a married woman, at which point Anne's female friends tend to disappear from the narrative.

While most of Montgomery's novels end with one or more couples planning to marry, they also depict the narrow range of options regarding both home and career for unmarried women in the communities they live in. In *A Tangled Web*, "old" Margaret Penhallow is "always overworked and snubbed and patronised" because of one of the dominant values of her extended family: "If you were married you were somebody. If not, you were nobody." Although she earns a living as a dressmaker, she is forced to live with her brother and his family, which includes "saucy and unattractive youngsters who made fun of her," because having a home of her own is socially and financially unthinkable. In *Mistress Pat*, Pat steps into the role of "mistress" at Silver Bush only because her mother is an invalid and her older sister has married and moved away. Once her older brother Sid marries, she becomes redundant as a figure in the household. In *Emily's Quest*, Emily can stay home and write for the time being, but the narrator mentions her awareness that New Moon will go to her spurned cousin Andrew after Aunt Elizabeth dies. Emily reacts badly to Andrew's "proprietary airs" about the grounds, prompting Aunt Elizabeth to remind Emily that "if you had married Andrew New Moon would have been yours" — even though, as Emily retorts, Andrew's changes "would have come just the same": "Andrew wouldn't have listened to me. He believes that the husband is the head of the wife."[8]

Several commentators have suggested that Montgomery tacked on obligatory "satisfying" endings solely to reassure her publishers and her readers of the dominant values her works otherwise undermine. Mary Rubio, for instance, notes that Montgomery wrote within the "very restrictive genre" of the domestic romance and accordingly "presented a surface reinforcement of all the prevailing ideologies which her early 20th century audience demanded," such as mixed-gender romantic bliss and female contentment within the domestic sphere. But in light of comments about writing and about gender that Montgomery made in essays and interviews as well as in her journals and letters, it may be necessary to reconsider the notion that these "happy" endings are solely the product of convention — and not simply due to her stated view, shown in a journal entry dated April 15, 1914, that "to be in the arms of a man whom I loved with all my heart and to whom I could willingly look up as *my master* is, after all, every woman's real idea of happiness, if she would be honest enough to admit it."[9]

— 2 —

In his review of *Emily's Quest*, published in the September 1927 issue of *The Canadian Bookman*, V.B. Rhodenizer states that "L.M. Montgomery's happy endings are dictated not so much by the wishes of readers and publishers, as by her philosophy of life." Public statements made by Montgomery throughout the 1920s certainly add credibility to this claim. In *Fiction Writers on Fiction Writing*, she responded to a question about "the elemental hold of fiction on the human mind" by declaring that "fiction redresses the balance of existence and gives us what we can't get in real life," a perspective that she universalized by referring to "the deep desire in every one of us for 'something better than we have known.'" In a 1925 interview published in the *Toronto Star Weekly*, she put forth the idea that "a woman may successfully combine a profession of her own with the oldest one in the world, that of wifehood and motherhood but only if she be able to pursue the career at home" — an idea that was evidently informed by her view that "girls have, if they be normal women, a desire for marriage in their hearts." And in a 1928 interview published in that same paper, in which she was asked if she believed that "the much-powdered and puffed, compacted and barbered, gay and daring young ladies of the present, generally speaking, will ultimately settle down to the humdrum business of marriage and all the responsibilities it entails," her "decided" response inadvertently echoed the wedding vow: "I do."[10]

Granted, Montgomery complained frequently in her journals that she'd been misquoted by the press, and certainly, the pressure she felt to conform to her second public role as the wife of a Presbyterian minister informed the writerly persona that she cultivated and that didn't always align with what she did and said in private. But we don't need to look too far in her fiction to find evidence of this world view about "normal" girls and the home. In *Rilla of Ingleside*, for instance, Rilla's contributions to the war effort consist almost exclusively of sewing, baking, cleaning, and child rearing — tasks that initially she has no aptitude for or interest in. Her few forays into the public sphere, such as organizing charity concerts and filling in for a shop-keeper, are hardly as radical as the labour done during the war years by numerous women in reality who did farm labour, worked in munitions plants, or joined the war effort as nurses. And in the Pat books, as well as in *Jane of Lantern Hill* (1937), much is made of Pat and Jane's "natural" abilities with all domestic tasks — not to mention the "natural" inability of Jane's father to look after himself.

It may be tempting to interpret this recurring view of the home as the default site for "normal" girls and women as old-fashioned, if not sexist and regressive — it certainly sounds that way when the narrator of *Jane of Lantern Hill* mentions that Jane's uncle William "never lost an opportunity of announcing his belief that a woman's place was in the home." Similarly, the idea of eleven-year-old Jane yearning for the "fun" of lighting the candles at the dinner table and polishing the silver might seem to strain credulity. Still, there's a fair amount of nuance here. Jane starts off as a girl with no self-confidence and little scholastic aptitude as a result of how much she's picked on and criticized by her maternal relatives. But her first summer spent keeping house in Prince Edward Island gives her social and organizational skills she takes back with her to Toronto, where her teachers suddenly marvel at her "executive ability." Montgomery's novels also depict the home as a place where female characters find fulfillment in terms of creativity and problem-solving, as cooks, hosts, and domestic artists. Most importantly, similar to Anne's decision to forego her undergraduate studies and stay home with Marilla at the end of *Anne of Green Gables*, her later books depict domestic work as something that Jane *wants* to do — and that Rilla *can* learn.[11]

— 3 —

Particularly since Montgomery's journals and letters entered the larger discussion about her fiction and her legacy, a number of commentators have weighed in about her feminism — including the question of whether or not she can be claimed retroactively as a feminist. Mollie Gillen refers to Montgomery as "independent" and "semi-feminist" in her 1975 biography, *The Wheel of Things*, whereas Cecily Devereux, in her introduction to a Broadview critical edition of *Anne of Green Gables*, historicizes Montgomery within the early feminist movement in imperial Canada in order to demonstrate that she was "clearly well on the conservative side of the early twentieth-century feminist spectrum." Mary Rubio and Elizabeth Waterston, introducing the third volume of Montgomery's selected journals, note that by the 1920s, "Maud Montgomery Macdonald was increasingly in a mood that we would now call feminist." More specifically, "Women could now vote (Montgomery did), could maintain a separate bank account (she did), could travel alone by train or by car to unfamiliar communities (she did). But patriarchal power in church, state, law, and home seemed undiluted still."[12] In short, Montgomery found ways to maximize her power without attempting to overthrow the social order — which makes sense given her dual role as a minister's wife and as a writer whose livelihood depended on her books appealing to a wide range of readers.

One way Montgomery negotiated patriarchal power involved the family's automobile, which was "really my car of course, since I paid for it," but was "registered in Ewan's name so was legally his," according to a journal entry dated December 9, 1922. This arrangement proved to be fortuitous — besides being practical, because she never learned how to drive — after she and her husband got into a minor accident with one of their parishioners, who promptly sued them for damages despite being primarily at fault. But because of a double standard at this time and in this place, Montgomery's earnings were legally considered hers, not part of the family's income, and so they remained out of bounds of the lawsuit against her husband. Moreover, it was thanks to her earnings that the family could afford an automobile to begin with, as well as a maid, a trained nurse when she gave birth, and eventually boarding school for their sons — all of which would have been unattainable on her husband's salary as a pastor.[13]

In spite of the family's material privileges, Montgomery's success as a writer appeared to irk her husband. As she noted in a journal entry dated March 25, 1922, "Ewan has never had any real sympathy with or intelligent interest in my literary work and has always seemed either incredulous or resentful when anyone has attributed to me any importance on the score of it." In another journal entry dated less than a month after this, she recalled the time when, early in their marriage, he reacted badly to the sight of a letter addressed to Miss L.M. Montgomery and, as she put it, "sulked for three days." She attributed this to her husband having internalized "the mediaeval feeling that a woman has no business to have any separate individuality in name or attainment from her lord and master." But because she had to live with this friction, not only in her own house but also in rural communities where people had high expectations of how members of the minister's family should comport themselves, she had several reasons to downplay the relative freedoms her wealth offered her.[14]

In December 1921, Montgomery published an autobiographical sketch entitled "How I Became a Writer" in the *Manitoba Free Press*. This piece repeats familiar anecdotes about her childhood in Prince Edward Island, her family, her schooling, her favourite British poets, and her developing ability as a writer, but it concludes with a remarkable revelation about Montgomery's sense of her work, her readers, and her nation: "In my latest story, 'Rilla of Ingleside,' I have tried, as far as in me lies, to depict the fine and splendid way in which the girls of Canada reacted to the Great War — their bravery, patience and self-sacrifice. The book is theirs in a sense in which none of my other books have been: for my other books were written for anyone who might like to read them: but 'Rilla' was written for the girls of the great young land I love, whose destiny it will be their duty and privilege to shape and share." By keeping its focus on Rilla at home, the novel demonstrates that her promise to "keep faith" with her late brother's vision of a new future, one in which "you will tell your children of the *Idea* we fought and died for," has just as much value as the contributions to the war effort of the men who fought.[15] At the same time, given Montgomery's later comments about the supposed desires of all "normal" women, it would seem that the destiny of "the girls of Canada" refers to work done within the home as wives and mothers, rather than to a wider range of options for women in all spheres.

But if being a wife and a mother is, for Montgomery, a cultural ideal for women, then a complication here is a convention that she experienced in her own life and that she shared with her characters — that only men could extend proposals of marriage. Or, to put it more bluntly, men within these cultural and fictional worlds decided whether or not women got to fulfill their destiny as wives and mothers. This notion is presented as so natural within Montgomery's fiction that, in *Anne of Avonlea*, seven-year-old Dora Keith is "shocked into speaking without being spoken to" when Davy, her twin brother who's less bothered by social convention, suggests that Marilla is unmarried because she never asked anyone to marry her. "It's the *men* that have to do the asking," Dora protests. Several of Montgomery's books dramatize some of the ways that this convention constrained women's agency. When Anne's offered the principalship at Summerside High School near the end of *Anne of the Island*, she doesn't know whether or not to accept because she's waiting to see if Roy Gardner will propose to her. "Naturally," the narrator acknowledges, "Anne's plans could not be settled until Roy had spoken" — phrasing that echoes the novel's earlier chapter "Gilbert Speaks," in which Gilbert proposes to her for the first time. In *Anne's House of Dreams*, Anne predicts that seventeen-year-old Dora "will probably marry young" since "she'll never miss her first chance for fear she might not get another." And in *Rainbow Valley*, Rosemary West declines John Meredith's proposal of marriage without explaining that she does do because she once promised Ellen, her domineering older sister, that she would never marry. When Ellen frees her from that promise, Rosemary is aghast at Ellen's suggestion that "it's not too late":

> "Have you quite lost your senses in *every* respect? Do you suppose for an instant that *I* am going to go to John Meredith and say meekly, 'Please, sir, I've changed my

> mind and please, sir, I hope you haven't changed yours.' Is that what you want me to do?"
>
> "No — no — but a little — encouragement — he would come back" —

It's revealing that even for the outspoken and forward-thinking Ellen, being direct in the matter of a reconsidered marriage proposal isn't to be thought of. Instead, offering "a little — encouragement" is as far as she recommends. Rosemary and Mr. Meredith do reconcile eventually, but in a way that doesn't breach propriety too severely. Una, the youngest Meredith daughter, proposes to Rosemary again on her father's behalf — but without her father's knowledge — despite the fact that she's been made to believe that Rosemary will turn her father against her and her siblings as soon as she becomes their stepmother.[16]

The choice of the word "natural," in *Anne of the Island*, to refer to Roy's prerogative to initiate a discussion about the future on his own timeline is followed by two more comments about male privilege in mixed-gender relationships that are presented as without question. When Roy's mother and his sisters pay Anne a visit that's a thinly veiled evaluation of her as a prospective addition to their family, Anne "remembered that Mrs. John Blythe was so fond of cats that she kept as many as her husband would allow." And when she returns to Avonlea and learns that her friend Jane Andrews is about to marry a Winnipeg millionaire, Jane's catty mother informs her that "Jane has only one trouble — she can cook so well and her husband won't let her cook." Even after Anne finally realizes her love for Gilbert, she feels unable to do anything — not even offer him any "encouragement" — except wait to see if he proposes again. If he does not, she must "reconcile herself to a future where work and ambition must take the place of love."[17]

It's worth noting that these moments are part of a broader system of patriarchal thinking that virtually all of Montgomery's characters have to contend with. In some cases, these forms of patriarchy are overt, such as the resistance and hostility Anne receives from many of her neighbours for being the first Avonlea girl to go to college, but this takes on more subtle forms as well. In *The Blue Castle*, when Valancy reflects on every form of injustice she's encountered in her twenty-nine years, one example that comes to mind is the time when, as a young girl, her cousin Byron pinched her during a dinner-table prayer, making her cry out, but then denied it. "He was *believed*. In the Stirling clan the boys were always believed before the girls." In *A Tangled Web*, Little Sam looks around the room at an extended family gathering and notices "William Y.'s Sara [who] was undeniably handsome, but she was a trained nurse and Little Sam always felt that she knew too much about her own and other people's insides to be really charming." And in three multi-chapter fiction serials that Montgomery published between 1903 and 1909 and entitled "The Bitterness in the Cup," "Four Winds," and "Una of the Garden," male characters' fixation on the notion of the "ideal woman" becomes an impossible standard for female characters to live up to — not to mention that all three narratives praise the adult women who are the objects of men's desire for being so childlike.[18]

Montgomery's younger characters are more likely to question the values that surrounding adults have internalized as unchangeable, as I noted earlier when I brought up Anne's question about why women couldn't be ministers. But by the time they're adults, these characters have by and large ceased to rebel against the heteronormative values that their communities appear to uphold as natural components of mixed-gender marriage. As a child in *Emily of New Moon*, Emily feels "an odd sensation of rebellion" after Dean saves her life and proclaims that "your life belongs to me henceforth." But once she's an adult in *Emily's Quest*, she isn't shown reacting to Dean's reminder of this ownership when he tells her that "I give your life back to you." Perhaps this shouldn't be surprising, since barely a few pages before this, Emily describes the bond she has with Teddy Kent using similar language of male ownership: "I belong to him. He doesn't love me — he never will — but I belong to him." At most, Montgomery's books depict her characters following her lead in finding relative freedoms within the existing social order. This includes several secondary characters who are afraid to do or say things that their fathers or their husbands wouldn't approve of but eventually find the courage to stand up for themselves. "If Joe can face the Huns I guess I can face father," Miranda Pryor announces when Rilla offers to go with her to break the news to her father that she's eloped without his consent. Perhaps Susan Baker says it best in that novel when she declares that "a man should be master in his own household and his women folk should bow to his decrees … but one can exercise a little gumption on the quiet now and then."[19]

— 4 —

A synopsis for *Mistress Pat* included in a list of books the Frederick A. Stokes Company published around the same time in 1935 calls it "a cheerful and lively story of charming 'Pat' of Silver Bush" who, "as she grows to womanhood, meets romance and chooses between two suitors." Such a description grossly misrepresents the contents of this novel. Although it ends with Pat and Hilary declaring their feelings for one another, Hilary otherwise makes only two brief appearances in the novel, and neither of them overlaps with Pat's ill-fated romance with the much older David Kirk. Moreover, the novel's eleven-year timeframe means that Pat ends the story at thirty-one. Perhaps this is why McClelland and Stewart, Montgomery's Canadian publisher, went a different route in its marketing campaign for this novel, judging by the fact that an ad in the *Toronto Daily Star* referred to the novel as being "filled with unique, charming, unexpected people."[20]

Besides, Hilary and David are only two of a large coterie of men Pat ends up dating — or fending off — throughout this book, all of whom are undeveloped as characters and dismissed through clever one-liners. These include Jem Robinson ("His face needs side-whiskers and he was born a generation too late"), Elmer Moody ("He breathes through his mouth"), Joe Merritt ("Our taste in jokes is entirely different"), Dwight Madison ("Pat said she thought he snored and Cuddles remarked that he looked like spinach"), Rex Miller ("When I asked him a question … I always knew exactly what he'd answer"), and Samuel Macleod ("He looked like a windmill in a fit"). And besides the sheer number of times, throughout the eleven-year span of the novel, that one secondary character remarks to another that it looks like Pat has no desire to marry and thereby leave Silver Bush, Pat's own perspective about courtship in general is worth paying attention to: "Judy, this love business is … just a nuisance. Life would be much simpler if there were nothing of the sort." Certainly, the novel seems to be setting Pat up to break convention and remain single, which would be nothing short of revolutionary, given not only the expectations of readers but also the limited number of options that Pat sees for herself by the novel's end.[21]

And so, Hilary's sudden reappearance in the final moments of the novel seems rather unbelievable, as does Pat's equally sudden realization that she does love Hilary after all. Or perhaps it seems unbelievable because it follows the highly similar resolutions to Rilla's and Emily's love stories — not to mention the ending to Leslie Moore's courtship with Owen Ford after an unrealistic turn of events frees her from her unhappy first marriage. The overlaps among all these plot points are noteworthy for three reasons. First, all four men travel great distances to declare their love: Kenneth from Toronto, Owen and Hilary from Vancouver, and Teddy from "thousands of miles away, in the Orient," as far as Emily knows. These are hardly short distances in the age before commercial airlines. To put their travel times in perspective, let's remember that Montgomery's 1890 journey from Cavendish to Prince Albert, in what is now Saskatchewan, involved twelve days of trains, boats, wagon rides, and stopovers; her return home the following year, which she wrote about in an essay published in the Charlottetown *Patriot*, took ten days. Granted, a face-to-face love declaration obviously makes for a more dramatic climactic moment in a work of fiction than a letter, a telegram, or even a telephone call, but once the dust settles, the fact remains that a tremendous amount of time elapses between the moment these male characters decide to make this declaration of love and them actually declaring it. Throughout that time, women in love remain in ignorance of what actions these men have set in motion.[22]

Second, while Kenneth and Teddy never explain what prompted their decision to show up unannounced after the women who love them have stopped receiving letters from them, the remaining resolutions come about because of third-party meddling. Gilbert reveals that Anne's former roommate Philippa wrote him a letter that "advised me to 'try again,'" whereas Hilary shows Pat a similar letter that Judy Plum sent to him on her death bed. In both cases, the stated reasons for trying again are because Anne and Pat have turned down proposals from someone else, not because either character has confided her romantic feelings for Gilbert and Hilary to the people who decide to intervene. In *Anne's House of Dreams*, Miss Cornelia suggests that Anne write to Owen Ford and "just mention, casual-like," that Leslie is now free to marry him. Anne's annoyed by Miss Cornelia's attempts at matchmaking — probably because she was already planning to do precisely that. But while Philippa and Judy wouldn't know whether or not Gilbert and Hilary would take their advice, the narrator hints that Anne has knowledge of "a certain thing that Leslie did not know" and that Leslie does not find out for several more chapters — namely, that Owen is on his way — and as a result, Anne "did not feel herself called upon to waste overmuch sympathy" on Leslie.[23]

Third, in their final scenes, Pat makes a vague plan to return to teaching, whereas Rilla, feeling "horribly lonely" after finding out from a paper that Ken has returned to Canada, ponders joining Una Meredith in taking a household science course (a program of study that Frederica Campbell had completed). These mentions of alternatives to marriage as viable options to women moments before a man reappears out of nowhere with a love declaration are part of a pattern I've noted before involving Leslie in *Anne's House of Dreams* and Nora Nelson in *Anne of Windy Poplars*, both of whom resolve — temporarily — to study nursing. But what's fascinating is that Pat and Rilla ponder these options at what are undeniably their lowest moments. And so, not only do the men, by declaring their love, permit these female characters to meet their destiny as women, but also, they rescue the protagonists from careers they don't really want.[24]

It might be tempting to see these overlaps between Montgomery's novels as an indication that she was simply following the same fiction conventions from book to book. But instances of more detailed overlaps between texts suggest a greater degree of intentionality on the author's part. Consider, first, Roy Gardner's marriage proposal in *Anne of the Island*:

> Roy asked Anne to marry him in the little pavilion on the harbour shore where they had talked on the rainy day of their first meeting.... The whole effect was quite flawless....

> When Roy paused for his answer she opened her lips to say her fateful yes.
>
> And then — she found herself trembling as if she were reeling back from a precipice.... She pulled her hand from Roy's.
>
> "Oh, I can't marry you — I can't — I can't," she cried, wildly.
>
> Roy turned pale — and also looked rather foolish. He had — small blame to him — felt very sure.
>
> "What do you mean?" he stammered.
>
> "I mean that I can't marry you," repeated Anne desperately. "I thought I could — but I can't."

Compare this to the scene in *Mistress Pat* detailing a similar proposal from Donald Holmes, who shares Roy's advantages in terms of position and social standing, but who, unlike Roy and certainly unlike Gilbert, is never developed as a character:

> [Donald] had come to ask her a certain question and he asked it, simply and confidently, as he had a right to ask it ... for if any girl had ever encouraged a man Pat had encouraged Donald Holmes that summer....
>
> She turned to Donald and opened her lips to say, "yes." She found herself trembling.
>
> "I'm ... I'm terribly sorry," was what she said. "I can't marry you. I thought I could but I can't."[25]

Much like instances in which the details in Montgomery's fiction match closely those in her journals, these two scenes share so many features that it seems hard to believe Montgomery didn't have a copy of *Anne of the Island* open in front of her when she wrote the new scene in *Mistress Pat*. Similarly, a conversation between Pat and her mother after Pat decides to marry David Kirk — whose surname, a Scots word for "church," is only one way this character brings to mind Dean Priest, except that *he's* the writer, not Pat — finds its source material in a similar discussion in *Emily's Quest* of Emily's decision to marry Dean:

> "Are you very sure you love him, Emily?" Aunt Laura asked that evening.
>
> "Yes — in a way," said Emily.
>
> Aunt Laura threw out her hands and spoke with a sudden passion utterly foreign to her.
>
> "But there's only one way of loving."
>
> "Oh, no, dearest of Victorian aunties," answered Emily gaily. "There are a dozen different ways. *You* know I've tried one or two ways already. And they failed me. Don't worry about Dean and me. We understand each other perfectly."

Pat's mother asks her the same unwanted question — whether or not she really loves David.

> "I do really, mother, but perhaps not in just the way you mean."
>
> "There's only the one way," said mother softly.
>
> "Then I'm one of the kind of people who can't love that way. I've tried … and I can't."
>
> "It doesn't come by trying either," said mother.
>
> "Mother dear, I'm terribly fond of David. We suit each other … our minds click. He loves the same things I do. I'm always happy with him … we'll always be good chums."[26]

Curiously, in addition to several details in common between these two scenes involving engagements that the protagonists eventually call off, they likewise recall similar circumstances that Montgomery wrote about in her journals: "Perfect and rapturous happiness, such as marriage with a man I loved intensely would give me, I have ceased to hope for. I would be content with a workaday, bread-and-butter happiness.... Again and again I asked myself did I care enough for [this man] to justify my marrying him.... I liked him — I respected him — I saw all his good qualities of heart and character; to put it plainly, I was *very* fond of him. But I knew that was all." But in stark contrast to Emily and Pat, who realize they'd rather be single than marry men for whom they feel only lukewarm affection, Montgomery's ponderings are from a journal entry dated October 12, 1906, in which she weighed the pros and cons of accepting a proposal from Ewan Macdonald — whom she married five years later. "I think I have done the wisest thing in assenting," she concluded in her journal. "I feel content."[27]

And so, when, in *Fiction Writers on Fiction Writing*, Montgomery wrote about how fiction "gives us what we can't get in real life," her work was once again informed by her experience.

— 5 —

Given that Anne, Rilla, Emily, and Pat do little to challenge the fixed idea that the man must speak first *and* that their approach to courtship and marriage mirrors what Montgomery herself experienced, it's tempting to presume that this was a world view that she endorsed — and that she offered to her readers for them to consider. But that's only one way of looking at this aspect of her work. Another way is to view her fiction as realistic depictions of young women doing their best to find a place for themselves in a world that has such narrow expectations about how women should behave. Besides, these four supposedly happy endings happen so quickly and are preceded by so much doubt and uncertainty — Rilla's hesitation about whether her promise to Ken even means anything makes her feel "idiotic and ashamed" — that they seem to have a cliffhanger aspect to them as well. After all, given the convention to end the story with wedding bells, a convention she broke with Anne but maintained with the three later protagonists, her writing never shows what married life for these characters actually looks like.[28]

And even if Montgomery really did believe — or wanted to believe — that an adult woman's freedom had to be found within the four walls of her house, she undercut that belief by delaying the "normal" girl's destiny as long as narratively possible. And at the end of *Emily's Quest*, once Emily and Teddy have finally pieced together that their years of mutual doubt were due to misunderstanding, Emily transforms her earlier sense of male ownership into one that's mutual: "Why, Teddy has always belonged to me and I to him. Heart, soul and body." Even so, Dean sends her as a wedding gift the deed to a house that has never known happiness, which Emily persists in seeing as a touching gesture despite Dean's earlier remark, when they abandon the house as part of walking away from their failed engagement, that "houses, like people, can't escape their doom, it seems."[29]

But whether destiny or doom, Montgomery's heteronormative romance plots allow readers to have it both ways — to claim the endings as "happy" or to ponder more troublesome patterns of actions and reactions across multiple texts.

# 10

# Returns to Anne

— 1 —

In early 1935, L.M. Montgomery published an article in *The Chatelaine* in which she shared her impressions of two feature-film adaptations of *Anne of Green Gables*: a silent film that had appeared in 1919 and a "talkie" that had just been released in November 1934. She was careful to make no mention of the fact that she'd received no compensation for either film or that she'd played no part in the adaptation process. But she was direct about what she'd liked and disliked about the films and found ways to signal to readers that she didn't consider either one to be connected to her own work. "At times," she wrote of the second film in particular, "I had the sensation of watching a story written by somebody else."[1]

Given that she'd sold all remaining rights to her first seven books, including *Anne of Green Gables*, to the Page Company in 1919, it would appear that publishing an article about the new film in a high-profile magazine was the most she could do to reinsert herself into the conversation about her best-known literary character. But in a journal entry dated March 9, 1935, she announced work on an unexpected project: "a new *Anne* book, having succumbed at long last to the urgency of publishers and 'fans.'" Her tone was positive — "If it proves possible to 'get back into the past' far enough to do a good book it ought to do well commercially after the film" — but the choice of the verb "succumb" did not make the project seem terribly promising, and in a letter to Ephraim Weber dated a few months later, she told him she'd yielded to the pressure from her publishers "very unwillingly." In public, however, she kept the focus away from her lack of enthusiasm and her need for funds. "It was most difficult at first to recapture the atmosphere of the past and to pick up the threads of the story first told many years ago, but now I find myself easily living again all the life-story of my Anne," she said in a speech given to the Canadian Women's Press Club, according to the *Toronto Daily Star*. "Only I must watch myself carefully lest such modernities as motor cars or radios or even a new-fangled sled creep into the story by mistake."[2]

The book in question, which fills the three-year gap between *Anne of the Island* and *Anne's House of Dreams* in which Anne works as the principal of Summerside High School, appeared in 1936. But this time, the continued demand for her work all over the English-speaking world led to an unexpected problem. The *Manning River Times* of Taree, Australia, quoted a letter that "Mr. Ronald Graham, of the staff of the Taree branch of the Commonwealth Bank," had received from Montgomery and that provided an explanation.

> It was very kind of you to send me such a nice letter and I assure you I appreciate it. I get a great many letters from boys and Stanley Baldwin, Premier of Great Britain, has written me, telling me how much he loved "Anne." So you are in quite good company! You may be interested in knowing that I've just published another "Anne" book. "Anne of Windy Poplars," in America and "Anne of Windy Willows" in England. The latter was my title, but my American publishers thought it was too much like "The Wind in the Willows." It filled in the gap between "Anne of the Island" and "Anne's House of Dreams" when Anne was teaching

> school in Summerside High School. I am very glad my books have given you pleasure, and I am delighted to send the autographs for you and your sister. With all good wishes, I am, yours faithfully, L.M. Montgomery Macdonald. P.S. — I get so many "for" letters that my replies have to be brief. — L.M.M.

Oddly enough, Montgomery overlooked the fact that her Australian publisher had likewise retained the *Windy Willows* title, whereas the book appeared in Canada as *Anne of Windy Poplars* as well. She also omitted the fact that the two versions had numerous minor differences between them, particularly in two scenes in which eccentric older women regale Anne with anecdotes about how all their relatives died. Montgomery's American publisher had suggested trimming some of the anecdotes on the pretext that they were "too gruesome," but they appeared in *Windy Willows* anyway.[3]

The fact that *Anne of Windy Poplars* was published two decades after *Anne of the Island* and *Anne's House of Dreams* is something that's downplayed in most reprint editions, especially in numbered sets of Anne books that are organized according to the chronology of Anne's life. Since Montgomery was writing a book whose story fit between two existing titles, she had an unusual creative challenge that would be akin to travelling in a time machine — she went back into her character's past but couldn't do anything that would have an impact on what happened after that, because technically, it had already happened. And so, she took advantage of Gilbert's absence as a medical student and wrote part of the novel in the form of Anne's letters to him. Similar to the excerpts from Rilla's and Emily's diaries in earlier books, these letters not only capture Anne's voice but also privilege her perspective. Curiously, in these letters Anne regularly shares with Gilbert secrets confided in her by her two landladies, "Aunt" Chatty and "Aunt" Kate, including their clever use of reverse psychology to manage their live-in housekeeper, Rebecca Dew.

But because the initial readers of this novel would have remembered that the books that followed this one chronologically had in fact been published long before, many of them likely noticed instances of dramatic irony within the text, whereby they had greater knowledge of what would happen later than the characters did. Near the beginning of the book, Anne looks toward the future in a letter to Gilbert and expresses the hope that one day they will find "our 'house of dreams'" — which of course they will — or did — and imagines "a few funny adventures to bring laughter in our old age. Old age! Can *we* ever be old, Gilbert? It seems impossible." Old age may seem impossible to Anne at this moment, but less so for readers in 1936, given that at the end of *Rilla of Ingleside*, published twenty years before, Anne and Gilbert are already in their fifties. And while there's no direct mention of the Great War since it's far in the future for the characters, the novel makes an indirect reference to this conflict when Anne writes to Gilbert about preparing to give a class on the War of 1812. "It seems so strange to read over the stories of those old wars … things that can never happen again. I don't suppose any of us will ever have more than an academic interest in 'battles long ago.' It's impossible to think of Canada ever being at war again. I am so thankful that phase of history is over." But in a journal entry dated August 21, 1935, when she was still writing the opening chapters in the novel, Montgomery was already fretting about talk of "another war scare" in Europe.[4]

This novel is in many ways a story about women's work, given that, as a twenty-two-year-old high school principal, Anne is belittled due to her gender and her age. But the animosity that Anne faces from the Pringles, the dominant family in Summerside, ends as abruptly as it starts, and while vice-principal Katherine Brooke openly resents having to report to someone who's younger than she is, Anne finds a way to defuse that tension as well. Otherwise, like in *Anne of Avonlea* and *Anne of the Island*, the school becomes the anchor for all the subplots about community, family, and love. But while some of these plot threads contain romantic resolutions, this novel goes against convention in several ways. Katherine Brooke's storyline ends not with a marriage proposal but with the decision to give up teaching, a profession she's never enjoyed, and take a secretarial course instead. And by the time the novel ends, she gets a job "as private secretary to a globe-trotting M.P.," complete with Anne's acknowledgement that marriage needn't be the right choice for all women: "That life will just suit Katherine." If anything, the book's big romantic resolution involves a different kind of love-related epiphany, except that in this case it's a father's love for his daughter. Toward the end of the novel, Anne worries about the future awaiting her young neighbour Little Elizabeth, who's being raised by two dour old ladies, and so she writes a letter to Elizabeth's father urging him to take responsibility for the daughter he hasn't seen since she was a baby. The scene in which Elizabeth overhears her father and Anne talking has several details in common with a similar scene at the end of *Jane of Lantern Hill*, which is no surprise, since both scenes draw on a shared source: a 1934 short story entitled "Tomorrow Comes."[5]

Although Montgomery recorded privately that she had "a rather poor opinion of that book," as she phrased it in a journal entry dated August 10, 1936, she was surprised to learn that the *Daily Mirror* of London had selected *Anne of Windy Willows*, with its extra "gruesome" bits, as its "romantic Book of the Month." And in 1940, RKO Radio Pictures went into production with a film adaptation of *Anne of Windy Poplars*. "I suppose they'll murder the book as per usual," Montgomery wrote to Weber in a letter dated May 8, 1939, drawing on her experience of being tremendously disappointed by film adaptations of books she'd enjoyed.[6] This film didn't do so well at the box office compared to the 1934 talkie that had preceded it, but at least Montgomery finally received payment for a film adaptation of her work.

## — 2 —

In the same letter to Weber in which she shared the news about the film adaptation of *Anne of Windy Poplars*, Montgomery mentioned that she'd recently finished another Anne book, "in compliance with urgings from four publishers in Canada, U.S., England and Australia." *Anne of Ingleside* fills the five-year gap between *Rainbow Valley* and *Rilla of Ingleside* and thus focuses on Anne as the busy mother of six young children, but her stated opinion about it was even lower than how she'd felt about *Windy Poplars*: "I will send you a copy," she promised him, "but you need not strain your conscience saying anything nice about it." In her journal, she told quite a different story, one that involved five months of outlining during an extended period of writer's block. "I *dread* trying to begin it," she wrote in an entry dated September 7, 1938. "What if I find I *cannot* write?" But on the following Monday, she went to work anyway. "On this hot dark muggy day I sat me down and began to write *Anne of Ingleside.* It is a year and nine months since I wrote a single line of creative work. But I can *still* write. I wrote a chapter. A burden rolled from my spirit. And I was suddenly *back in my own world* with all my dear Avonlea and Glen folks again. It was like going home."[7]

*Anne of Ingleside* is in many ways a troublesome book. Most of the episodes that centre on Anne's young children end with them becoming disillusioned with the world around them, either because friends turn out to be two-faced or because appearances prove to be deceptive. In one chapter, young Walter overhears a group of women gossiping about a scandal that occurred long ago at the funeral of a man named Peter Kirk, but when he asks Anne if she'll tell him what happened, she puts him off — just before the entire episode unfolds on the page in a rare flashback. As Mary Henley Rubio notes of this scene, Montgomery "bundles up all the hypocrisy she has witnessed over a lifetime of funerals, takes aim at decorous piety, and delivers herself of an immense amount of anger at men who were tyrants in their own homes." Moreover, "though Maud took aim at male tyranny, she also criticized women's gossip." In the end, Anne decides that "the story of what happened at Peter Kirk's funeral is one which Walter must never know. It was certainly no story for children." And yet, it appears within a novel that today is published in editions aimed at child readers, just like the remainder of Montgomery's books.[8]

Susan returns in this novel as the Blythes' maid-of-all-work, and several of the characters introduced in *Anne of Windy Poplars* visit Ingleside in this book. While in *Rainbow Valley* Susan is bitterly opposed to Walter writing poetry, here she appears to have a far more generous reaction to a series of letters he writes from the perspective of two chipmunks in the yard, to the point that she brags about them in letters to Rebecca Dew: "At least these compositions are not poetry." In this late addition to the overall story, it's Anne who reluctantly becomes a poet, when neighbour Mrs. Mitchell browbeats her into agreeing to write an obituary poem for her recently departed husband. "Occasionally I do write a little story," Anne explains.

"But a busy mother hasn't much time for that. I had wonderful dreams once but now I'm afraid I'll never be in Who's Who, Mrs. Mitchell." Still, Anne consents to give it a try — and ends up writing a poem entitled "The Old Man's Grave," whose text happens to match that of a poem that Montgomery first published in *The Youth's Companion* in 1906 and that had already been included in two anthologies edited by John W. Garvin and in Montgomery's book-length collection, *The Watchman and Other Poems*. But much like what keeps happening to her kids in this book, Anne ends up being disillusioned when her poem appears in the paper the next week — along with an extra verse tacked on by Mrs. Mitchell's dubiously talented nephew.[9]

Near the end of the novel, Anne starts to worry when Gilbert, who seems emotionally distant all of a sudden, appears to have forgotten their wedding anniversary. This nagging feeling intensifies when the couple is invited to a dinner party that will reunite them with "Mrs. Andrew Dawson of Winnipeg, *née* Christine Stuart." Whereas in *Anne of the Island* Gilbert's friendship with Christine turned out to be reassuringly platonic, *Anne of Ingleside* intensifies the drama by retroactively adding all kinds of distressing details to earlier stages of Anne's life. Anne now remembers receiving a spiteful comment about Gilbert and Christine's relationship from a character whose name never appears in *Anne of the Island*, followed by the recollection that "not long after her marriage she had found a small photograph of Christine in an old pocketbook of Gilbert's." Anne has an increasingly miserable time at the dinner party, and by the time they return home, she's convinced herself that Gilbert has stopped loving her:

> And now … Gilbert had grown tired of her. Men had always been like that … always would be. She had thought Gilbert was an exception but now she knew the truth. And how was she going to adjust her life to it?
>
> "There are the children, of course," she thought dully. "I must go on living for them. And nobody must know … *nobody*. I will not be pitied."[10]

*Anne of Ingleside* ends much like the four novels I discussed earlier that depict a female protagonist experiencing her lowest moments just before the man she loves reappears out of nowhere. But in this case, because Anne and Gilbert are already married, the reasons for Anne's temporary misery must come from elsewhere. As it turns out, Gilbert has been preoccupied by a patient in critical condition, and he simply pretended to forget about their anniversary because he felt bad that the gift he'd purchased for Anne hadn't arrived yet. And so, once Anne and Gilbert have found each other again, she spends the last scene checking up on her slumbering children — including Walter, who "was smiling in his sleep as someone who knew a charming secret. The moon was shining on his pillow through the bars of the leaded window … casting the shadow of a clearly defined cross on the wall above his head." The narrator then provides a glimpse past Anne's perspective and into the future — that is to say, the past: "In long after years Anne was to remember that and wonder if it were an omen of Courcelette … of a cross-marked grave 'somewhere in France.' But tonight it was only a shadow … nothing more."[11]

And in the book's final moments, the narrator describes Anne as entirely unchanged despite the passage of time. "In her white gown, with her hair in its two long braids, she looked like the Anne of Green Gables days … of Redmond days … of the House of Dreams days. That inward glow was still shining through her."[12]

Montgomery may have dismissed this book as a potboiler, but she nevertheless went to great pains to link this story to those that had come before, chronologically or not, even if that meant introducing some minor continuity problems. Another way that she connected this later Anne book to those that preceded it, something that wouldn't have been apparent to readers prior to the publication of her journals, was in her dedication to "W.G.P.," who presumably was Will Pritchard, a close friend from Saskatchewan who'd died young and the brother of Laura Pritchard Agnew, to whom Montgomery had dedicated *Anne's House of Dreams*. These links are fitting, because with the exception of one new poem and a few reprinted pieces, *Anne of Ingleside* would be the last piece of writing she would publish before her death.

## — 3 —

In a letter dated November 4, 1939, to a reader she addressed as Mrs. Aitken, Montgomery offered a rare hint about a project she was contemplating for the future. "My publishers want me some day to fill in the gap between 'Rainbow Valley' and 'Rilla of Ingleside,' and perhaps I may. But I can't somehow bear the thought of making Anne a grandmother. I want her to remain immortally young. One can keep up that illusion through her motherhood but I am afraid it could not be done through grandmotherhood!" The reason for this concern about Anne's immortal youth is unclear, since the only feasible way for Anne to become a grandmother would have been for Montgomery to write a book set after *Rilla of Ingleside* rather than one set before, but what this letter nevertheless shows is that the publication of *Anne of Ingleside* the preceding July hadn't quenched the appetite for more books about Anne.[13]

But in September of that year, war broke out again between England and Germany, much to her distress. While on a visit to Prince Edward Island that month, she sent a postcard to G.B. MacMillan in Scotland. "Come for a walk with me on this shore tonight," she wrote, "and we will forget for an hour the nightmare that has been loosed on the world. It is unfair that we should have to go through this *again*." Making a similar statement about the unfairness of this second war in a letter to Ephraim Weber dated February 13, 1940, she acknowledged that her attitude was "childish," but "it is exactly how I feel." In that same letter to Weber, she mentioned that she'd begun work on a sequel to *Jane of Lantern Hill*, but no details about this project have survived.[14]

At some point in the last few years of her life, Montgomery completed the manuscript of yet another Anne book, which she called *The Blythes Are Quoted* and which she divided into two parts, one set before and one set after the Great War of 1914–1918. At first glance this would appear to be the book Montgomery wrote to Mrs. Aitken about, except that it doesn't fill the gap between *Rainbow Valley* and *Rilla of Ingleside*. An early vignette mentions that Walter is twelve, the same age he is at the start of *Rainbow Valley*, which means that part of this book overlaps with the time period of an earlier volume.[15] For this book, she returned to the format L.C. Page had suggested to her thirty years earlier and that had led to the publication of *Chronicles of Avonlea*: She took fifteen existing short stories that featured unrelated characters and revised them to include mentions and appearances of a grown-up Anne and her family. But what makes this project unique is what she added to bind the stories together: vignettes depicting the Blythe family members discussing forty-one poems that are attributed within the text to Anne or to Walter but that, like "The Old Man's Grave" in *Anne of Ingleside*, were poems that Montgomery had published under her own name. While parts of this book appeared in 1974 as *The Road to Yesterday*, it wasn't published in its entirety until my edition came out in October 2009, a little over a year after the publication of Butler's *Globe and Mail* essay in which she revealed her family's interpretation of Montgomery's death as a suicide.

Ever since I first read the typescripts of *The Blythes Are Quoted* at the University of Guelph archives in 1999, I've pondered how Montgomery's final contribution to literature functions as a capstone to her earlier work. The absence of any concrete mention of this project in her journals or in her surviving correspondence adds to the mystery of when she wrote it and what she hoped to achieve with it, but that's in keeping with another strategic silence in her life writing — the drafting, three-and-a-half decades earlier, of *Anne of Green Gables*. And yet, the circumstances of her life had changed immeasurably between the publication of her first novel and the point at which she worked on her final book. As Mary Rubio and Elizabeth Waterston note in their introduction to the last volume of Montgomery's selected journals, "Her final entries are those of a clinically depressed woman who is contemplating an ending — an ending of the lived-life and an ending for the written-life."[16] Perhaps not surprisingly given this frame of mind, *The Blythes Are Quoted* takes up such topics as adultery, illegitimacy, misogyny, revenge, murder, despair, aging, hatred, and death — elements that aren't wholly absent from her fictional worlds yet aren't characteristic of her work.

I also became intrigued by a clue that I came across during the early stages of my work, long before the publication of Butler's essay: Montgomery's obituary in the *Globe and Mail*, which mentioned that a new collection of stories had been "placed in the hands of a publishing firm" on the very day of her death.[17]

Was that a coincidence? Or does it suggest a certain degree of intentionality on Montgomery's part?

There's no way to answer such a question with certainty. After all, as Rubio has argued in her subsequent contribution to the conversation about Montgomery's death, "If Maud was indeed writing until the end of her life, we could infer that she was determined to replenish her falling income with another novel — not something that one would necessarily expect from a person contemplating suicide later the same day." And after all, the closing section of *The Blythes Are Quoted* is entitled "Au Revoir," which means "till we meet again," keeping open the possibility that Montgomery did not mean for this book to be the ultimate end.[18]

But another way to interpret this book in the context of Montgomery's life and death is to consider that *The Blythes Are Quoted* is as much a suicide note as the single sheet of paper found on her nightstand after she died. Neither document points conclusively to premeditated suicide (let alone elucidate what might have been her specific motive for taking her own life), but each suggests despair and a willingness to be done with living.

I mentioned in the introduction to this book that there's no way, with the evidence available, to prove beyond a shadow of a doubt whether or not Montgomery's death was deliberate. Even so, I like to think that the creative choices revealed in her final book, as in all her work, had some intention behind them — especially since, unlike preceding books that survive in handwritten manuscript form, this one exists as three separate, but highly different, typescripts. Much like with her journals, where it stands to reason that Montgomery intended for her handwritten ledgers *and* her abridged typescript to stand as the definitive versions of her journal, despite all the discrepancies between them, the existence of three completed but undated typescripts suggests that Montgomery wanted posterity to understand the care with which she considered the text and the arrangement of these materials before she submitted copies of the typescript to her publishers.

And so, if we accept the fact that *The Blythes Are Quoted* was a completed work and if we're open to the possibility that the submission of this manuscript to Montgomery's publishers on the day of her death was not coincidental, then what does this final book contain about her beloved Anne characters that, much like her journals, she wouldn't publish while she was alive?

— 4 —

Let's begin with the book's form — the blending of short fiction, poetry, and dialogue.

Montgomery's decision to weave so many of her own poems into the typescript makes for a fascinating experiment in terms of genre — or perhaps she was motivated to do so simply because she didn't have enough recent material for another collection of poems. But for this idea to work, regardless of the reason behind it, she had to revise some of the continuity in the preceding books. While *Anne of Ingleside* establishes that "The Old Man's Grave" consists of Anne's first attempt at writing poetry, *The Blythes Are Quoted* offers a retroactive revision of Anne's writing life. "Before her marriage Anne wrote occasional stories but gave this up when her children were babies," the narrator explains in the first vignette. And now, in her forties, Anne "sometimes reads her occasional poems to the family circle at twilight." As the book progresses, she reveals not only what inspired her to write these poems but also during what periods of life she wrote them: while teaching school in Avonlea (in *Anne of Avonlea*), while attending Redmond College (in *Anne of the Island*), the night before her wedding day (in *Anne's House of Dreams*). Her comment that "Remembered" was a poem she "never could get an editor to accept" reveals that she not only wrote poems but also attempted to have them published. The poems discussed in part one of the book receive a range of responses from Gilbert (approving or disapproving depending on each poem's subject matter), their sons Jem and Walter, and from Susan, who revises her earlier opposition to poetry writing to be more gender specific: as she tells Walter, "I wish you would remember that while writing poetry is a very good amusement for a woman it is no real occupation for a man."[19]

Revising existing short stories for this volume led to some challenges in terms of repetition. She selected a four-chapter fiction serial entitled "Some

Fools and a Saint," first published in the *Family Herald and Weekly Star* in 1931, as the opening story in the collection, but she ran into trouble with the last two sentences: "Lucia twisted herself from Curtis' grasp and ran. But before she ran Curtis heard the most charming sound in the world … the little yielding laugh of a woman caught by her lover." Montgomery evidently concluded that there was too much overlap with the final line in *Mistress Pat* (1935), which I mentioned earlier in this book, because she changed it:

> Lucia twisted herself from his grasp and ran. But before she ran Curtis caught a look in her eyes. He was suddenly a very happy man.
>
> "What will Dr. Blythe say?" he wondered. He knew quite well what Mrs. Blythe would say.

That was one problem solved, but in the original version of "The Road to Yesterday," published in *Canadian Home Journal* in 1934, Jerry makes a bold declaration to Susette — "I've made you mine with that kiss. You can never belong to anyone else" — that likewise recalls the final scene in *Mistress Pat.* Evidently that one escaped her notice or she didn't think it was sufficiently problematic, because it appears intact in the revised version of that story.[20]

Similar problems occurred when Montgomery used stories that were originally set more or less in the present as the basis for revised stories set before the Great War. In the original version of "An Afternoon with Mr. Jenkins," published in the *Family Herald and Weekly Star* in 1933, Timothy wants to buy some flowers and put them "at the base of the soldiers' monument. Because my father was a brave soldier" — a statement that Mr. Jenkins presumes means that Timothy's father was "killed at the front." In *The Blythes Are Quoted*, Mr. Jenkins changes this to "killed in South Africa," implying that Timothy's father served in the South African War, an amendment that suits the story's revised chronology. In the original version of "The Twins Pretend," published in the *Toronto Star Weekly* in 1937, one of the games that ten-year-old Jill suggests to her twin brother involves pretending to be "Edith Cavell at her execution." Cavell was executed on October 12, 1915, and yet, in the version of this story in *The Blythes Are Quoted*, now set before the war, this game is still mentioned. Moreover, the short story "A Dream Comes True" involves a character who drives an automobile recklessly on the highway to Charlottetown, even though automobiles were not nearly that prevalent in Prince Edward Island before the Great War. In a chapter in *Rilla of Ingleside* set well into the war years, the Blythes purchase their first automobile, which is such a newfangled contraption that Susan quotes a naysayer neighbour who avows that "the Government should be turned out of office for permitting them to run on the Island at all."[21]

Like so many of her novels, many of the stories in this book end with the promise of wedding bells. But many of the love stories take on a new tone, to say the least. In "Penelope Struts Her Theories," Penelope Craig keeps turning down marriage proposals from Roger Galbraith because she's more interested in him as a friend than as a husband, but after Penelope runs herself ragged trying to raise two boys on her own, Roger loses his patience. "You are going to marry me inside of three weeks. I'm not asking you … I'm telling you." In "Brother Beware," Timothy kidnaps Alma Winkworth in a desperate attempt to prevent his brother from proposing to her, only to fall in love with her himself. But when he does propose, the narrator shifts to Alma's point of view and reveals that what she feels is not only the delight in marrying "the fine-looking man she had admired so much the first time she had seen him in Glen St. Mary Church" but also "relief" that she can stop working and can say good-bye to "lean vacations in cheap boarding houses."[22]

And although Montgomery had largely ignored her publishers' urging to include Anne as much as possible when she'd put together *Chronicles of Avonlea* thirty years before, in this case, she arguably went a bit overboard with the mentions and appearances of the Blythe characters. And yet, for every character who has only good things to say about the Blythes, one or more characters find their praise excessive — "I think you worship those Blythes," Chrissie points out reproachfully of her former governess, "Aunty" Clack. "You are always quoting them." And occasionally, the narrator reveals some uncharitable opinions about Anne: Clarissa Wilcox, in "Retribution," calls her "that stuck-up Mrs. Blythe," whereas Miss Shelley, in "The Reconciliation," finds her shallow ("She had been heard to say that it was a pity Dr. Blythe had not selected a woman of deeper nature for his wife"). Or as Aunt Lilian puts it in "The Cheated Child," although thankfully not out loud, "That Mrs. Dr. Blythe makes me sick." Montgomery's *Anne of* titles place Anne at the centre of the story in relation to place, but the title "The Blythes Are Quoted" flips the emphasis around so that Anne and her family members are the objects of community gossip, and the results of that shift in focus are fascinating. Clarissa Wilcox mentions that "*I* could tell Mrs. Blythe a few things about Dr. Blythe and his nurses ... yes, and about him and Mrs. Owen Ford if I wanted to." These allegations are never referred to again, let alone substantiated or dismissed. The point seemingly isn't whether or not these allegations about Gilbert being unfaithful are true, but rather, the emphasis in this final book is on the gossip that circulates throughout the community about the Blythes, regardless of truth.[23]

## — 5 —

Two more facets of this final book need to be mentioned, especially given how pervasive they are throughout the book: death and war.

Death is persistently present throughout *The Blythes Are Quoted.* The short stories "Retribution" and "A Commonplace Woman" consist of elaborate deathbed scenes, and even the more comedic stories contain an abundance of casual mentions of characters' relatives and friends who have died. The omnipresence of death is not entirely new for Montgomery — you'll recall the two scenes in *Anne of Windy Poplars/Willows* in which eccentric women regale Anne with witty anecdotes about the deaths of all their family members — but what's most noticeable here is how all these passing mentions of death add to the event that's at the heart of this final book. Walter Blythe, whose death in *Rilla of Ingleside* is something the family members do their best to accept as part of a sacrifice for a new postwar world, returns in this final book, only to die again. "He had destroyed most of his poems before going overseas," the narrator mentions, "but left a few with his mother." And in the second half of the book, poems attributed to Anne alternate with poems attributed to Walter, including the final poem, "The Aftermath," in which the speaker talks about bayonetting another man and having to live

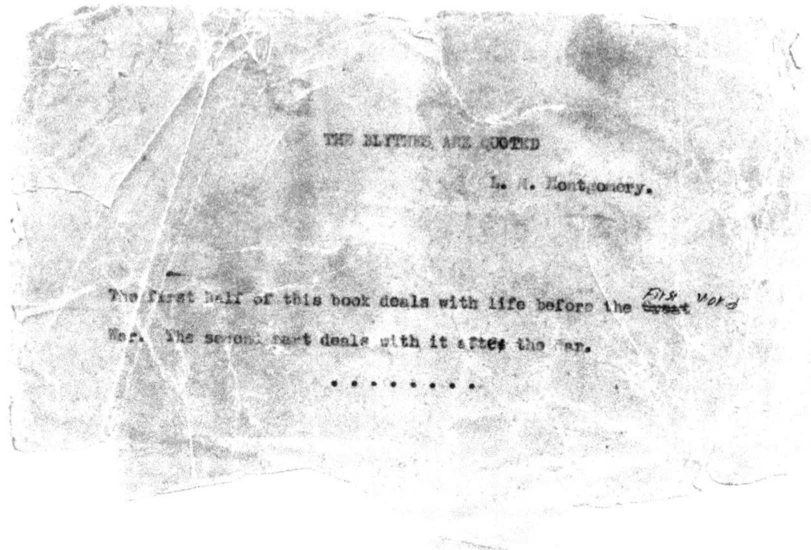

THE BLYTHES ARE QUOTED

L. M. Montgomery.

The first half of this book deals with life before the ~~Great~~ First World War. The second part deals with it after the War.

.........

Fragment of the title page of one of the typescripts of *The Blythes Are Quoted*, with an emendation in ink.

with that memory. Unlike the remaining poems attributed to Walter, this one he wrote "'somewhere in France' in the year of Courcelette and sent home to his mother with the rest of his papers." Anne waits until years later, in the midst of the Second World War, before she shares it with anyone — and even then, she shows it only to her oldest son, Jem. And Anne's response to the poem reveals that not only are the family members still mourning the loss of Walter, but they've also had to revise their understanding of the meaning they once attributed to his death. "I am thankful now, Jem, that Walter did not come back. He could never have lived with his memories … and if he had seen the futility of the sacrifice they made then mirrored in this ghastly holocaust …"[24]

But while this newfound realization occurs at the end of *The Blythes Are Quoted*, Montgomery provided a tangible clue about it on the title page of the typescript that was submitted to her publishers, which reads as follows: "The first half of this book deals with life before the Great War. The second part deals with it after the War."[25]

On this page, the word "Great" is crossed out and replaced with "First World" in ink.

It would have taken only a few minutes for Montgomery to type out a new sheet of paper with this correction. But again, if we allow for the possibility that all markings on the page are intentional, even if we can't prove what the intention was, I've always wondered if Montgomery wanted to signal this change in ink, as a last-minute acknowledgement that the Great War she'd believed in as the war to end all wars had proven, by 1942, to be futile.

— 6 —

Two copies of one of the typescripts for *The Blythes Are Quoted* are in the McClelland and Stewart archives at McMaster University in Hamilton, indicating that, one way or another, Montgomery did submit them. But I have not yet found any other textual record from the period that mentions this project, let alone explains why, despite her publishers' apparent request for another Anne book after they published *Anne of Ingleside* in 1939, they opted not to publish it. Possibly they concluded that the blend of genres made the book difficult to describe or that the criticism of the war would alienate some readers. As with the cause of Montgomery's death, we can speculate, but unless concrete evidence turns up, it's difficult to say for sure.

But even at the end of her life, Montgomery carried on with a strategy she'd been using throughout her career — to test out her work in periodical form prior to book publication. Three weeks before her death, she submitted a poem to *Saturday Night* magazine along with a note that matches almost perfectly the headnote found at the start of part one of *The Blythes Are Quoted*: "In one of my books, *Rilla of Ingleside*, a poem is mentioned, supposed to have been written and published by Walter Blythe before his death in the Great War. Although the poem had no real existence hundreds of people have written me asking me where they could get it. It has been written but recently, but seems to me even more appropriate now than then."

> One day the Piper came down the glen,
> Sweet and long and low played he …

The children followed from door to door
No matter how those who loved might implore,
So wiling the song of his melody
As the song of a woodland rill.

Some day the Piper will come again
To pipe to the sons of the maple tree …
You and I will follow from door to door,
Many of us will come back no more!
What matter that if Freedom still
Be the crown of each native hill?[26]

Sometimes I wonder how many astute readers of *Saturday Night* in 1942 picked up on the fact that this poem entitled "The Piper" does not really resemble the poem implied in *Rilla of Ingleside* — and not simply due to the mention of "again" or the absence of the phrase "keep faith." At the very least, there's no mention here that this poem has any connection to a book-length work that will follow. This magazine published Montgomery's note and poem, along with an obituary tribute to her, in its issue dated two weeks after her death, as her final published poem.

# Conclusion

## After Life's Fitful Fever

In a journal entry dated December 7, 1919, L.M. Montgomery wrote down the epitaph she'd selected for the tombstone for her cousin and dearest friend, Frederica Campbell McFarlane: "After life's fitful fever she sleeps well," a quotation (with an adjusted pronoun) from Shakespeare's *Macbeth*. "It is the one I want on my own when I die," she added. "And I trust I shall sleep well — and dreamlessly. For I think it will take me a long while to get rested."[1]

When Montgomery died more than two decades later, on April 24, 1942, her family members evidently had no awareness of this choice of epitaph, since it did not appear on her tombstone. But there could be no doubt that Montgomery wanted to be buried back in Cavendish, Prince Edward Island. "I like Ontario very much," she wrote in a short biographical statement that appeared in *Twentieth Century Authors: A Biographical Dictionary of Modern Literature*, released the same year as her death, "but anyone who has once loved 'the only island there is' never really loves any other place. And so the scene of all my books save one has been laid there. And in my dreams I go back to it."[2] And so, as countless newspapers across North America paid tribute to her and to her work, she was interred on April 30, 1942, a few steps away from the grave where her mother and her maternal grandparents are buried. New editions of *Anne of Green Gables*, *Anne of Avonlea*, and *Anne of the Island*, dated April 1942, were published by the Ryerson Press (Toronto), the first of innumerable reprint editions available to subsequent generations of Montgomery readers in North America and beyond.

Less than six months later, W.J. Hurlow wrote, in the "Under the Reading Lamp" column of the Ottawa *Citizen*, about a trip to Green Gables, which since the late 1930s had become part of the Prince Edward Island National Park. As Hurlow noted of the farmhouse that had recently been renovated to have a greater resemblance to the house described in *Anne of Green Gables*, "In its general aspect and surroundings it was exactly as we had pictured it for thirty years." But then the focus shifts away from the house and toward the cemetery nearby: "In the little cemetery a new grave has been dug among tombs some of which are more than a century old. On that summer day two

Cover of the Ryerson Press edition of *Anne of Green Gables*, published in 1942.

wreaths of marigolds and nasturtiums were wilting in the hot sunshine on Lucy Maud Montgomery's last resting place. But her fame as an imaginative genius shows no withered fronds. Canadians who have thoughtlessly fallen into the unpatriotic habit of discounting the value and permanence of our national literature might recover a sense of proportion by the sun-kissed, windswept, sea-washed shores of Avonlea."[3]

In the decades since Montgomery's death, the critical conversation about her work has changed immeasurably, perhaps even more so than the technologies that her readers use to engage with her work and with each other. But her grave — where her husband was buried with her, following his own death in December 1943 — remains essentially unchanged. It is a place to pay tribute, to give thanks, and to contemplate not only the existing body of work that means so much to so many people, but also the work that Montgomery might have written, had the circumstances of her life differed from what they were.

In volume 1 of *The L.M. Montgomery Reader*, I included an essay by Montgomery that I'd come across in a scrapbook owned by the Campbell family in Park Corner, Prince Edward Island, home of some of her emotionally closest relatives and the place where she married Ewan Macdonald in 1911. At the time, I estimated that the essay had been published sometime around 1933. A few years after the publication of that book, I came across this essay in the May 1931 issue of *Canadian Home Journal*, where it appeared as part of a larger round table entitled "Looking Back on Life" that asked "eight representative Canadian women" the following question: "Would you if you had the opportunity, make any change in life as you have found it?"

This piece allows us to reflect on Montgomery's lasting legacy as an internationally acclaimed writer whose popularity shows no sign of abating more than seven decades after her death. Much like the continued digitization of older print sources allows readers and researchers to look back on her life and her work with increased appreciation for all its complexities and nuances, this essay demonstrates Montgomery's view that "looking backward" can change our perspective on past events and perceptions:

Looking backward is not, I think, a peculiarly pleasant business for anybody, but it is an intriguing one. It is, for one thing, amazing to see how values have shifted. Things and events, which at the time seemed of tremendous importance, have shrunk to insignificance and are clearly seen to have had no real influence on my life at all. Whereas, on the other hand, many things which at the time seemed of no importance at all are now seen to have been of cataclysmic influence and to have changed the whole trend and tenor of my existence and career. One lesson that "looking backward" has brought home to me is the power of seeming trifles.

Another thing that strikes me is the bitter flavour that many old joys have acquired and the strange enchanting sweetness of recollection that has come to old sorrows. I see humour now in many things that seemed unrelieved tragedy at the time and many comic memories have revealed an inner core of tragedy. I am amazed at the wise things I did which turned out to be foolish and at the foolish things that have turned out to be wise. And I can now trace very clearly a manifest destiny "shaping my ends" in despite [*sic*] of all my futile resistances and struggles.

I was ambitious in youth and I have realized some of my ambition. I had a certain knack of picking friends which I took as a matter of course but can now see to have been a very vital endowment. I wanted to drain the cup of life fully, whether its brewage was bitter or sweet, and I have done it. So I look back on my life with a certain feeling of satisfaction, despite a still unsated thirst.

Yet I would not want to live it again, just as, having finished a book, I do not want to start in and read it over again no matter how interesting it was. I want a different book.

But this one *has* been interesting![4]

# Acknowledgements

Writing a book is in many ways a solitary venture, but I'm grateful to several friends and colleagues who offered support, suggestions, and conversation, all of which helped make this book possible. I offer my sincere thanks to Michelle Baumtrog, Gini Bechtel, Vanessa Brown, Kate Macdonald Butler, Mary Beth Cavert, Sally Keefe Cohen, Carolyn Strom Collins, Evan Coole, Cecily Devereux, Jason Dickson, Kelly Norah Drukker, Owen Dudley Edwards, Elizabeth Rollins Epperly, Melanie J. Fishbane, Irene Gammel, Carole Gerson, Sarah Goff, Daniela Janes, Caroline E. Jones, Yuka Kajihara, Kate Lawson, Joanne Lebold, Jennifer H. Litster, Simon Lloyd, Andrea McKenzie, Rachel McMillan, Bernadeta Milewski, E. Holly Pike, Lisa Richter, Laura M. Robinson, Mary Henley Rubio, Tamara Shantz, Cynthia Soulliere, Margaret Steffler, Kate Sutherland, Steve Wood, Debra Worth, the late Christy Woster, Emily Woster, and Lorraine York. I also offer a shout-out to the thirteen hundred or so members of the L.M. Montgomery Readathon, a Facebook discussion group that Andrea McKenzie and I founded at the start of the Covid-19 pandemic — it's been such a pleasure learning more about Montgomery's life, work, and legacy alongside you all. Special thanks to Jacob Letkemann, my partner, and to our families, particularly my mother, Claire Pelland Lefebvre.

Thanks as well to Chris Casuccio, my agent at Westwood Creative Artists; the entire team at Dundurn, particularly Meghan Macdonald, Janna Green, and Jess Shulman; and the staff at Archives and Special Collections, University of Guelph library, particularly Graham Burt and Gillian Manford.

I delivered parts of some of these chapters as papers at public events hosted by the Lucy Maud Montgomery Society of Ontario in Leaskdale and by the L.M. Montgomery Institute at the University of Prince Edward Island in Charlottetown. Thanks to the organizers of those events for everything they contribute to the public conversation about L.M. Montgomery's life, work, and legacy.

I dedicate this book to the memory of Elizabeth Hillman Waterston (1922–2024), a pioneering L.M. Montgomery scholar whose work, encyclopedic knowledge, and personal encouragement meant a great deal to me, as they no doubt did to so many fellow Montgomery scholars.

# Appendix

## Books by L.M. Montgomery

### Books Published Within Montgomery's Lifetime

*Anne of Green Gables* (1908)
*Anne of Avonlea* (1909)
*Kilmeny of the Orchard* (1910)
*The Story Girl* (1911)
*Chronicles of Avonlea* (1912)
*The Golden Road* (1913)
*Anne of the Island* (1915)
*The Watchman and Other Poems* (1916)
*Anne's House of Dreams* (1917)
*Rainbow Valley* (1919)
*Further Chronicles of Avonlea* (1920)
*Rilla of Ingleside* (1921)
*Emily of New Moon* (1923)
*Emily Climbs* (1925)
*The Blue Castle* (1926)
*Emily's Quest* (1927)
*Magic for Marigold* (1929)
*A Tangled Web* (1931)

*Pat of Silver Bush* (1933)
*Courageous Women* (1934), with Marian Keith and Mabel Burns McKinley
*Mistress Pat: A Novel of Silver Bush* (1935)
*Anne of Windy Poplars* (1936)
*Jane of Lantern Hill* (1937)
*Anne of Ingleside* (1939)

## Posthumous Collections of Shorter Works

*The Road to Yesterday* (1974)
*The Alpine Path: The Story of My Career* (1974)
*The Doctor's Sweetheart and Other Stories* (1979), selected by Catherine McLay
*The Poetry of Lucy Maud Montgomery* (1987), selected by John Ferns and Kevin McCabe
*Akin to Anne: Tales of Other Orphans* (1988), edited by Rea Wilmshurst
*Along the Shore: Tales by the Sea* (1989), edited by Rea Wilmshurst
*Among the Shadows: Tales from the Darker Side* (1990), edited by Rea Wilmshurst
*After Many Days: Tales of Time Passed* (1991), edited by Rea Wilmshurst
*Against the Odds: Tales of Achievement* (1993), edited by Rea Wilmshurst
*At the Altar: Matrimonial Tales* (1994), edited by Rea Wilmshurst
*Across the Miles: Tales of Correspondence* (1995), edited by Rea Wilmshurst
*Christmas with Anne and Other Holiday Stories* (1995), edited by Rea Wilmshurst
*The Way to Slumbertown* (2005)
*The Blythes Are Quoted* (2009), edited by Benjamin Lefebvre
*Una of the Garden* (2010), edited by Donna J. Campbell and Simon Lloyd
*After Many Years: Twenty-One "Long-Lost" Stories* (2017), edited by Carolyn Strom Collins and Christy Woster
*A Name for Herself: Selected Writings, 1891–1917* (2018), edited by Benjamin Lefebvre
*A World of Songs: Selected Poems, 1891–1921* (2019), edited by Benjamin Lefebvre
*Christmas with L.M. Montgomery* (2021)
*Around the Hearth: Tales of Home and Family* (2022), edited by Joanne Lebold (originally selected by Rea Wilmshurst)
*Twice upon a Time: Selected Stories, 1898–1939* (2022), edited by Benjamin Lefebvre

*A Chapter of Accidents: Twenty-Seven Rediscovered Stories* (2025), edited by Carolyn Strom Collins

*Schooled with Briars: Collected Serials, 1903–1913* (2025), edited by Benjamin Lefebvre

## Life Writing

*The Green Gables Letters from L.M. Montgomery to Ephraim Weber, 1905–1909* (1960), edited by Wilfrid Eggleston

*My Dear Mr. M: Letters to G.B. MacMillan from L.M. Montgomery* (1980), edited by Francis W.P. Bolger and Elizabeth R. Epperly

*The Selected Journals of L.M. Montgomery* (5 vols., 1985–2004), edited by Mary Rubio and Elizabeth Waterston

*After Green Gables: L.M. Montgomery's Letters to Ephraim Weber, 1916–1941* (2006), edited by Hildi Froese Tiessen and Paul Gerard Tiessen

*The Complete Journals of L.M. Montgomery* (2 vols., 2012–2013), edited by Mary Henley Rubio and Elizabeth Hillman Waterston

*L.M. Montgomery's Complete Journals* (5 vols., 2016–2019), edited by Jen Rubio

# Notes

## Abbreviations

### WORK BY L.M. MONTGOMERY

*AA*: *Anne of Avonlea* (L.C. Page and Company, 1909)

*AfGG*: *After Green Gables: L.M. Montgomery's Letters to Ephraim Weber, 1916–1941*, ed. Hildi Froese Tiessen and Paul Gerard Tiessen (University of Toronto Press, 2006)

*AGG*: *Anne of Green Gables* (L.C. Page and Company, 1908)

*AHD*: *Anne's House of Dreams* (McClelland, Goodchild, and Stewart, 1917)

*AIn*: *Anne of Ingleside* (McClelland and Stewart, 1939)

*AIs*: *Anne of the Island* (Page Company, 1915)

*AWP*: *Anne of Windy Poplars* (McClelland and Stewart, 1936)

*BC*: *The Blue Castle* (McClelland and Stewart, 1926)

*BQ*: *The Blythes Are Quoted*, ed. Benjamin Lefebvre (Viking Canada, 2009)

BQ ts.: "The Blythes Are Quoted" (typescript; L.M. Montgomery Collection, Archival and Special Collections, University of Guelph Library)

*CA*: *Chronicles of Avonlea* (L.C. Page and Company, 1912)

*CJLMM*, 1: *The Complete Journals of L.M. Montgomery: The PEI Years, 1889–1900*, ed. Mary Henley Rubio and Elizabeth Hillman Waterston (Oxford University Press, 2012)

*CJLMM*, 2: *The Complete Journals of L.M. Montgomery: The PEI Years, 1901–1911*, ed. Mary Henley Rubio and Elizabeth Hillman Waterston (Oxford University Press, 2013)

*EC*: *Emily Climbs* (McClelland and Stewart, 1925)
*ENM*: *Emily of New Moon* (McClelland and Stewart, 1923)
*EQ*: *Emily's Quest* (McClelland and Stewart, 1927)
EVLMMJ: Edited Version of L.M. Montgomery Journals (typescript; L.M. Montgomery Collection, Archival and Special Collections, University of Guelph Library)
*FCA*: *Further Chronicles of Avonlea* (The Page Company, 1920)
*GGL*: *The Green Gables Letters from L.M. Montgomery to Ephraim Weber, 1905–1909*, ed. Wilfrid Eggleston (Ryerson Press, 1960)
*GR*: *The Golden Road* (L.C. Page and Company, 1913)
*JLH*: *Jane of Lantern Hill* (McClelland and Stewart, 1937)
*KO*: *Kilmeny of the Orchard* (L.C. Page and Company, 1910)
LGBM: Letters to G.B. MacMillan (George Boyd MacMillan fonds, Library and Archives Canada)
*LMMCJ*, 1: *L.M. Montgomery's Complete Journals: The Ontario Years, 1911–1917*, ed. Jen Rubio (Rock's Mills Press, 2016)
*LMMCJ*, 2: *L.M. Montgomery's Complete Journals: The Ontario Years, 1918–1921*, ed. Jen Rubio (Rock's Mills Press, 2017)
*LMMCJ*, 3: *L.M. Montgomery's Complete Journals: The Ontario Years, 1922–1925* (Rock's Mills Press, 2018)
*LMMCJ*, 4: *L.M. Montgomery's Complete Journals: The Ontario Years, 1926–1929*, ed. Jen Rubio (Rock's Mills Press, 2017)
*LMMCJ*, 5: *L.M. Montgomery's Complete Journals: The Ontario Years, 1930–1933*, ed. Jen Rubio (Rock's Mills Press, 2019)
*MDMM*: *My Dear Mr. M: Letters to G.B. MacMillan from L.M. Montgomery*, ed. Francis W.P. Bolger and Elizabeth R. Epperly (McGraw-Hill Ryerson, 1980)
*MM*: *Magic for Marigold* (McClelland and Stewart, 1929)
*MP*: *Mistress Pat: A Novel of Silver Bush* (McClelland and Stewart, 1935)
*NH*: *A Name for Herself: Selected Writings, 1891–1917*, ed. Benjamin Lefebvre (University of Toronto Press, 2018)
*PSB*: *Pat of Silver Bush* (McClelland and Stewart, 1933)
*RI*: *Rilla of Ingleside* (McClelland and Stewart, 1921)
*RV*: *Rainbow Valley* (McClelland and Stewart, 1919)
*SB*: *Schooled with Briars: Collected Serials, 1903–1913*, ed. Benjamin Lefebvre (University of Toronto Press, 2025)
*SG*: *The Story Girl* (L.C. Page and Company, 1911)
*SJLMM*: *The Selected Journals of L.M. Montgomery*, vol. 1: *1889–1910*; vol. 2: *1910–1921*; vol. 3: *1921–1929*; vol. 4: *1929–1935*; vol. 5: *1935–1942*, ed.

Mary Rubio and Elizabeth Waterston (Oxford University Press, 1985, 1987, 1992, 1998, 2004)

*TT*: *Twice upon a Time: Selected Stories, 1898–1939*, ed. Benjamin Lefebvre (University of Toronto Press, 2022)

*TW*: *A Tangled Web* (McClelland and Stewart, 1931)

*W*: *The Watchman and Other Poems* (McClelland, Goodchild, and Stewart, 1916)

*WS*: *A World of Songs: Selected Poems, 1894–1921*, ed. Benjamin Lefebvre (University of Toronto Press, 2019)

### SECONDARY SOURCES

*Reader*: *The L.M. Montgomery Reader*, vol. 1: *A Life in Print*; vol. 2: *A Critical Heritage*; vol. 3: *A Legacy in Review*, ed. Benjamin Lefebvre (University of Toronto Press, 2013, 2014, 2015)

## Epigraphs

*ENM*, 317, 318; L.M. Montgomery, "[Seasons in the Woods]," in *Reader*, 1: 92 (all ellipses but the first in original).

## Introduction: The Glory and the Dream

1 Kate Macdonald Butler, "The Heartbreaking Truth About Anne's Creator," *Globe and Mail*, September 20, 2008, F1.

2 "'I Am So Glad You Told Us the Truth,'" *Globe and Mail*, September 27, 2008, F5.

3 *LMMCJ*, 2: 248.

4 James Adams, "Happy 100th Birthday, Anne," *Globe and Mail*, February 9, 2008, R9.

5 Faye Hammill, *Women, Celebrity, and Literary Culture Between the Wars* (University of Texas Press, 2007), 100.

6 *SJLMM*, 5: 350; Mary Rubio and Elizabeth Waterston, in *SJLMM*, 5: 399.

7 Laura M. Robinson, "Tragedy of Everyday Life," review of *Marian Engel: Life in Letters*, ed. Christl Verduyn and Kathleen Garay, and *The Selected Journals of L.M. Montgomery*, vol. 5: *1935–1942*, ed. Mary Rubio and Elizabeth Waterston, *Canadian Literature* 189 (Summer 2006): 145.

8 "The Dead Shall Have Their Dominion," *Globe and Mail*, October 29, 1977, Weekly Magazine supplement, 16; Stuart Macdonald, "L.M. Montgomery," *Globe and Mail*, November 3, 1977, 6; Cynthia Brouse, "The Maud Squad," in *Reader*, 2: 294; Irene Gammel, review of *The Selected Journals of L.M. Montgomery*, vol. 5: *1935–1942*, ed. Mary Rubio and Elizabeth Waterston,

and *Anne of Green Gables*, ed. Cecily Devereux, *University of Toronto Quarterly* 75, no. 1 (Winter 2006): 326; *MDMM*, 204; *AfGG*, 263, 260.

9 Jim Day, "Suicide Took Life of Anne Creator, Expert on Author Not Surprised," *Guardian* (Charlottetown), September 23, 2008, A1.

10 Mary Henley Rubio, *Lucy Maud Montgomery: The Gift of Wings* (Doubleday Canada, 2008), 575–76. See also "Is This Lucy Maud's Suicide Note?," *Globe and Mail*, September 24, 2008, A1.

11 Adams, "Lucy Maud Suffered 'Unbearable Psychological Pain,'" *Globe and Mail*, September 24, 2008, A7; Rubio, untitled talk, From Canada to the World: The Cultural Influence of Lucy Maud Montgomery, University of Guelph, October 25, 2008.

12 Rubio, *Lucy Maud Montgomery*, 575.

13 "Behind Green Gables," *Globe and Mail*, September 25, 2008, A16; Paul Tiessen, "The Death of Lucy Maud," *Globe and Mail*, September 30, 2008, A20; Gammel, "The Fatal Disappointments of Lucy Maud," review of *Lucy Maud Montgomery: The Gift of Wings*, by Mary Henley Rubio, *Globe and Mail*, November 15, 2008, D4. See also *AfGG*, 105; *LMMCJ*, 3: 32.

14 Vanessa Brown and Benjamin Lefebvre, "Archival Adventures with L.M. Montgomery; or, 'As Long as the Leaves Hold Together,'" in *Reader*, 2: 380.

15 Rubio, *Lucy Maud Montgomery*, 578.

16 Gammel, "Introduction: Life Writing as Masquerade: The Many Faces of L.M. Montgomery," in *The Intimate Life of L.M. Montgomery*, ed. Gammel (University of Toronto Press, 2005), 4.

17 Jerry Jacobs, "A Phenomenological Study of Suicide Notes," *Social Problems* 15, no. 1 (Summer 1967): 62.

18 Edwin Shneidman, *Voices of Death* (Harper and Row, 1980), 68; Rubio, *Lucy Maud Montgomery*, 28.

19 Montgomery, "Book Price Record Book, 1908–1942" (L.M. Montgomery Collection, Archival and Special Collections, University of Guelph Library); Montgomery, comp., Scrapbooks 1–12 (University Archives and Special Collections, University of Prince Edward Island Library); Montgomery, comp., "Scrapbook of Reviews from Around the World Which L.M. Montgomery's Clipping Service Sent to Her, 1910–1935" (L.M. Montgomery Collection, Archival and Special Collections, University of Guelph Library).

20 I discuss this fiction serial, entitled "The Luck of the Tremaynes" and appearing in *The American Home* in 1907, in the afterword to *Schooled with Briars*.

21 *Anne of Green Gables*, adapt. Kevin Sullivan and Joe Wiesenfeld, dir. Kevin Sullivan (Sullivan Films, 1985); *Anne of Green Gables: The Sequel*, writ. and dir. Kevin Sullivan (Sullivan Films, 1987); *Road to Avonlea*, developed by Fiona McHugh (Sullivan Entertainment, 1990–1996); *Anne with an "E,"* created by Moira Walley-Beckett (Northwood Entertainment, 2017–2019).

22 Montgomery, *The Road to Yesterday* (McGraw-Hill Ryerson, 1974); Montgomery, *The Alpine Path: The Story of My Career* (Fitzhenry and Whiteside, n.d.); Francis W.P. Bolger, *The Years Before "Anne"* (Prince Edward Island Heritage Foundation, 1974). For reviews of posthumous Montgomery titles, see Lefebvre, "Epilogue: Posthumous Titles, 1960–2013," in *Reader*, 3: 353–90.

23 Elspeth Cameron, "Split Personality," *Saturday Night*, November 1985, 73; Janet Saunders, "Green Gables Creator Tells All to Her Diary," review of *The Selected Journals of L.M. Montgomery*, vol. 1: *1889–1910*, *Winnipeg Free Press*, February 22, 1986, 72. Saunders's quotation is from a journal entry dated February 11, 1910, that the editors quoted in their introduction to the first volume and that appeared in the second volume, released in 1987. See Rubio and Waterston, introduction to *SJLMM*, 1: xxi; *CJLMM*, 2: 286.

24 Alexandra Heilbron, *Remembering Lucy Maud Montgomery* (Dundurn Press, 2001), 15, 14–15.

25 "Will Address Authors," *Toronto Daily Star*, November 5, 1928, 1.

26 *The Poetical Works of Wordsworth: The "Albion" Edition* (Frederick Warne, n.d.), 314.

27 *AIs*, 244. The sentence in "The Woods in Winter" alluding to Wordsworth's poem reappears in slightly different form at the end of chapter 28 of *The Golden Road* (see *GR*, 335).

28 *CJLMM*, 2: 173.

## 1 Things Readers Want to Know

1 "Author of 'Anne of Green Gables' Dies in Toronto," *Boston Globe*, April 25, 1942, 5; "L.M. Montgomery, Noted Canadian Writer, Passes," *Evening Citizen* (Ottawa), April 25, 1942, 11; "Author of 'Anne' Stories Succumbs," *Belvidere (IL) Daily Republican*, April 25, 1942, 2; "'Anne of Green Gables' Author Expires at 67," *Watertown (NY) Daily Times*, April 25, 1942, 17.

2 "Author of Anne of Green Gables Taken by Death," *Hamilton Spectator*, April 25, 1942, 21.

3 *SJLMM*, 5: 331, 332. See also the frontispiece in vol. 1 of *The L.M. Montgomery Reader.*

4 "Noted Author Dies Suddenly at Home Here," in *Reader*, 1: 361, 362n8, 359.
5 See chapters 72–75 in vol. 1 of *The L.M. Montgomery Reader*.
6 "L.M. Montgomery," *Windsor (ON) Daily Star*, April 27, 1942, 4; W.L. Clark, "As We See It," *Windsor (ON) Daily Star*, April 27, 1942, 2.
7 "Lucy Maud Montgomery," in *Reader*, 1: 363; "Dealt with Life in Canada," *Ontario Intelligencer*, April 27, 1942, 4.
8 "In Ancestral Scenes," *Ontario Intelligencer*, May 1, 1942, 4. The quotation "echoes roll from soul to soul" is from part 3 of *The Princess: A Medley*, a long poem by Alfred, Lord Tennyson.
9 J.J. Kerr, "'Anne of Green Gables,'" *Vancouver Daily Province*, May 8, 1942, 4.
10 Montgomery, "The Way to Make a Book," in *Reader*, 1: 141–42. See also *MDMM*, 141; Rubio, *Lucy Maud Montgomery*, 227–30.
11 *Anne of Green Gables*, adaptation by Donald Harron, produced by Norman Campbell (Canadian Broadcasting Corporation, 1958).
12 "'Anne's' Doings Remain Popular," *Saskatoon Star-Phœnix*, May 1, 1942, 4; Freda Laight, "Green Gables Children," *Leader-Post*, April 29, 1942, 11.
13 J.O. Trainor, "My Literary Friends," *The Catholic Record*, May 15, 1909, 5; review of *Emily of New Moon*, *The Congregationalist*, September 20, 1923, 371; Jane Spence Southron, "After Green Gables," review of *Anne of Ingleside*, *New York Times*, July 30, 1939, Book Review section, 7. "Cranford" refers to a mid-nineteenth-century novel of that name by Elizabeth Gaskell.
14 "To Rest in 'The Blue Haze Yonder,'" *Gazette* (Montreal), April 29, 1942, 8; Aida B. McAnn, "Life and Works of L.M. Montgomery," *The Maritime Advocate and Busy East*, June–July 1942, 20; *Arkansas Gazette* (Little Rock), "The Book Case Corner," September 20, 1942, 3rd section, 13.
15 "Things Readers Want to Know," *Winnipeg Evening Tribune*, April 4, 1923, 4.
16 "Questions and Answers," *Middletown (NY) Times Herald*, January 18, 1935, 4; "Ask the Witch Doctor," *Auckland Star*, February 11, 1933, 2.
17 "Look for Your Answer Here," *Cleveland Plain Dealer*, September 14, 1927, 20; ibid., September 17, 1932, 6; Flora MacFarland, "Is Your Question Answered Here?," *Cleveland Plain Dealer*, August 21, 1943, 6.
18 Edward M. Tuttle, "Boys and Girls," *The Rural New-Yorker*, October 25, 1924, 1355; ibid., November 29, 1924, 1485; ibid., December 27, 1924, 1586.
19 Kathleen Kaye, "The Heartitorium," *Salt Lake Telegram* (Salt Lake City), February 3, 1918, 2nd section, 4; ibid., February 12, 1922, Society section, 3.
20 "Why She Refused to Offer Her Opinions," *Toronto Star Weekly*, December 17, 1921, general, fiction, and woman's section, 14; "Emotional Actress

Lost When She Became Author," *Toronto Star Weekly*, March 1, 1924, 35; *LMMCJ*, 3: 2, 225.

21 Kerr, "'Anne of Green Gables,'" 4; "The Creator of 'Anne,'" in *Reader*, 1: 373; "L.M. Montgomery's 'Anne,'" in *Reader*, 1: 365, 366; "[L.M. Montgomery's Last Poem]," in *Reader*, 1: 375.

## 2 The Visionary Gleam

1 "Author Tells How He Wrote His Story," in *Reader*, 1: 33–34.

2 Montgomery, "How I Became a Writer," *Manitoba Free Press*, December 3, 1921, Christmas Book Section, 3. See also Montgomery, "An Autobiographical Sketch," in *Reader*, 1: 255–56.

3 *NH*, 272; *CJLMM*, 2: 118.

4 Montgomery, "How I Began to Write," in *Reader*, 1: 68–69.

5 *CJLMM*, 2: 10; *NH*, 275.

6 Florence R. Livesay [F.R.L.], "There's Only One Island, P.E.I.," *Toronto Star Weekly*, October 29, 1927, 41 (ellipsis in original); *MDMM*, 131.

7 Montgomery, "Blank Verse? 'Very Blank,' Said Father," in *Reader*, 1: 181.

8 Montgomery, "An Autobiographical Sketch," 257; Montgomery, "How I Began," in *Reader*, 1: 145–46; *CJLMM*, 1: 314; *NH*, 281, 44–46.

9 Montgomery, "An Autobiographical Sketch," 257.

10 Montgomery, "On Cape Le Force," *Daily Patriot* (Charlottetown), November 26, 1890, 1; *NH*, 263–65, 341–42n3.

11 Montgomery's poem "The Wreck of the 'Marcopolo,' 1883" is presumed to have appeared in the Charlottetown *Daily Patriot* in August 1892, but due to a gap in the copies of this newspaper that survive, those details can't be confirmed. A clipping of that publication appears in Montgomery's Scrapbook 7.

12 "Report on Copyright Situation at Meeting of Toronto Branch," *The Canadian Bookman*, February 1928, 59.

13 *NH*, 4–6; "Noted Author Dies Suddenly at Home Here," 360.

14 See *NH*, 11–57.

15 *NH*, 60, 61; editorial, *Progress* (Saint John, N.B.), May 2, 1896, 4.

16 *NH*, 80, 81, 140.

17 Montgomery, "Don't," *The Children's Visitor*, August 18, 1907, 5 (ellipsis in original).

18 *WS*, 85; Montgomery, "Comparisons," *Munsey's Magazine*, April 1901, 16. "Comparisons" appeared in *The Watchman and Other Poems* as "My 'Longshore Lass" (*W*, 33).

19 "Two Songs of Love," *Arizona Republican* (Phoenix), December 18, 1898, 5.
20 "Books and Reading," *Evening Post* (New York), June 26, 1906, 8. See also Montgomery, "Midsummer," *The Outing Magazine*, July 1906, 486.
21 Montgomery, "Irrevocable," *The Congregationalist*, November 10, 1898, 652; also, unsigned and as "Beyond Recall," in *Brown County World* (Hiawatha, KS), July 7, 1899, 1.
22 Montgomery, "An Old-Fashioned Woman," *The Congregationalist and Christian World*, August 31, 1901, 314; "Seen and Heard," *Lowell (MA) Sun*, March 3, 1903, 6; "Women Replace Men: They Make Better Tellers in Savings Banks," *Northern Wisconsin Advertiser* (Wabeno), November 21, 1901, 4.
23 Montgomery, "Marian's Choice," *Days of Youth*, July 31, 1904, 5, 6.
24 *AGG*, 419, 422.
25 Montgomery, "The Prize Competition," *Days of Youth*, September 29, 1907, 5, 6, 7.
26 Montgomery, "Mock Sunshine," *The Home Journal*, February 14, 1900, 1.
27 See Scrapbook 6.
28 *LMMCJ*, 3: 390–91.
29 Montgomery, "An Invitation Given on Impulse," *Times* (Philadelphia), April 22, 1900, 32.
30 Montgomery, "How I Began," 146.
31 *NH*, 289–90.

## 3 Such Simple Little Tales

1 *CJLMM*, 2: 192.
2 Montgomery, "Let Us Walk with Morning," *East and West: A Paper for Young Canadians*, June 20, 1908, 195.
3 "Week-End Book Notes," *Boston Herald*, June 27, 1908, 7; "Mid-Week Book Notes," *Boston Herald*, August 12, 1908, 6; ibid., August 26, 1908, 6.
4 "From L.C. Page & Company's Announcement List of New Fiction," in *AGG*, back matter.
5 "The Busy Man's Book Shelf," *The Busy Man's Magazine*, September 1908, 144; ibid., October 1908, 146.
6 *CJLMM*, 2: 198–99; *LMMCJ*, 5: 23.
7 *AGG*, 249, 71, 72; M.G. Hesse, introduction to *Childhood and Youth in Canadian Literature*, ed. Hesse (Macmillan of Canada, 1979), 2.
8 *AGG*, 113, 115–16.
9 *AGG*, 334, 350–51.

10 *GGL*, 73; Carolyn Strom Collins, introduction to *Anne of Green Gables: The Original Manuscript*, ed. Collins (Nimbus Publishing, 2019), 5; Collins, introduction to *The Blue Castle: The Original Manuscript*, ed. Collins (Nimbus Publishing, 2024), 8–9; Montgomery, *Readying Rilla: L.M. Montgomery's Reworking of "Rilla of Ingleside,"* ed. Elizabeth Waterston and Kate Waterston (Rock's Mills Press, 2016), 9, 13–14, 20, 24.

11 *GGL*, 70–71.

12 "*Anne of Green Gables*," in *Reader*, 3: 52; "Oops!," *New York Times*, October 6, 1996, Book Review section, 119.

13 "Notes on Travellers and Their Lines," *The Publishers' Weekly*, February 29, 1908, 953; "List of New Books," *The Athenaeum*, January 23, 1909, 104; "From Sir Isaac Pitman and Sons," *The Bookseller*, February 12, 1909, 230.

14 "Two New Novels," in *Nonconformity and Politics*, by A Nonconformist Minister (Sir Isaac Pitman and Sons, 1909), n.pag.

15 Review of *Anne of Green Gables*, *Daily Telegraph* (London), January 22, 1909, 12; "A Selection of Newly Published Books from Sir Isaac Pitman and Sons' Spring List," *The Bookman*, Spring 1909, 21; *CJLMM*, 2: 220; "*Anne of Green Gables*," 66.

16 *CJLMM*, 2: 196, 199; ad for *Anne of Green Gables*, *The Publishers' Weekly*, December 26, 1908, 1917.

17 *CJLMM*, 2: 193; *NH*, 47–49, 200–202; *TT*, 25–34.

18 *AA*, 366–67 (ellipses in original); *GGL*, 90.

19 Notice for *Kilmeny of the Orchard*, *The Bookseller, Newsdealer and Stationer*, April 1, 1910, 227; review of *Kilmeny of the Orchard*, *Press* (Christchurch), November 19, 1910, 7; review of *Kilmeny of the Orchard*, *Otago Daily Times*, November 25, 1910, 2. For more on the transformation from "Una" to *Kilmeny*, see my afterword to *Schooled with Briars*, which reprints this serial.

20 *SG*, 165–66.

21 *CJLMM*, 2: 316; ad for Canada Drug and Book Co., *Daily News* (Nelson, B.C.), July 8, 1911, 4; "Selected Reading," *The Youth's Companion*, October 20, 1910, 562; "Book Chat and Anecdote," *Montreal Daily Star*, May 9, 1911, 6.

22 "Published Today: From Page's List," *Sun* (New York), July 24, 1915, 10.

23 *CA*, 204, 84–85, 290–91.

## 4 In Lands Afar

1 *NH*, 237, 309–11.

2 See *NH*, 234, 310.

3 Rubio, "Why L.M. Montgomery's Journals Came to Guelph," in *The Lucy Maud Montgomery Album*, comp. Kevin McCabe, ed. Alexandra Heilbron (Fitzhenry and Whiteside, 1999), 474; "L.M Montgomery's Ideas," in *Reader*, 1: 269.

4 *CJLMM*, 2: 396.

5 "Look for Your Answer Here," *Cleveland Plain Dealer*, September 17, 1932, 6; *CJLMM*, 2: 404.

6 Thomas Guthrie Marquis, *English-Canadian Literature* (Glasgow, Brook), 564; "A Talented Authoress," *Toronto Star Weekly*, July 8, 1911, 3.

7 *CJLMM*, 2: 367, 417; "Old-Timers' Stories Source for Author," *Globe and Mail*, November 11, 1937, 5; "L.M. Montgomery Finds Ontario Drab," *Varsity*, November 15, 1935, 1.

8 *LMMCJ*, 1: 51, 55.

9 *LMMCJ*, 1: 100, 130; *MDMM*, 68.

10 *WS*, 20.

11 *WS*, 21; Montgomery, "When I Go Home Again," *The American Messenger*, September 1914, 157.

12 *LMMCJ*, 1: 119.

13 Elizabeth Rollins Epperly, *Through Lover's Lane: L.M. Montgomery's Photography and Visual Imagination* (University of Toronto Press, 2007), 160; J.D. Logan and Donald G. French, *Highways of Canadian Literature: A Synoptic Introduction to the Literary History of Canada (English) from 1760 to 1924* (McClelland and Stewart, 1924), 301. See also Lefebvre, headnote to "[Seasons in the Woods]," in *Reader*, 1: 73–74.

14 Epperly, *Through Lover's Lane*, 160.

15 Montgomery, "[Seasons in the Woods]," 89–90 (ellipses in original).

16 *RI*, 112; *EC*, 210, 127; *MP*, 254; *GR*, 37; *BC*, 228–29; *MP*, 208.

17 Montgomery, "[Seasons in the Woods]," 78–79.

18 *AHD*, 230, 231.

19 Lefebvre, headnote to "[Seasons in the Woods]," 74.

20 *AHD*, 62.

21 *TT*, 177.

22 *AHD*, 345–46.

23 *NH*, 25–26.

24 Montgomery, "Prince Edward Island," in *Reader*, 1: 353; "The Annual Dinner," *The Canadian Bookman*, October 1939, 32.

25 *LMMCJ*, 4: 141.

## 5 The War at Home

1 *LMMCJ*, 1: 202, 220.

2 *LMMCJ*, 1: 224, 230–31.

3 *LMMCJ*, 1: 254; LGBM, January 18, 1917, 12–13.

4 Review of *The Watchman and Other Poems*, *The Teachers Monthly*, February 1917, 124.

5 Ad for *The Watchman and Other Poems*, *Globe* (Toronto), November 22, 1916, 2; *W*, n.pag.; LGBM, March 29, 1916, 12–13.

6 John W. Garvin, ed., *Canadian Poets* (McClelland, Goodchild, and Stewart, 1916); ad for *Canadian Poets*, *Toronto Star Weekly*, December 16, 1916, 31.

7 Garvin, ed., *Canadian Poets and Poetry* (Frederick A. Stokes, 1916); Garvin, ed., *Canadian Poets*, rev. ed. (McClelland and Stewart, 1926); Garvin, ed., *Canadian Poems of the Great War* (McClelland and Stewart, 1918); *WS*, 52.

8 "Published Today," 10; Commonwealth of Massachusetts Superior Court, "Lucy M. Montgomery Macdonald v. The Page Company et al." (Lucy Maud Montgomery Collection, Library and Archives Canada), 7.

9 *Anne of Avonlea* contract (Lucy Maud Montgomery Collection, Library and Archives Canada), n.pag.; "Best-Selling Books," *The Publishers' Weekly*, December 1, 1917, 1890; ibid., December 15, 1917, 2066.

10 *AfGG*, 67.

11 Katherine Hale, "Canadian Novelists, as a Rule, Apparently Untouched by the War," *Toronto Star Weekly*, December 15, 1917, general section, 10; Alfred S. Clark, "The World of Books," *Boston Post*, September 1, 1917, 9.

12 *AHD*, n.pag., 4, 37; LGBM, January 18, 1917, 16.

13 *RI*, 7, 17.

14 "Common Sense and Cheerfulness," *New York Times*, September 7, 1919, Review of Books section, 453; ad for *Rainbow Valley*, *The Publishers' Weekly*, August 16, 1919, 462; "*Rainbow Valley*," in *Reader*, 3: 217.

15 *LMMCJ*, 1: 267, 283, 294.

16 *LMMCJ*, 2: 90.

17 *LMMCJ*, 2: 215; LGBM, April 7, 1918, 12–13.

18 "The Book and the Film," in *Reader*, 1: 347.

19 *FCA*, 270.

20 Montgomery, "Only a Common Fellow," *American Agriculturist*, January 11, 1908, 50; *MDMM*, 124.

21 *LMMCJ*, 2: 128.

22 "*Rilla of Ingleside*," in *Reader*, 3: 233; *RI*, 9.

23 *LMMCJ*, 1: 183, 162–63, 165–66; *AHD*, 177–78; *RI*, 16, n.pag.

24 *AfGG*, 61; *RI*, 77.

25 LGBM, March 29, 1916, 4–5; see also *LMMCJ*, 1: 214.

26 *RI*, 221–22.

27 "Canadian Writers on Canadian Literature — A Symposium," in *Reader*, 1: 49; *LMMCJ*, 2: 178.

28 *LMMCJ*, 2: 279; "No More of 'Anne' Books, Says Author," *Evening Times and Star*, July 30, 1921, 2; *LMMCJ*, 2: 335; ad for *Rilla of Ingleside*, *Boston Herald*, September 10, 1921, 5.

29 "*Rilla of Ingleside*," 236; review of *Rilla of Ingleside*, *Rochester Democrat and Chronicle*, September 4, 1921, 3rd section, 7.

## 6 With Hamlet Left Out

1 *CJLMM*, 1: 3; *AGG*, 45, 50.

2 See *CJLMM*, 1: 64, 141.

3 *CJLMM*, 1: 130, 140.

4 *LMMCJ*, 1: 269, 275.

5 *CJLMM*, 1: 170; *GGL*, 51.

6 *NH*, 270; *ENM*, 7.

7 *CJLMM*, 1: 377–78; *EQ*, 67.

8 *EQ*, 67.

9 Rubio and Waterston, introduction to *SJLMM*, 5: xxi.

10 Adams, "The Full Lucy," *Globe and Mail*, January 17, 2004, R12.

11 *CJLMM*, 2: 286.

12 Rubio and Waterston, introduction to *SJLMM*, 1: xxi; Rubio, "'A Dusting Off': An Anecdotal Account of Editing the L.M. Montgomery Journals," in *Working in Women's Archives: Researching Women's Private Literature and Archival Documents*, ed. Helen M. Buss and Marlene Kadar (Wilfrid Laurier University Press, 2001), 60–61.

13 Ad for *The Selected Journals of L.M. Montgomery*, vol. 1: *1889–1910*, Ottawa *Citizen*, November 16, 1985, C2.

14 Rubio, "'A Dusting Off,'" 52–56; Alyce Durham, "Lucy Maud Books in for Evening," *Burlington (ON) Gazette*, December 17, 1985, 26.

15 Mark Abley, "The Girl She Never Was," *Saturday Night*, November 1987, 52, 54; J.M. Bumsted, *A History of the Canadian Peoples* (Oxford University Press, 1998), 264–65, 247; J.M. Bumsted and Michael C. Bumsted, *A History of the Canadian Peoples*, 5th ed. (Oxford University Press, 2016), 326; Carol Shields, "Loving Lucy," review of *The Selected Journals of L.M. Montgomery*, vol. 4: *1929–1935*, *Globe and Mail*, October 3, 1998, D18.

16 Epperly, "L.M. Montgomery and the Changing Times," *Acadiensis* 17, no. 2 (Spring 1988): 181, 185; Rubio and Waterston, introduction to *SJLMM*, 5: xxiv.
17 *LMMCJ*, 2: 179.
18 *CJLMM*, 2: 192; *NH*, 295; *EQ*, 232. See my notes in *A Name for Herself* for discrepancies between "The Alpine Path" and the journal entries Montgomery had borrowed from to create this text.
19 Rubio and Waterston, introduction to *SJLMM*, 1: xxiv. In their introduction to the first volume, Rubio and Waterston describe their process of transcribing and editing the text of Montgomery's handwritten ledgers (see ibid., xxiii–xxiv).
20 *CJLMM*, 2: 283, 287. See also Rubio and Waterston, introduction to *SJLMM*, 5: xxi–xxii.
21 *LMMCJ*, 3: 25; *ENM*, 351.
22 *LMMCJ*, 5: 188.
23 EVLMMJ, 1: n.pag. See also Brown and Lefebvre, "Archival Adventures with L.M. Montgomery," 380–81.
24 *LMMCJ*, 5: 188; *SJLMM*, 5: 185, 258.
25 Rubio and Waterston, introduction to *SJLMM*, 1: xxiii; EVLMMJ, 3: 77–78 (ellipses in original).
26 *CJLMM*, 1: 368, 371; EVLMMJ, 2: 3a, 3b.
27 *CJLMM*, 1: 388. As Rubio and Waterston note, here Montgomery misquoted Sir Walter Scott's *The Talisman*: "The tragedy of Hamlet, the character of the Prince of Denmark being left out" (*CJLMM*, 1: 388n1).
28 *CJLMM*, 1: 397.
29 Rubio, *Lucy Maud Montgomery*, 102; *LMMCJ*, 2: 248; EJLMMV, 2: 21 (ellipses in original).
30 EJLMMV, 2: 41, 53.
31 In her biography, Rubio notes that after the publication of the first volume of Montgomery's selected journals, readers connected to the Leard family took issue with her depiction of Herman Leard as uncultured and unintelligent (Rubio, *Lucy Maud Montgomery*, 100–102).
32 EJLMMV, 2: 47; see also *CJLMM*, 1: 430.

## 7 A Fiction Writer on Fiction Writing

1 *CJLMM*, 2: 172; T.S. Stribling, "Everybody's Advice to Writers," *The Editor*, December 22, 1923, 89, 90.
2 "From *Fiction Writers on Fiction Writing: Advice, Opinions and a Statement of Their Own Working Methods by More Than One Hundred Authors*," in *Reader*, 1: 189, 190, 194, 195.

3 Phoebe Dwight, "Want to Know How to Write Books? Well Here's a Real Recipe," in *Reader*, 1: 54; Owen McGillicuddy, "A Sextette of Canadian Women Writers," in *Reader*, 1: 178.
4 Montgomery, "The Way to Make a Book," 138; "Proud That Canadian Literature Is Clean," in *Reader*, 1: 200; "English Union Hears Author of Noted Book," *Globe* (Toronto), October 4, 1935, 9.
5 "A Bystander at the Office Window," *Globe* (Toronto), February 7, 1923, 5; "Who Are the 12 Greatest Canadian Women?," *Toronto Star Weekly*, March 24, 1923, 19; *LMMCJ*, 3: 121, 130.
6 *NH*, 235, 240, 247, 269, 272; Mary Josephine Trotter, "The Novelist of the Isle: L.M. Montgomery," *Everywoman's World*, September 1914, 11.
7 *AHD*, 21–22; Genevieve Wiggins, *L.M. Montgomery* (Twayne Publishers, 1992), 60.
8 Arlene Perly Rae, *Everybody's Favourites: Canadians Talk About Books That Changed Their Lives* (Viking, 1997), 91.
9 Montgomery, "Novel Writing Notes," in *Reader*, 1: 198.
10 *AIs*, 115, 118.
11 *AIs*, 116; Montgomery, "The Adventures of a Story," *Times* (Philadelphia), October 28, 1900, 32.
12 *AIs*, 119, 120, 153.
13 *AIs*, 120; *CJLMM*, 2: 348; "Week-End Book Notes," *Boston Herald*, October 24, 1908, 9; *NH*, 290.
14 Epperly, *The Fragrance of Sweet-Grass: L.M. Montgomery's Heroines and the Pursuit of Romance* (University of Toronto Press, 1992), 63.
15 *AIs*, 279; *NH*, 277.
16 *AIs*, 280; *AA*, 206.
17 *AIs*, 322; Montgomery, "The Adventures of a Story," 32.
18 *NH*, 283. See also *CJLMM*, 2: 19.
19 *AHD*, 206, 207.
20 *AHD*, 159.
21 *AHD*, 216.
22 *LMMCJ*, 1: 329–31; *AHD*, 84.
23 *TT*, 85, 93; *AHD*, 222.
24 *AHD*, 224, 335; *RV*, 20, 25–26.
25 *RV*, 26, 27, 184, 77, 166.
26 *RI*, 161, 163, 226–27.
27 *RI*, 259, 258; *RV*, 340.
28 *EC*, 1.

29 *AfGG*, 88, 114–15.
30 Ad for Frederick A. Stokes Company, *The Publishers' Weekly*, August 11, 1923, 474; ibid., August 18, 1923, 533; ibid., August 25, 1923, 598.
31 *ENM*, 57, 16, 11, 48–49.
32 *EC*, 81, 82, 81.
33 *EQ*, 3, 13–25.
34 *EQ*, 66, 70, 221–24.
35 "My Best Piece of Work," *Toronto Star Weekly*, November 2, 1929, general section 1, 9, 10.
36 *MM*, 15; *TW*, 13, 11; *PSB*, 128; *TW*, 48; *MP*, 133; *AWP*, 46, 59; *JLH*, 119.
37 *JLH*, 90, 296 (ellipses in original).
38 *TW*, 213, 215.
39 *AfGG*, 149, 149n8.

## 8 A Writer and Her Critics

1 *LMMCJ*, 4: 233, 234. In this journal entry, Montgomery also transcribed the poem, which appears in *The Blythes Are Quoted* as "I Wish You" (see *BQ*, 70–71).
2 "Canadian Authors Turn Many Away from Big Meeting," *Globe* (Toronto), November 7, 1928, 14.
3 H. Napier Moore, "In the Editor's Confidence," *MacLean's Magazine*, October 1, 1929, 92; Montgomery, "A Question of Acquaintance," *MacLean's Magazine*, October 1, 1929, 12–13, 81–83.
4 Maude Petitt Hill, "The Best Known Woman in Prince Edward Island," *The Chatelaine*, May 1928, 8–9, 65; ibid., June 1928, 23, 41–42; V.B. Rhodenizer, "Who's Who in Canadian Literature: L.M. Montgomery," in *Reader*, 1: 237–40; Hale, "About Canadian Writers: L.M. Montgomery, the Charming Author of 'Anne,'" in *Reader*, 1: 241–43; Livesay, "There's Only One Island, P.E.I."; Margaret Ray, "A Canadian Bookshelf for American Tourists," *The Publishers' Weekly*, June 23, 1928, 2527.
5 "Inside Stuff," *The Canadian Bookman*, August 1927, 251. See also *AfGG*, 156–57.
6 See *LMMCJ*, 4: 230, 231–32.
7 Logan and French, *Highways of Canadian Literature*, 299, 298.
8 Mary Vipond, "Best Sellers in English Canada, 1899–1918: An Overview," *Journal of Canadian Fiction* 24 (1979): 97, 98.
9 Logan and French, *Highways of Canadian Literature*, 300; Vipond, "Best Sellers in English Canada," 104.

10 Logan and French, *Highways of Canadian Literature*, 301; Archibald MacMechan, *Head-Waters of Canadian Literature* (McClelland and Stewart, 1924), 211; Lionel Stevenson, *Appraisals of Canadian Literature* (Macmillan, 1926), 31–32; Lorne Pierce, *An Outline of Canadian Literature (French and English)* (Louis Carrier, 1927), 38.

11 Waterston, *Kindling Spirit: L.M. Montgomery's "Anne of Green Gables"* (ECW Press, 1993), 19; William Arthur Deacon, *Poteen: A Pot-Pourri of Canadian Essays* (Graphic Publishers, 1926), 169. For more on shifts in Montgomery's critical reputation throughout her career, see Lefebvre, "Introduction: A Life in Print," in *Reader*, 1: 16–24.

12 Leslie McGrath, "Reading with Blitheness: *Anne of Green Gables* in Toronto Public Library's Children's Collections," in *Anne's World: A New Century of Anne of Green Gables*, ed. Irene Gammel and Benjamin Lefebvre (University of Toronto Press, 2010), 104; *Books for Boys and Girls, Being a List of Two Thousand Books Which the Librarians of the Boys and Girls Division of the Toronto Public Library Deem to Be of Definite and Permanent Interest* (Boys and Girls House, Public Library of Toronto, 1927), 154; MacMechan, *Head-Waters of Canadian Literature*, 215, 211–12.

13 French, "Canada's Jane Austen," *The School*, December 1914, 268, 270.

14 French [D.F.], "Rilla, Daughter of 'Anne,'" *Globe* (Toronto), October 8, 1921, 19; French, "Canada's Jane Austen," 268; French, "When the Critic Smiles," *The Canadian Magazine*, October 1919, 514.

15 Logan and French, *Highways of Canadian Literature*, 299–302; *LMMCJ*, 3: 142. See also Lefebvre, "Introduction: A Life in Print," 17–18.

16 Leslie Horner, *Famous Canadian Stories: Re-Told for Children*, ed. French (McClelland and Stewart, 1923); French, ed., *More Famous Canadian Stories: Retold for Boys and Girls* (McClelland and Stewart, 1926), 216; French, ed., *Famous Canadian Stories: The Romance of Discovery, Exploration and Development* (McClelland and Stewart, 1945), 329.

17 Janet E. Baker, "Archibald MacMechan: Canadian Man of Letters" (Ph.D. dissertation, Dalhousie University, 1977), 120, 254.

18 Stevenson, "Overseas Literature: From a Canadian Point of View," *The English Review*, December 1924, 877, 881; Stevenson, *Appraisals of Canadian Literature*, 31–32, 157, vii.

19 Rubio, *Lucy Maud Montgomery*, 354, 461, 466.

20 Clara Thomas and John Lennox, *William Arthur Deacon: A Literary Life* (University of Toronto Press, 1982), 37.

21 Deacon, "Canadian Literature," *The Saturday Review of Literature*, December 20, 1924, 399.

22 "*Anne of Ingleside*," in *Reader*, 3: 348, 352n2; Rubio, *Lucy Maud Montgomery*, 463.

23 Deacon [W.A.D.], "The Fly Leaf," *Globe and Mail*, March 27, 1937, 27; ibid., March 30, 1946, 10; ibid., June 12, 1954, 14; ibid., May 14, 1960, 17.

24 Deacon [W.A.D.], "The Fly Leaf," *Globe and Mail*, March 18, 1939, 8; ibid., February 22, 1941, 11; ibid., September 20, 1941, 8; April 1, 1950, 10.

25 Deacon [W.A.D.], "The Fly Leaf," *Globe and Mail*, August 8, 1942, 8.

26 Deacon [W.A.D.], "The Fly Leaf," *Globe and Mail*, September 27, 1941, 8.

27 "Mr. Gomery Makes Plea for Authors," *The Ubyssey*, February 18, 1927, 2.

## 9 The Scarce Hints of Love

1 *MP*, 338 (ellipsis in original).

2 "*Rilla of Ingleside*," 227; *MP*, 333 (ellipsis in original).

3 *RI*, 201–2, 243; *EC*, 301.

4 *MDMM*, 118. See also *LMMCJ*, 3: 197.

5 *CJLMM*, 1: 78, 277, 278.

6 *AIs*, 84.

7 *AIs*, 156.

8 *TW*, 20, 21; *EQ*, 204, 205.

9 Rubio, "Subverting the Trite: L.M. Montgomery's 'Room of Her Own,'" in *Reader*, 2: 117; *LMMCJ*, 1: 155.

10 "*Emily's Quest*," in *Reader*, 3: 288; "From *Fiction Writers on Fiction Writing*," 195; Norma Phillips Muir, "Famous Author and Simple Mother," in *Reader*, 1: 225, 227; C.L. Cowan, "Minister's Wife and Authoress," in *Reader*, 1: 251.

11 *JLH*, 15, 14, 201.

12 Mollie Gillen, *The Wheel of Things: A Biography of L.M. Montgomery, Author of "Anne of Green Gables"* (Fitzhenry and Whiteside, 1975), 88; Cecily Devereux, introduction to *Anne of Green Gables*, ed. Devereux (Broadview Editions, 2004), 30; Rubio and Waterston, introduction to *SJLMM*, 3: xii.

13 *LMMCJ*, 3: 101, 110, 133–34.

14 *LMMCJ*, 3: 21, 27.

15 Montgomery, "How I Became a Writer," 3; *RI*, 259.

16 *AA*, 318; *AIs*, 298, 184; *AHD*, 306; *RV*, 317–18, 333–35.

17 *AIs*, 286, 308, 322.

18 *BC*, 60; *TW*, 49. These serials appear in *Schooled with Briars*, in whose afterword I discuss this narrative thread shared among them.

19 *AGG*, 350; *ENM*, 281; *EQ*, 129, 128; *RI*, 220, 274.

20 Hermann B. Deutsch, *The Wedge: A Novel of Mexico* (Frederick A. Stokes, 1935), back cover; ad for *Mistress Pat*, *Toronto Daily Star*, December 11, 1935, 28.

21 *MP*, 14, 58, 94, 114, 159, 164, 159.

22 *EQ*, 306; *CJLMM*, 1: 35–41, 92–98; *NH*, 17–26.

23 *AIs*, 325; *MP*, 338; *AHD*, 278, 285.

24 *RI*, 368. For more on this common thread between these texts, see my afterword to *Schooled with Briars*.

25 *AIs*, 299–300; *MP*, 219–20 (first and third ellipses in original).

26 *EQ*, 82; *MP*, 271–72 (ellipses in original).

27 *CJLMM*, 2: 156–57, 158.

28 *RI*, 244.

29 *EQ*, 309, 132.

## 10 Returns to Anne

1 Montgomery, "Is This My Anne," in *Reader*, 1: 325; *Anne of Green Gables*, screenplay by Frances Marion, dir. William Desmond Taylor (Realart Pictures Corporation, 1919); *Anne of Green Gables*, screenplay by Sam Mintz, dir. George Nicholls, Jr. (RKO Radio Pictures, 1934).

2 *SJLMM*, 4: 356, 357; *AfGG*, 227; "Creator of 'Anne' Addresses Women," *Toronto Daily Star*, January 8, 1936, 25.

3 "Letter from Popular Author," *Manning River Times* (Taree), October 17, 1936, 8; Lefebvre, afterword to *TT*, 270, 286–87n23.

4 *AWP*, 15, 144 (ellipsis in original); *SJLMM*, 5: 32.

5 *AWP*, 226, 298, 293–94; *JLH*, 293–97; *TT*, 212–26.

6 *SJLMM*, 5: 82; *AfGG*, 248; *Anne of Windy Poplars*, screenplay by Michael Kanin and Jerry Cady, dir. Jack Hively (RKO Radio Pictures, 1940).

7 *AfGG*, 248; *SJLMM*, 5: 277, 278.

8 Rubio, *Lucy Maud Montgomery*, 547; *AIn*, 259.

9 *AIn*, 136, 143–44, 146–47; *WS*, 81.

10 *AIn*, 302, 303, 316 (ellipses in original).

11 *AIn*, 322 (ellipses in original).

12 *AIn*, 323 (ellipses in original).

13 "A Letter from Maud," *The Road to L.M. Montgomery* 2 (June 1996): 11.

14 *MDMM*, 199; *AfGG*, 255.

15 *BQ*, 69.

16 Rubio and Waterston, introduction to *SJLMM*, 5: xxiii.

17 "Noted Author Dies Suddenly at Home Here," 359.

18 Rubio, "Uncertainties Surrounding the Death of L.M. Montgomery," in *Anne Around the World: L.M. Montgomery and Her Classic*, ed. Jane Ledwell and Jean Mitchell (McGill-Queen's University Press, 2013), 53; *BQ*, 502.

19 *BQ*, 68, 174, 255.

20 Montgomery, "Some Fools and a Saint," *Family Herald and Weekly Star*, June 10, 1931, 22 (ellipsis in original); Montgomery, "The Road to Yesterday," *Canadian Home Journal*, January 1934, 48; *BQ*, 67, 499.

21 Montgomery, "An Afternoon with Mr. Jenkins," *Family Herald and Weekly Star*, August 2, 1933, 20; Montgomery, "The Twins Pretend," *Toronto Star Weekly*, August 21, 1937, general section 2, 2; *BQ*, 85, 123; *RI*, 284.

22 *BQ*, 249, 394 (ellipsis in original).

23 *BQ*, 339, 110, 261, 276, 110 (ellipsis in original).

24 *BQ*, 363, 510 (ellipses in original).

25 BQ ts., n.pag.

26 "[L.M. Montgomery's Last Poem]," 376–77 (ellipses in original).

## Conclusion: After Life's Fitful Fever

1 *LMMCJ*, 2: 212.

2 "Montgomery, Lucy Maude [*sic*]," in *Twentieth Century Authors: A Biographical Dictionary of Modern Literature*, ed. Stanley J. Kunitz and Howard Haycraft (H.W. Wilson, 1942), 974.

3 W.J. Hurlow, "Under the Reading Lamp," *Evening Citizen* (Ottawa), September 5, 1942, 18.

4 "Looking Back on Life," *Canadian Home Journal*, May 1931, 6. The quotation "shaping my ends" is from Shakespeare's *Hamlet*.

# Index


Abley, Mark, 126
Adams, James, 2, 6, 7, 124
*Anne of Avonlea* (Montgomery), 75–78, *76*, 80, 153, 190, 204, 220
  contract, 104
  reception, 78
  screen adaptations, 11, 14
  writing process, 75–76
*Anne of Green Gables* (Montgomery), 35, 57, 65–67, 69–71, 72–74, 75, 80, 118, 128, 153, 159–60, 169
  as career-defining work, 2, 27, 179
  centenary, 1–2
  contract, 99, 121
  editions, *68*, 71, 188, 220, *220*
  reception, 25, 31–32, 66–67, 69, 73–75, 169, 171
  screen and stage adaptations, 11, 12, 14, 24, 30, 101, 108–9, 201
  target audience, 31, 67–69, 73–74
  writing process, 62–63, 71, 121, 160, 174, 210
*Anne of Ingleside* (Montgomery), 205–8, 209, 210, 212, 217
  reception, 32, 177
  target audience, 206
  writing process, 205–6
*Anne of the Island* (Montgomery), 80–81, 99, 100, 104, 150–54, 161, 184, 185, 190, 191, 194–96, 198, 204, 207, 220
  screen adaptation, 11, 14, 152, 153
  writing process, 87, 104
*Anne of Windy Poplars* (Montgomery), 61, 163, 164, 195, 201–5
  screen adaptations, 11, 14, 178, 205
  writing process, 201–2
*Anne's House of Dreams* (Montgomery), 31, 91–92, 94–96, *105*, 105–7, 111, 147, 154–56, 190, 194, 195, 208
  reception, 106
  writing process, 100, 104
archival documents, 8, 10–11, 117, 131–32
Austen, Jane, 32, 173, 174
authorial signatures, 48, 50–51, 85

biographical information, requests for, 33–35, 37, 39, 84
*Blue Castle, The* (Montgomery), 31, 71, 89, 91, 126, 191–92
*Blythes Are Quoted, The* (Montgomery), 13–14, 25–26, 209–12, 214–18, 243n1

abridged edition, 12, 14, 210
typescripts, 211, *216*, 216–17
Bolger, Francis W.P., 12
book contracts, 99–100, 104, 121
book dedications, 102, 106, 111, 208
books. *See individual titles*
international circulation, 24, 29, 178
Brooke, Rupert, 107
Brouse, Cynthia, 4
Brown, Vanessa, 8
Butler, Kate Macdonald, 1–3, 4–5, 6, 7, 210–11

Canadian Authors Association, 176, 178, 179
Canadian literature
Montgomery's assessment of, 114
Montgomery's work as, 10, 27–29, 30–31, 102, 169–74, 177, 179–80
Carman, Bliss, 25
*Chronicles of Avonlea* (Montgomery), 80, 81–82, 87, 151, 210, 214
Collins, Carolyn Strom, 71

Deacon, William Arthur, 170, 172, 176–80
Devereux, Cecily, 188
didacticism and moralizing, 59, 61, 154

early writing and publications, 40, 42–44, 45, 48–49, 96–97, 153
*Emily Climbs* (Montgomery), 10, 91, 101, 158, 160, 183, 184
*Emily of New Moon* (Montgomery), 10, 45, 101, 116, 122, 131, 147–48, 159–61, 162, 192
reception, 32, 174, 175
*Emily's Quest* (Montgomery), 10, 101, 123, 128, 161–62, 185, 186, 192, 194, 196–97, 198–99
Epperly, Elizabeth Rollins, 4–5, 89, 127, 151–52

First World War, 87, 102, 106–8, 110–15, 157–58, 189, 204, 213–14
Frederick A. Stokes Company, 103, 193
French, Donald G., 89, 168–70, 172–74, 176
*Further Chronicles of Avonlea* (Montgomery), 109–10, 168

Gammel, Irene, 4, 7–8, 9
Garvin, John W., 103, 106, 207
Gillen, Mollie, 188
*Golden Road, The* (Montgomery), 80–81, 87, 88, 91, 233n27
Gomery, Percy, 179–80

Hale, Katherine, 106, 107
Hammill, Faye, 2
Heilbron, Alexandra, 13
honours, 24, 145–46

*Jane of Lantern Hill* (Montgomery), 163, 164, 187, 205, 209
journals, *3*, 3–4, 10, 12, 41, 118–19, 130
and "The Alpine Path," 120, 122, 128
edited typescript, 8, 132–36, *133*, *134*, 138–41, *139*
handwritten ledgers, 6, 128, 130–32, 137–38, 140
as private/public documents, 12–13, 124–25, 131–32, 167
published volumes, 6, 12–13, 125–27, 131, 241n31
as record of Montgomery's life, 13, 124, 128, 130, 167–68

*Kilmeny of the Orchard* (Montgomery), 78–79, 80, 237n19

L.C. Page and Company, 29–30, 66, 67, 77, 80–81, 82, 99, 104, 168, 201
Leard, Herman, 137–41, 241n31

letters to/from readers, 2, 202–3, 209
Logan, J.D., 89, 168–70, 172, 174, 176

Macdonald, Chester, 24, 84, 87
Macdonald, Ewan, 24, 84, *120*, 121, 130, 188–89, 197–98, 221
Macdonald, Stuart, 4, 7, 8, 9, 24, 84, 132
MacMechan, Archibald, 170–72, 174–77
MacMillan, G.B., 4, 9
*Magic for Marigold* (Montgomery), 84, 163–64
manuscripts, 29, 71–72, 143
McClelland and Stewart, 100, 193, 217
McCrae, John, 107
McLay, Catherine, 14
miscellaneous pieces, 10, 46, 47, 117
  "Alpine Path, The: The Story of My Career," 12, 120–21, 122, 128, 146–47
  "Around the Table," 50
  "Autobiographical Sketch, An," 46
  "Blank Verse? 'Very Blank,' Said Father," 45
  "Canadian Writers on Canadian Literature," 114
  "Crooked Answers," 76
  in *Fiction Writers on Fiction Writing*, 143–44, 186, 198
  "From Prince Albert to P.E. Island," 48, 96–97
  "Half an Hour with Canadian Mothers," 76
  "How I Became a Writer," 39–40, 189
  "How I Began," 46
  "How I Began to Write," 42–44
  "Is This My Anne," 201
  "Looking Back on Life," 221–22
  "My Best Piece of Work," 162
  nature essays, 21, 89–91, 93
  posthumous collections, 14, 48
  "Prince Edward Island," 97
  in *Twentieth-Century Authors*, 219
  "Way to Make a Book, The," 30, 145
  "Western Eden, A," 48
*Mistress Pat: A Novel of Silver Bush* (Montgomery), 91, 163, 164, 181–82, 185, 187, 193–95, 196–97, 198, 213
Montgomery, L.M.
  ancestry, 40
  burial place, 4, 219, 220–21
  death, 1, 3–4, 5, 7, 8–9, 23, 26, 210
  early life and schooling, 25, 39–45, 48–50, 118–19, 160
  funeral and burial, 219–20
  mental health, 1, 3, 4, 5–7, 8
  as minister's wife, 1, 86, 108, 187, 188
  note found on deathbed, 5–6, *6*, 8–9, 10
  photographs of, *41*, *49*, *54*, *93*, *119*, *120*
  romantic relationships, 123, 136–41, 183–84, 197–98
  teaching career, 132–34, 137
  wedding, 135
  writing career, 21–22, 41, 75, 127, 146

obituaries, 23–26, 48, 210–11
Ontario, 83–85, 86, 93–94
  Leaskdale, 25, 83–84, *86*
  Norval, 25, 97
oral storytelling, 95

Page, Lewis C., 99–100, 108–10
*Pat of Silver Bush* (Montgomery), 163, 187
patriarchal thinking, 191–92
Pierce, Lorne, 170, 171
poems, 10, 20, 46, 50–55, 62, 99–104, 117
  in *Anne of Ingleside*, 207
  in anthologies, 103–4, 207
  "Autumn," 40

in *The Blythes Are Quoted*, 210, 212
"Comparisons," 52, 235n18
"Don't," 51
"Exile, The," 87–88
"If Love Should Come," 52
"Irrevocable," 53
"I Wish You," 165, 243n1
"Let Us Walk with Morning," 66
"Midsummer," 53
"Old-Fashioned Woman, An," 53–54
"Old Man's Grave, The," 207
"On Cape Le Force," 46–47
"Our Women," 103–4
"Piper, The," 38, 217–28
posthumous collections, 12, 14
"Summons, The," 88
"When I Go Home Again," 88
"Wreck of the 'Marcopolo,' 1883, The," 47, 235n11
popular writing, Montgomery's work as, 10, 37–38, 75, 146, 167, 169–70, 178, 188
posthumous tributes and reception, 11, 12–13, 26–29, 37–38, 221
Prince Edward Island, 27, 81, 83–86, 88, 95
Cape Leforce, 47
Cavendish, 24, 25, 40, 86–87, 118–19, 137
Lover's Lane, 89
print materials, digitization and preservation, 17–19, 22, 89
profiles and interviews, 36–37, 115, 144–45, 168, 186
public appearances, 19, 85–86, 109, 145, 165–68

*Rainbow Valley* (Montgomery), 106, 107–8, 156–57, 160, 175, 190–91
writing process, 105–6
reception, 11, 13, 20, 26, 31–32, 89, 146, 167, 168, 170–80, 186
retrospection and self-analysis, 44–45, 130, 221–22
*Rilla of Ingleside* (Montgomery), 71, 91, 106, 111, 113–14, 115, 157–58, 160, 182, 184, 187, 189–90, 192–93, 194, 195, 198, 204, 209, 214, 215, 218
reception, 107, 111, 115–16, 173, 175, 181
writing process, 105–6, 110, 111, 114–15
*Road to Avonlea* (television series), 11, 14–15, 16
Robinson, Laura M., 3
Rubio, Mary Henley, 4, 6, 7, 12, 126, 127, 185–86, 241n19
biography of L.M. Montgomery, 5, 7–9, 10, 84, 137, 177, 211, 241n31
commentary on Montgomery's journals, 3, 4, 124, 125, 130, 135, 188, 210

sales and earnings, 10, 29–30, 65, 80–81, 101–2, 103, 105, 108, 115, 117–18, 163, 168, 188–89, 201
Scott, Walter, 40, 241n27
scrapbooks, 10–11, 17, 94, 117, 235n11
Second World War, 204, 209, 216
Shakespeare, William, 219, 247n4
short stories and serials, 10, 20, 46, 50–51, 55–60, 62
"Adventures of a Story, The," 149–50, 153–54
"Afternoon with Mr. Jenkins, An," 213
"Bitterness in the Cup, The," 192, 245n18
"Four Winds," 192, 245n18
"Hurrying of Ludovic, The," 81
"Invitation Given on Impulse, An," 61–62
"Life-Book of Uncle Jesse, The," 156
"Luck of the Tremaynes, The," 11, 232n20

"Marian's Choice," 56–57, 72
"Miss Marietta's Jersey," 76
"Mock Sunshine," 58–59
"Only a Common Fellow," 109–10
"Our Charivari," 46
"Passing Confidence, A," 59
posthumous collections, 12, 14, 15, 210, 232n20, 237n19, 245n18
"Prize Competition, The," 57–58
"Question of Acquaintance, A," 167
"Road to Yesterday, The," 213
"Schoolmaster's Bride, The," 95–96
"Some Fools and a Saint," 212–13
"Tomorrow Comes," 205
"Twins Pretend, The," 213–14
"Una of the Garden," 78, 192, 237n19, 245n18
shorter works. *See* miscellaneous pieces; poems; short stories and serials
Simpson, Edwin, 123, 136–37, 140
speeches, 145, 165–68, 202
Stevenson, Lionel, 170–71, 175–76
*Story Girl, The* (Montgomery), 78, 79–80, 95, 111
suicide notes, 9–10

*Tangled Web, A* (Montgomery), 31, 163–64, 185, 192
target audience, 16–17, 29, 30–33, 51, 67–69, 73–74, 79, 189, 206
Tennyson, Lord Alfred, 40, 46, 234n8
Tiessen, Hildi Froese, 164
Tiessen, Paul Gerard, 7, 164
Twain, Mark, 25
typescripts, 211, *216*, 216–17

unfinished or unpublished writing projects, 60–61, 209

*Watchman and Other Poems, The* (Montgomery), 100–103, 207, 235n18
Waterston, Elizabeth Hillman, 12, 71, 127, 171, 241n19
commentary on Montgomery's journals, 3, 4, 124, 125, 130, 135, 188, 210
Waterston, Kate, 71
Weber, Ephraim, 4, 9
Wiggins, Genevieve, 147
Wilmshurst, Rea, 15, 117
Wordsworth, William, 21, 46, 62, 89, 233n27
writing process, 10, 85, 105, 121, 123–24, 143–45, 146–47